THE KOREAN ECONOMIC SYSTEM

The Korean Economic System
Governments, Big Business and Financial Institutions

JAE-SEUNG SHIM
BaekSeok University, South Korea

and

MOOSUNG LEE
The University of Myongji, South Korea

ASHGATE

Published by
Ashgate Publishing Limited
Gower House
Croft Road
Aldershot
Hampshire GU11 3HR
England

Ashgate Publishing Company
Suite 420
101 Cherry Street
Burlington, VT 05401-4405
USA

Ashgate website: http://www.ashgate.com

British Library Cataloguing in Publication Data
Shim, Jae-Seung
 The Korean economic system : governments, big business and
 financial institutions. - (Asian finance and development)
 1. Korea (South) - Economic conditions 2. Korea (South) -
 Economic policy 3. Korea (South) - Foreign economic
 relations - Japan 4. Japan - Foreign economic relations -
 Korea (South)
 I. Title II. Lee, Moosung
 330.9'5195

Library of Congress Cataloging-in-Publication Data
Shim, Jae-Seung.
 The Korean economic system : governments, big business and financial institutions / by
 Jae-Seung Shim and Moosung Lee.
     p. cm. -- (Asian finance and development)
 Includes bibliographical references and index.
 ISBN 978-0-7546-7078-0
 1. Korea--Economic conditions--1945- 2. Economic development--Korea. 3. Big
 business--Government policy--Korea. 4. Korea--Economic policy. 5. Financial
 institutions--Korea. 6. Korea--Foreign economic relations--Japan. 7. Japan--Foreign
 economic relations--Korea. I. Lee, Moosung. II. Title.

 HC467.S448 2008
 330.9519--dc22

2008015807

ISBN 978-0-7546-7078-0

Mixed Sources
Product group from well-managed
forests and other controlled sources
www.fsc.org Cert no. SA-COC-1565
© 1996 Forest Stewardship Council
FSC

Printed and bound in Great Britain by
MPG Books Ltd, Bodmin, Cornwall.

Contents

List of Figures

List of Tables

Chapter 1

Introduction[1]

Although a large number of developing countries in the Third World today have purported to achieve growth through industrialisation, most of their experiences have revealed growth to be a 'myth' of economic development. With the hope of building a self-sustaining economy, these countries have tried to get over long-standing economic backwardness by introducing foreign capital and technology. However, such a move has fallen far short of expectation and little progress has still been witnessed in most of the developing countries. Faced with continued economic stagnation and political instability, despite efforts at industrialisation, the hope of economic independence and stability has sometimes faded away.

The so called Four Tigers, namely, Hong Kong, the Republic of Korea, Singapore and Taiwan,[2] however, have been considered exceptional to this general rule. They have indeed achieved an astonishing rate of economic growth and prolonged development. As a World Bank report (1993) illustrated, annual growth in these countries over the past three decades was approximately 5.5 per cent, faster than in all other regions of the world. Among these newly industrialized countries, the Republic of Korea, actually South Korea, has succeeded in transforming herself into an economic powerhouse. As the 11th largest trading country in the world, Korea has succeeded in manufacturing and exporting such advanced goods as automobiles and semiconductors. Ascribed to these export-oriented development policy, Korea has achieved a strikingly high growth performance for a prolonged period and has finally become a member of a 'rich countries' club, such as the Organisation for Economic Cooperation and Development (OECD), at the turn of the twentieth century.

The rapid economic development achieved by Korean can easily be grasped if the growth rates between Korean and Japan (which was considered another model of economic miracle of the post World-War II era) are compared. Between 1970 and 1997, Korean GDP grew at an annual average of 8.4 per cent (*The Economist*, 1998), drawing economists and others to explain what led to her economic success. Compared with advanced countries today, for example, Japan which attained economic growth only after at least 100 years of accumulated effort, Korea's economic growth in less than five decades has attracted much attention.

Against this backdrop, we are forced to ask a number of important and also intriguing questions: what has made the Korean economy work? How can the

---

1   The whole argument of this research draws on the PhD thesis of Jae-Seung Shim, but it has reviewed and updated afterwards. The first author is Jae-Seung Shim.

2   The definition of four tigers draws on the opinion of the World Bank. For more details, see World Bank (1993).

country's remarkable economic development be explained? Are there lessons from this for other developing countries?

Various theoretical approaches have shown their relevance and limitations in explaining Korea's success, some more than others. Prominent amongst the louder voices are the neoclassical, focusing on the free market system; the developmental-statist, stressing the effective role of government; and the dependency approach, focusing on continued dependence on foreign capital and technology.

Neoclassical economists, mainly supported by the World Bank (1987, 1993) and the IMF (1996), point out the importance of an efficient allocation of resources corresponding to market forces and outward-oriented strategies. Based on the law of comparative advantage, neoclassical economists contend that Korea has attained rapid and sustained economic growth by adopting an outward-oriented policy since the mid-1960s. However, just as the developmental-statists severely criticize, neoclassical economists seem not to understand the role played by the government in the Korean economy. In fact, they argued that the market would be allowed to play a part in the distribution of resources when the government was highly interventionist (Amsden 1989; Wade 1990).

On the other hand, a critique of dependency theorists should not go unchecked. Influenced by Latin American radical economists, dependent theorists assert that successful economic development in Korea has been achieved by heavy dependence on foreign capital, technology and trade (Evans 1979; Kim 1988; Castley 1997, 1998). Since the fortune of Korea's economic development ties with that of external forces, the ups and downs of the global economy have ample chances of leading Korean economy to stagnation and even to underdevelopment (Cardoso 1977). However, the argument of dependency scholars does seem to underestimate the dynamics of changes in the relationships. Indeed, Korea's economic relationship with Japan has changed gradually from vertical to horizontal by reflecting a convergence to interdependence, which is mutually beneficial. Moreover, Korea has experienced continued high economic performance without any alarming signs of significant stagnation or underdevelopment, apart from a relatively short period of financial crisis which started in 1997 and officially ended around 2000.

The common factor for the neoclassical and the developmental-statist analysts is the importance which they both place on internal factors, particularly focusing on whether or not the government has followed market principles. In the analyses of these two perspectives, external factors have been relatively neglected (Castley, 1997). By contrast, dependency economists have focused on external factors while internal factors have been given relatively less weight.

None of the existing theories of economic development is sufficient, in itself, to explain the economic success of Korea. Indeed, there is considerable controversy over the factors which have most contributed to it. This research, therefore, aims to derive a different explanation by combining and modifying elements in the existing theoretical perspectives with a view to fitting the special features of the Korean experience. A middle way is chosen: based on a cautious use of the developmental-state view which is seen as particularly relevant to Korea, this research combines all of the relevant explanations of the three perspectives mentioned so far, in particular bearing in mind the assumption that most of the internal factors affecting development have been chosen and determined by government.

Korea's rapid and sustained economic performance can be explained by a complex interplay of many variables such as political stability, a favourable international environment, competent bureaucrats, a skilled labour force, timing, and dependency. The relationship between these variables has changed over time. In analysing economic development, it is meaningless to focus on several particular factors in a particular period in the sense that various factors have various facets. Economic development is an evolutionary process of institutions mixed with internal and external factors and to explain it adequately, the focus of attention should be on the institutions of development rather than on the selection of specific factors considered most relevant to rapid economic development.

In addition, the argument on the Korean model[3] is the method of universalisation, teaching us that we can learn from Korean economic development negatively as well as positively. Here some questions will be raised for the study of Korean economic development. Can economic development be explained in a different way from the main three perspectives and if so, what is the best way to explain the process of Korean economic development? And is the Korean economic development model applicable as a strategy for other developing countries?

Purpose

There are three main explanations of economic development: the neoclassical view, the developmental-state view and the dependency view. The former two see government and market as alternative mechanisms for the allocation of resources, whereas the latter focuses on the cut-off of an unequal exchange relationship from the core as an alternative way of breaking away from dependency. The neoclassical view is that Korea has attained astonishing economic growth in spite of heavy government intervention, while the developmental-state view sees Korea's success as a consequence of heavy government intervention (World Bank 1993; Amsden 1989; Jwa 1999). In other words, the former does not abandon its belief in market efficiency while the latter insists on the efficiency of government intervention. However, if a country based on a market economy achieved rapid and sustained economic development despite market inefficiencies caused by government intervention, two possible assumptions will be proposed: 1) the market is more efficient than government intervention; 2) there are some other

---

3 Papanek (1990) believes that among East Asia countries Japan has become the advanced nation, Taiwan is in an unstable political position in international society, while Hong Kong and Singapore are small city-state countries facing different problems with no agricultural sectors. Therefore the 'East Asian Model' is typified by Korea. However, in many ways Korea and Taiwan have affinities such as similar colonial experiences and export-promotion policies.

factors that compensate for the failure of government intervention. In other words, under the condition that the market needs a certain level of visible hand, it can be said that the evolution of institutions not only trades off the distortion of resource allocation caused by government intervention, but results in economic development (North 1990; Aoki 1995). Here, interest is focused on an evolutionary process of institutions affected by internal and external factors. Indeed, there is no more revealing argument concerning the process of economic development than the synergy between internal and external factors.

Internal factors are an insufficient condition for economic development in general and for an economy with poor natural resources and a small domestic market, in particular. By the same token, external factors are insufficient for an economy which hardly possesses a receptacle for the adaptation of the external factors. Thus, economic development is likely to be caused by the interplay of internal and external factors rather than by internal or external factors alone. Indeed, a positive linkage between internal and external factors results in a favourable pattern of economic development. In particular, in the course of economic development, the role of internal and external factors becomes symbiotic initially, but can become competitive over time. For example, the role of government as the main internal factor has its own limits in overcoming market malfunctions.[4] To solve market malfunctions, government chooses strategic alliances with private institutions. However, private institutions are not capable of solving various market malfunctions in general and this is particularly obvious for less developed countries. This is why an initially complementary relationship between government and other institutions may become competitive over time. Furthermore, external factors can become gradually embedded into domestic economic institutions creating certain patterns of a unique economic system. In this process, each institution grows and evolves, leading to economic development. For that reason, an analysis of the evolutionary process of each institution by exploring the interaction between internal and external factors through time will be needed.

The purpose of this book is to analyse the process of Korean economic development, especially in the period from post-World War II to 2002 when Kim Dae-Jung government claimed to have successfully overcome the financial crisis hitting Korea in 1997. The book does not cover the years since 2002 when the Noh Moo-Hyun government started its reign because it is still too early to assess rapidly changing political economic environments in Korea. The book focuses on an analysis of the evolutionary process of institutions by exploring the interplay of internal factors, particularly the role of government and external factors, and the influence of Japan in the process of Korean economic development. Specifically, the book intends to:

1) examine the formation and the workings of the economic system, with an emphasis on the close interaction between government, private institutions (chaebol and financial institutions) and the influence of Japan;
2) analyse the outcomes of the economic system;

---

4   More details will be provided in Chapter 3.

3) assess the progress of Korea's economic system and the changing relationship with Japan.

In doing so, the study will suggest some important implications for other developing countries. Korea has experienced a unique process of economic development with mechanisms and outcomes that are different from those suggested by the three major perspectives. Furthermore, in this study, it will be shown that Japan has had a much deeper effect than the US on the formation of the Korean economic system (see Table 1.1).

Table 1.1   Japan: characteristics favourable to the Korean Economy

	Characteristics favourable to Korea
	1) Geographical proximity (reduction of transaction costs)
	2) Colonial experience (mutual understanding of cultural, social, political and economic structure)
	3) Timing
	4) Japan's industrial policy (favourable to Korea's exports)
	5) Provision of the Japanese development model
Japan	6) Different industrial structure (one generation behind Japan's industrial structure)
	7) Intensive and sustained contribution of capital, FDI and technology
	8) Supplier of production goods in manufacturing industries suitable for different industrial structure
	9) Supplier of technology suitable for different technological ladder
	10) Absorber of and distributor for Korean exports

For example, Japan's foreign investment mainly by small and medium sized firms concentrating on labour-intensive industries was much more suitable for the creation of employment and for technology transfer than that of American firms which centred on capital-intensive industries. According to Kojima (1977) and Ozawa (1972), American firms produce consumer goods, requiring economies of scale and high technology that are less appropriate for developing countries, at the stage of downstream technology and with a shortage of capital. Castley (1997) and Hattori (1988) argue that unlike the US, Japan sent industries to Korea that produce products in the declining stage of the product cycle. Korea was able to accept and benefit from such industries.

Theoretical Explanations

The basic theoretical explanations for understanding Korean economic development in this study stem from a review of the theories of the three major perspectives. The previous studies in connection with this one are very helpful in deriving a model of economic development. They include studies on the free market approach in the international economy (World Bank 1986, 1987, 1993;

Balassa 1971, 1981, 1988; Little 1982; Krueger 1978, 1980, 1990; Westphal 1990; Hong 1976; Corbo and Suh 1992; Sachs 1987; Krause 1992; IMF 1996); on the effective role of government (Amsden 1989; Jones and Sakong 1980; Sakong 1981, 1993; Deyo 1987; Haggard and Moon 1990; Haggard 1990; Taniura 1989; Wade 1990; Johnson 1982, 1987; Weiss and Hopson 1995; Kim 1997; Whang 1997); on dependency and development (Cardoso 1977; Evans 1979; Frank 1969, 1979; Nurkse 1959; Kim 1988; Honda 1990; Nakagawa 1987; Park 1990; Bernard 1995; Castley 1997); and on comparative institutional analysis (Aoki 1988, 1992; Aoki and Dore 1994; Aoki and Okuno-Fujiwara 1997; Aoki and Okuno 1996; Jwa 1999; North 1990, 1992; Eggertsson 1990; Fukagawa 1997).

In particular, the evolutionary analysis of each institution in explaining economic development needs a historical perspective. Historical observation allows an explanation of the interplay of internal and external factors. In particular, it helps to focus on the ways in which economic development has formed the Korean economic system by a deepening economic relationship with Japan. If there were no institution capable of expanding the Korean economy, it would have been impossible to industrialise itself by dependence on foreign capital and technology alone. Japan's presence with capital, advanced technology and previous experience has been beneficial to the Korean economy.

This case study of South Korea analyses how the country internalised her dependent position in order to become a self-sustaining economy. Indeed, the long historical observation adopted in this case study provides a deeper and more accurate understanding of Korea's economic development. It should be significant for other developing countries and for the theory of development economics to find out how the success story of the Korean economy can be explained and for an understanding of public policy in relation to the evolution of the economic system.

Research Methods

An Evolutionary Analysis of the Economic System

This study assumes that with the existing theories, it is difficult to explain the process of economic development as well as changing structural characteristics of institutions, while each theory shows its own relevance. Thus, an analysis is introduced of the economic system, which is formed in a gradual evolutionary process of institutions. In addition, Korea's political economic relationship with Japan is emphasised because Japan's influences have been progressively integrated into the formation of the Korean economic system.

Five arguments are offered in this research, which differ from the three main views of economic development.

1) In the case of Korea, economic development is achieved by a strategic alliance between a strong government and a leading economic institution (chaebol) in the market system. This alliance is complementary (symbiotic) initially and competitive over time. It plays as an independent variable that affects the

whole economy in the process of economic development. Other economic institutions are relatively excluded by the strategic alliance from enjoying the benefits of economic growth. The existence of the strategic alliance goes against arguments made in the three views of development that government and market have a zero-sum relationship with one group's interest being at the expense of the other's.

2) As the economy becomes mature, another independent variable (financial institutions)[5] emerges, affecting the process of economic development, as a response to market maturity.

3) In contrast to earlier studies, it is not assumed that the relationship between government and institutions is a constant one: it changes in the process of economic development.

4) It is assumed that institutions develop and evolve through competition and in turn, the evolutionary process of institutions contributes to economic development.

5) External factors including, both 'hardware' such as capital and technology and 'software' such as business culture, are assumed to have an influence on the formation of the economic system in a country; and it is expected that, over time, these factors will become internalised (or incorporated) into the economic system. In addition, the influence of external factors on the formation of the economic system changes through time and therefore, the economic system itself changes gradually.

Application to the Korean Economy

Internally, there are the three main institutions in the Korean economic system: government, chaebol[6] and finance. Externally, Japan's influence on the Korean economy has been gradually internalised into the institutions. Over time, with the influence of the Japanese economy on the Korean economy, the Korean economic system has been increasingly formed. The Korean government played a central role by designating the direction of industrialisation. In guiding development, the Korean government also put financial institutions under its powerful hand so that chaebol (business sector) were subordinate to the government. However, chaebol played an increasingly greater role over time as both an implementor of industrial policy and an agent of evolutionary institutions that adapted to changing economic environments mainly created by government. As the market became mature, the Korean economic system needed another institution that affects the market structure. The financial institutions that were put under the government's control have gradually developed in response to this need.

---

5   Importantly, this is not confined to a particular institution but any institution can become an independent variable through time.

6   Large, family-owned conglomerates, similar to the Japanese Zaibatsu. See Chapter 5 for more information.

A central assumption in the analysis of government, chaebol and financial institutions is that, as economic development proceeds, all three changed in their internal structure and in response to Japan's influence on the Korean economy. This has resulted in the unique Korean economic system, formed by the mixed role of internal and external factors.

Data Sources

Data for this study is derived from secondary sources including statistical and historical documents from companies, private think-tanks, including the Samsung Economic Research Institute, the Korea Economic Research Institute, government-sponsored institutes, such as the Korea Development Institute, the Bank of Korea, and the Korea International Trade Association. Data have come also from government ministries, including the MOCI (Ministry of Commerce and Industry), the MOST (Ministry of Science and Technology) and the MOFE (Ministry of Finance and Economy). The time horizon is from the late 1940s, when the Korean economy started to stand on its own feet, to 2002 when the Kim Dea-Jung government overcame the Korean financial crisis of 1997.

Some dynamic data come from my own calculations. More detailed statistical data were obtained through the KAMI (Korea Association of Machinery Industry), and the KEIA (Korea Electronics Industries Association). Data for external factors associated with Japan's influences are the Japanese EPA (Economic Planning Agency), the MOF (Ministry of Finance), the MITI (Ministry of International Trade and Industry) and the MOFA (Ministry of Foreign Affairs).

Organisation of the Book

The book is organised into two parts, with an introduction (Chapter 1) and a conclusion (Chapter 8). Part 1 consists of Chapters 2, 3 and 4 and is mainly designed to provide a theoretical understanding of the economic development process. The discussions in this part are centred on an evolutionary theory of economic institutions. Part 2, consisting of Chapters 5–7, applies that theory to the Korean case. Part 2 is an in-depth analysis of each institution (government, chaebol and the financial institutions) and of the influence of Japan on the Korean economic system.

Specifically, the second chapter reviews the literature on existing Korean economic development. The three perspectives on economic development are reviewed and described, namely the neoclassical perspective, the developmental-state perspective, and the dependency perspective. It is argued that we cannot fully accept any of these three perspectives.

In the third chapter, we look for a more relevant theoretical framework for understanding the unique economic development of Korea. The first section analyses how internal and external factors interact in the course of economic development. The second section focuses on how internal and external factors create an economic system in a country and analyses how it has been formed, and in the case of Korea how it has evolved into creating the present economic system. This provides some insights into the question of applicability for other developing countries.

In Chapter 4, we apply our theory of economic development to the process of Korean economic development and attempt to break away from the existing three views. The nature and origin of the Korean economic system is examined and in particular, the Chapter analyses how the system has functioned.

Chapter 5 explores government-business relationships, which have played a crucial role in the process of Korean economic development. The combination of government and chaebol has been a determining factor in the Korean economic system. In particular, as the economy has become mature, the relationship between government and chaebol has changed from being symbiotic to one of competition. In this chapter, we analyse the relationship between government and chaebol in terms of their structures and how the role of government has been intertwined with chaebol in terms of economic growth.

In Chapter 6, the emerging role of another determining factor is discussed. As the economy has become mature, the partnership between government and chaebol in the Korean economic system has gradually required another partner to supplement the strategic alliance and to maximise market demand. Naturally, in the process of economic growth, financial institutions, which were under heavy government intervention and regulation, have continued to grow and evolve in order to respond to such a market request and in this way, financial institutions have emerged as a determining factor affecting the direction of Korean economic development. Thus, we focus on how financial institutions have emerged as an independent factor alongside government policy.

Chapter 7 explores the influence of Japanese capital, Japanese direct investment, technology and trade networks along with the role of the Korean government. Capital and technology explain the ability of the Korean economy to increase output, improve productivity and to upgrade the entire economy one step further. Despite a poor supply basis for production goods as well as poor technology, Korea has pursued an export-first policy based on a growth-oriented policy since the early 1960s. Thus, she needs high quality production to meet the demanding tastes of the world market. We analyse where these goods come from; how the changes in trade dependence have affected the entire economy; and how the role of Japanese capital and technology has contributed to and changed the Korean economy. Over time, the Japanese economy has become embedded into the Korean economy, so that the more Korea exports to the world, the more she needs to import from Japan.

Finally, in Chapter 8, we assess whether or not the evolutionary process of institutions, composed of internal and external factors, leads to economic development. The questions raised in the present chapter are answered and the applicability to other countries of the model of Korean economic development in this research is discussed.

PART 1

Chapter 2

Existing Explanations for Korean Economic Development

Since the early 1960s Korea has grown faster than any other economy in the world. In fact, among the *Four Tigers* Korea's economic performance is particularly noteworthy. In per capita terms the annual growth rate Korea sustained over three decades was well over eight per cent with relatively equitable distribution[1] of the gains between the haves and the have-nots, while growth in most developing countries was at an annual rate of 1 to 3 per cent. Some even posted minus growth. In addition, in 1996 the amount of exports reached approximately $130 billion compared with $55 million in 1962, while imports grew from $420 million to over $150 billion during the same period (Korea International Trade Association 1996; BOK 1997). This indicates that in 1996 the volume of Korean exports had increased by 2,360 times that of 1962, accounting for an annual average growth of 28 per cent, while in 1997 the volume of imports was 357 times higher than that of 1962. Also, the share of the manufacturing sector in GNP increased from 16.4 per cent to 28.5 per cent. This growth performance of Korea, in becoming the world's

---

1 It is, however, doubtful how exact statistical data are in reflecting and explaining the entire Korean economic development. Joo (1983) revealed statistical problems likely to occur in the process of surveying, aggregating and publishing in the Korean economy. He argued that: (1) price indices were very often manipulated by policy-makers who were in charge, in order to get points for future promotion favourable to themselves and to please their bosses. According to him, even President Chun who wanted to boast of Korea's rapid growth by announcing manipulated statistics to the people, in order to justify his illegal capture of political power, later ordered the policy-makers responsible to submit more reliable data; (2) throughout the 1960 and 1970s, like other statistics, agricultural statistics did not reflect actual economic performance because the government wanted to show off its competence so that Korea could cut a better figure in the international arena. In particular, it is not widely known, but very famous in academic circles that some scholars were severely scolded by President Park for revealing some statistical fairy tales. For example, in the survey of urban income of working men, the bureau in question excluded the highest and the lowest income strata and, in contrast, in the survey of regional working men's income it did not exclude the highest and the lowest income strata so that the income disparity between urban and regional working men could be reduced although the average income of urban working men went down a little. However, such statistical tricks still prevail in the whole economic sector throughout the entire economic process. It is still a vivid memory that President Kim Dae-Jung called for candid data from policy-makers immediately after the Korean financial crisis at the end of 1997. For more details, see Joo (1983) and Bae (1977).

11th largest trading partner (KDI 1997), has drawn considerable attention along with the term 'miraculous,' generating an intense academic debate as to the causes of the 'Korean miracle,' that is, 'The Korean Model' (World Bank 1993).

Accordingly, much has been written about the economic success of Korea, although there is no generally accepted explanation for it (Lee 1998).[2] Up to the early 1980s, the outward-looking development strategy of Korea was seen as a successful case of economic development strategy, especially after overcoming the first oil shock. In particular, the neoclassical economists in the World Bank and IMF supported this strategy. According to them, Korea could have achieved rapid and sustained industrialisation by correcting the distortion of domestic price mechanisms and by shifting its policy to an outward looking strategy from import substitution. Balassa (1981, 1988), Westphal (1978), and Hong (1976, 1981) are the proponents of this view. They argued that in the early 1980s, while many developing countries in Latin America and Eastern Europe had struggled to restructure their economies, Korea succeeded not only in escaping from the second oil shock and foreign debt problems, but also in upgrading its economic structure due to policy suggestions, for example, a tight monetary and deregulation policies as recommended by the IMF. Many neoclassical economists such as Corbo and Suh (1992), Sachs (1987), and Krause (1992) have paid attention to the economy.

However, debates on the causes of Korean economic development since the early 1980s have not always reflected what the neoclassical school argued. For example, the developmental statists (Amsden 1989; Wade 1990; Whang 1997) argued that Korea did not follow many of the policies supported by the IMF, such as rapid deregulation, a tight monetary policy and minimum government intervention. Rather, they argued that the Korean government not only adopted gradual policies, but also determined the direction of development (Whang 1997; Weiss and Hobson 1995). Naturally, the role of government has been focused upon. Amsden (1989), the proponent of the developmental state, is so negative about the free market system which is supported by the neoclassical school. She insisted that strong government in Korea determined the direction of economic policies by using market-violating administrative measures to attain the goals set for development.

On the other hand, unlike these two schools, dependency economists emphasise a dark side of the Korean economy (Park 1994). The economy was dominated by a developmental dictatorship until the late 1970s and by a military regime until the early 1990s. Korea also has depended on the Japanese and US economies (Castley 1997, 1998). Some go further to argue that the economy has produced a corpulent contradictory structure dominated by chaebol that conspired with government at the expense of small and medium sized enterprises and workingmen (Park 1991).

Explanations of Korean economic success have emphasised several other factors. Some stress a value system, Confucianism as a means of political and

---

2   Esho argues that the Korean model is not a pure theoretical model but a policy suggestion derived from a historical economic development process. For more details, see Esho (1989).

social mobilisation compatible with a high-performing economy (Vogel 1991; Yoo 1997; Rozman 1991). Others emphasise economic success as the by-product of capitalist defence against communism (Eckert 1990; Doran 1993). Still others emphasis a deep understanding of the interaction between the enterprise, and the initiative and creativity of policy makers (Johnson 1987; Haggard 1990).

While other factors including Confucianism in explaining the economic success of the Korean economy are supported by relevant literature, disagreement on the ingredients of Korean economic success prevails between economists who emphasise the gravity of a market-centred policy; academic scholars who focus on the role of government in guiding economic development; and the dependency theorists who stress the strong dependent development caused by the core. In general, their viewpoints reflect different degrees of emphasis, although every paradigm has its own convincing argument on development strategies.

In this Chapter, the three major perspectives that have dominated traditional development strategies in explaining the ingredients of Korea's economic success – namely the neoclassical, the developmental state, and the dependency – are briefly reviewed.

The Neoclassical Perspective

Most developing countries experienced prolonged stagnation of their primary products during the 1950s and 1960s. This phenomenon brought about arguments on development strategies as to whether the stagnation was generated by the trade polices of developing countries themselves or by world wide recession, that is, demand side. Kravis (1970) argued that unsatisfactory economic growth in developing countries after World War II was caused by the failure of supply in developing countries themselves, in contrast to Nurkse (1959) who said it was caused by the failure of world demand.

The controversy over these phenomena led to the rise of the structuralist approach. This assumes the existence of a peculiar structural rigidity of the price system in developing countries themselves. Chenery (1975) noted that the equilibrating price mechanism, which not only increases favourable income distribution, but also maintains stable growth, does not work in these countries because of different price mechanisms between advanced and underdeveloped countries. This distrust of the price mechanism in developing countries was used to justify government intervention and public investment planning for industrialisation, as a substitute for market failure[3] (Nurkse 1954; Esho 1989). Linder (1981) argued that unstable market conditions in primary products forced

---

3   Arndt (1985) traced the historical origin of the structural approach. By observing the industrial process of England during the 1930s and 1940s, he concluded the main thread of the approach: 1) the price may give the wrong signal due to oligopoly or distortion by other factors; 2) production factors (labour, capital, and land) may react inadequately or wrong to the price signal; 3) the factors may not move swiftly because they are less movable, although they can react correctly to the signal.

productive structures to transform, however, this required some protectionism caused by the difficulty in importing parts and intermediate goods needed for exports. Little (1982) pointed out that economic development has been achieved by strong government intervention, which allocates resources, controls market behaviour and plans the economy. However, the structuralists' perspective, which hinted at an unlimited government capacity for effective economic policies, became the main counter-attack by neoclassical scholars when government errors in economic policy appeared in developing countries (Shapiro and Taylor 1990, quoted in Weiss and Hobson 1995: 137). When the Asia NICs boasted of their rapid and sustained economic development towards the international arena, the neoclassical school embraced them as a suitable economic model based on the principle of the market.

The neoclassical perspective aims to explain internal barriers to political and economic development in developing countries. Its theoretical perspective originated from traditional economic development viewpoints based on Euro-centric and ahistorical views for developing countries. The central argument of the neoclassical counter-attack is that underdevelopment is caused by the misallocation of resources because of unstable price mechanisms and unlimited state intervention by strong government activity in developing countries (Balassa 1981; Bhagwati 1987). Neoclassicists believe that economic development in a country is achieved as a result of the effective allocation of resources corresponding to market forces and outward-oriented strategies. They argue that it is state intervention in economic performance that retards the pace of economic growth in developing countries (Bhagwati 1978; Balassa 1988; Lal 1985). They contend that both economic efficiency and economic growth are stimulated and achieved by allowing competitive markets to foster free trade and export expansion. In doing so, they argue, excessive government intervention should be eliminated and foreign direct investment should be welcomed. Balassa (1982) pointed out that underdevelopment in developing countries is brought about by the heavy hand of the state and by the inefficiency that prevails in these countries. In other words, as pointed out by Krueger (1980), economic growth results from economic efficiency attained by policies based on the principle of the free market and minimal government intervention. For the neoclassical school, underdevelopment is the result of excessive government intervention and it is found in places where the economic orthodoxy of Adam Smith[4] does not exist. In this regard, underdevelopment and stagnation result in internal barriers rather than external ones.

When export pessimism, caused by prolonged stagnation in primary goods as well as world recession, had worsened terms of trade between advanced and

---

4   According to Adam Smith, government intervention is regarded as an impediment, saying that 'little else is requisite to carry the state to the highest degree of opulence but peace, easy taxes and tolerable administration of justice; all the best being brought about by the natural course of things' (quoted in Castley 1997: 5).

underdeveloped countries,[5] the neoclassical school supported outward-looking policies in developing countries (Keesing 1967; Balassa 1983; Hong 1981; Krueger 1979; Nam 1981; Kim 1987). They claimed that the world-wide stagnation was caused by trade policies in developing countries themselves, that is, supply side but not demand side. As a result, the effectiveness of policies shifting from import substitution to export-oriented policies was emphasised. Keesing (1967) stressed that outward-looking policies are compatible with export-oriented policy as well as import substitution policy. Balassa (1983) said that an outward-looking strategy meant 'the equal treatment of sales in domestic and foreign markets', the difference being distinguished according to whether sales in domestic and export markets received similar incentives, or if import substitution was favoured over exports. Lal (1983) argues that production incentives for domestic and overseas markets are the same and sales from exports are no less profitable than sales to the domestic market. Thus, as pointed out by Balassa (1983), adopting the outward-looking strategy can lead to a reduction in the bias of the incentive system against primary activities. In a word, export as well as import substitution in primary goods can be promoted by changes in incentives. The aim of adopting these policies is to strengthen the competitiveness of developing countries' commodities on the international market through technology transfer from advanced countries. Bhagwati (1978) in his suggestion on the apparent association between high and rapidly growing exports and rapid growth of manufacturing goods in developing countries argued that exports could improve investment and growth rates as well efficiency, through multiplier efficient allocation of resources as well as by stepping up the dynamic efficiency of the economy (Balassa 1981; Krueger 1978). In addition, Keesing (1967) maintained that to transform export-oriented policies led by manufacturing goods should be carried out from the initial stage of economic development with no experience of an import substitution period. To achieve this, according to him, devaluation of the currency and the various types of preferential tariff treatment are needed. Hewitt (1992) clarified the difference between outward-looking trade policy and inward-looking trade policy (see Table 2.1).

According to the neoclassical perspective, export-oriented industrialisation policies exploit the economies of scale in the world market, develop new technology and enlarge social capabilities as a result of openness to the world market. These policies enable factor endowments and technology to achieve maximum production in the form of comparative advantage. For the neoclassical school, economic development in developing countries results from export-

---

5   Structuralists argue that primary dependent trade in developing countries did fail to lead to economic development and rather, it widened the gap between advanced countries and developing countries because: (1) international trade market for primary goods was not stable so that this caused the poor income from exports in developing countries; (2) the terms of trade in primary products in developing countries is less profitable from the long-run view point than advanced countries, which centred exports on manufactured goods and thus, this caused income disparity between the advanced and the underdeveloped; (3) rapid technical innovation in primary goods lowered the price resulting in the shrinkage of income.

Table 2.1   The character of trade policy

Outward-looking trade policy	Inward-looking trade policy
Low level of protection	High level of protection
Less quota and import licence	Wide trade regulation
Export incentives	Less incentives for new exports
Reasonable exchange rate	Overvalued exchange rate

Source: Hewitt et al. (1992): 156. By permission of Oxford University Press.

oriented industries supported by fair trade, cheap labour, the principle of the free market and minimal government intervention. Indeed, the World Bank and IMF forced developing countries to adopt such outward-looking policies.

Thus, there is the virtuous circle of economic development caused by the adoption of export-oriented industrialisation. Exports encourage an increase in domestic production. Higher domestic production brings about an increase in income and this leads to an increase in employment. Above all, income increases through exports not only raises consumption expenditure but also increases savings. As a result, exports results in higher investment and in further expansion of domestic products and income through the multiplier effects (see Figure 2.1).

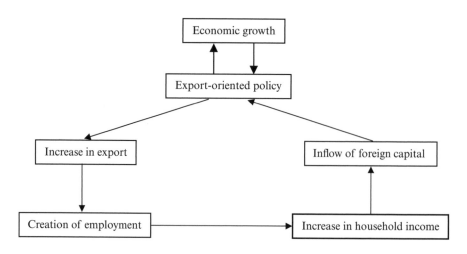

Figure 2.1   A neoclassical explanation of economic growth and export-oriented policy

In addition, export-oriented policy engenders higher household income which in turn generates higher savings. Savings may result in more investment which provides additional products and thus leads to further economic growth. The prolonged high economic performance attracts foreign capital that results in an increase in exports. The increase in products and income by way of exports creates employment. However, compared with capital-intensive industry it is obvious that labour-intensive industry creates more employment. Thus, at the initial stage of the economic development process the promotion of labour-intensive industry should be more effective than that of capital-intensive industry. Through this circulation of expansionary mechanisms the economy develops further and results in economic growth. According to the neoclassical perspective, the possibility of economic growth in a certain period is determined by the availability of resources and technical innovation and in the long term by the rate of technical improvements, which results from sharp competition in a liberal economic system.

Until the late 1980s, the neoclassical school believed that economic development could primarily be explained by macroeconomic stability that provided not only high human capital accumulation but also proper incentives for investment and savings, while the intervention of government in selected industries was at best irrelevant or, worse, had a detrimental or distorting effect on the allocation of resources. However, with the advent of a 'market friendly' approach supported by the World Bank and IMF, the neoclassical economists reluctantly admitted the intervention of government.

Indeed, it was not until the early 1990s that the World Bank (1993) lowered its voice, recognising there were many market imperfections in developing countries. In order to correct these, it was argued that government has a key role to play in making markets function properly through a market-friendly approach (World Bank 1993). This approach accepts the view that it is better for government to provide a favourable environment, for example, by investing in infrastructure, health care facilities, educational institutions, and natural security, that is, the 'moderated function of automatic adjustment of market'. However, the market friendly approach does not encourage government to act strongly in the market. It approves only of those government actions that facilitate development and market efficiency, although it is recognised the minimum government intervention can never maximise national welfare.

On the other hand, the argument on market failure has been changed to the argument on the failure of intervention, the failure of non-market factors, or the failure of government. These arguments claim an effectiveness for market mechanisms and supported the introduction of an active private sector (Lall 1985; Arndt 1987; World Bank 1988). In other words, the neoclassical school regards the private sector as a trouble-solving broker in order to resolve inadequacies in the market. Arndt (1987) argues that nobody can say that government policies are always effective to maximise market function. Chakravarity (1987) maintains that an economy that works imperfectly by externalities is better than an economy worked imperfectly by government. Meier (1987) points out that a 'poor country' results from the poor policies of government rather than the vicious circle of poverty. Accordingly, 'small' government should be introduced in developing countries to correct the distortions caused by the policy errors of government. It is thus concluded that minimal government is the best government.

Application to the Korean Economy

When Korea throughout the 1960s and 1970s appeared as a centre of attention with its striking economic performances compared with both advanced and developing countries, the neoclassical school regarded Korea as an economic model for developing countries by emphasising the effectiveness of outward-looking policies based on the principle of the market. They noted that Korea started economic takeoff around the early 1960s, by shifting her economic structure away from import-substitution industrialisation to export-oriented industrialisation, which laid the foundation for sustained economic growth. Little (1979) pointed out that by the middle of 1960s, Korea changed its policy to an export-oriented policy. It was combined with selective protection for certain import competing sectors along with a virtual free trade regime for exporters at world market prices, while the effective exchange rate for exporters was close to that which would have worked under free trade.

He further argued that an effective protection for industry was zero for Korea. This implied that incentives in exports and imports are the same so that there was no biased policy between the two. Balassa (1983) pointed out that on average, the NICs provided similar incentives to exports and import substitution. He goes further to argue that adopting the outward looking strategy would also involve reducing the bias of the incentive system against primary policies. Such a change in incentives would not only foster import substitution but also exports in major products. So Korea fell into his categories.

Krueger (1978) pointed out the importance of an efficient allocation of resources corresponding to market forces and outward strategies. According to him, the Korean government by minimising its role allowed markets to arbitrate in the allocation of resources. Ranis (1989) argued that the East Asian model, described by Cline (1982) as 'exporting as much as possible' was misunderstood. Rather the model was one of 'moving in the direction of market liberalisation as quickly as possible.' From the neoclassical point of view, the market was central in explaining the Korean economic success, and in contrast, the role of government was much less important.

The World Bank (1993) pointed out that active Korean government intervention during the period of heavy and chemical industry (HCI) promotion brought about market inefficiency by claiming that

> the Korean government promoted individual firms more often to rectify perceived entrepreneurial and skill deficiencies, using export performance to determine whether firms deserved continued promotion ... and in Korea, the selectively promoted sectors were the heavy and chemical industries: iron and steel, metal products, machinery, electronics, and industrial chemicals ... the costs of the HCI drive are still not fully known, but they were high. (308)

Furthermore, the World Bank (1993) argued the costs of government intervention by noting that the Korean government's intervention policy, most notably HCI promotion, has often been evaluated from the perspective of the success or failure of industrial policy. Another important approach in evaluating intervention policy, however, would be to estimate the fiscal/financial cost associated with intervention. Government intervention incurred direct costs in the form of subsidies to strategic sectors through policy loans and tax exemptions, especially during the 1973–79 period of HCI promotion. Intervention also incurred indirect costs in the form of accumulated nonperforming loans and the resulting portfolio difficulties of commercial banks. (309)

Accordingly, the World Bank advised that direct government intervention in the market that distorts the relative price mechanism brings about the deterioration of resource allocation. Clearly, from the neoclassical view, the role of the Korean government is limited to supplying public goods and social infrastructure since the market works effectively. Balassa (1983) pointed out that, at a micro-economic level, the government played a role in avoiding the heavy burden of taxation, price control, and the distortion of other relative prices whilst at the macro-economic level, it maintained a stable and low inflation rate, avoided excessive financial deficits, promoted the stabilisation of the financial and banking systems, provided an open market, and tried to keep stable and realistic exchange rates. This implies that the school does not support anarchy but rather a limited role for government.

Accordingly, for the neoclassical school it is quite natural that the economic success of Korea results from such careful policies. In other words, the primary role of government in Korean economic success is to improve various laws and regulations in such a way as to meet realistic market circumstances in order to distribute resources effectively. From the viewpoint of the neoclassical school, to explain the process of Korean economic development, the role of government is limited, whereas the market is seen as central.

The Developmental State[6] Perspective

Since the mid-1980s the neoclassical perspective has regarded Korean economic success as a showcase of a development paradigm for other developing countries. However, this view has been severely dented by the developmental-state view that emphasises the central role which government has played in attaining high economic growth (Johnson 1984, 1987; Amsden 1989; Wade; 1990; Weiss and Hobson 1995). The developmental-state view starts from criticism of the neoclassical perspective. It argues that economic development has been achieved by powerful government-led economic policy and intervention where market distortion prevailed. In short, the existence of market failure justifies government

---

6   They are also called as the statist, revisionist, government interventionist, industrialist and institutionalist. Indeed, as pointed out by Aoki and Okuno-Fujiwara (1997), this view has gained more support among political scientists and public forums, but has never become a mainstream view in economics, for more details, see Aoki and Okuno-Fujiwara (1997).

intervention. According to this view, market failure associated with coordinating resource mobilisation, allocating investment, and promoting technological catch-up at the developmental stage is so pervasive that state intervention is necessary to heal it. The point is that government is able to accelerate economic growth by artificial distortion of the price mechanism (Amsden 1989; Haggard 1990; Wade 1990; Weiss and Hobson 1995; Taniura 1989; Fukagawa 1997). Kim (1989) argues that the state not only allocates the amount of capital but also indicates the direction of investment in private firms directly and indirectly. Amsden (1989) notes that the state initiates fund-raising for industrialisation, plans industrial structure and intervenes in the market price mechanism. According to Kim (1989), the state is a substantial body that enables the industrial structure to move up artificially. The state is not a functional body based on substructure but a determining body affecting the whole economy. Thus, the developmental statists assume that government intervention is the *cause* of economic growth, with government as the driving force for positive change. Especially, they seek the causes from the effectiveness of national institutions and the efficiency of industrial policy (Jones and Sakong 1980; Johnson 1984, 1987; Amsden 1989; Wade 1990; Kim 1997; Aoki and Okuno-Fujiwara 1997; Fukagawa 1997). They claim that an authoritarian, government-led system minimises sectoral discords and thereby a country can overcome the problem of the allocation of resources, which are major obstacles to economic development. The developmental statists insist that the market functions imperfectly, especially in underdeveloped countries. Products in these countries bring about externalities and the constraint of credit. Accordingly, the developmental-state view emphasises the active role of government that not only distributes resources, which enables business to secure profitable gains and business expansion but also helps to adjust less effective market functions by the use of technology. As Westphal (1990) pointed out, government selects industrial policy to achieve international competitiveness. Indeed, from the developmental-state point of view, government is central for understanding economic development in a country. Government not only promotes economic development but also works alongside the dominant economic groups. Amsden (1989) maintains that economic development is the result of authoritarian leadership and a synergy between government and industry, though with government always in the leading position. Government plans, distributes and indicates but firms follow. In addition, even though the government maintains a cosy relationship with the firms, the relationship is always hierachical and top-down (Amsden 1989; Johns and Sakong 1980).

The developmental-state view stresses the activities, influence and capacity of state institutions in economic development. The developmental statists are negative about the free market system. They maintain that, contrary to the view of the neoclassical economists, in which the NICs are presented as free market economies approaching the US style, they were hardly paragons of free trade. The developmental-state view represents that the state is certainly significant, particularly in the developmental stage requiring expansion of infrastructure and provision of incentives. Amsden (1989) noted that economic expansion varies in accordance with government intervention so as to create price distortion which determines economic activity.

The developmental-state view maintains relative autonomy to other sectors in society, intervenes in the allocation of resources and engages in investment decision of the business. Haggard's (1990) comparison of the NICs with Latin America in explaining the economic success of the Asian NICs suggests that their uniqueness lies in: a relatively autonomous state; an economy which is highly centralised with interventionist economic policies; and a weak left-wing and tamed labour movement. He states that rapid economic development in East Asia lies in active government policy through export-led growth of manufactured goods. In other words, economic development can be achieved through comparative advantage resulting from effective government policies. Kuznet (1994) argued that international trade is critical for economic growth indicating both visible and invisible trade. According to him, government intervention is sufficient condition for bringing about economic growth.

In the neoclassical market model, producers who can employ the cheapest wage earners have without doubt comparative advantage in labour-intensive industry because the production function is the same at each point (Amsden 1989). Thus, industrialisation is nothing but a matter of decision of specialisation to correct factor price. Like Korea, in late industrialisation in a country, it is less effective to devalue substantial wage by way of exchange rate adjustments because technology is, in general, embedded in production equipment. Rather it is more effective to give various incentives to input because the economies of scale not only bring down production costs but also improve competitiveness. Thereby, the role of government can be justified. In these terms, the Korean model is rather a showcase of the developmental-state view than of the neoclassical school.

Application to the Korean Economy

According to the developmental-state view, the neoclassical interpretation of Korean economic growth is criticised due to the lack of factual validity when applied to Japan, Korea, and Taiwan. The developmental-state view argues that governments in these countries promoted the growth of individual industries selectively. The level of protection in these industries and the bias of protection between industries were much greater than the neoclassical scholars envisaged. The developmental statists argued that the Korean government adjusted not only the whole economy through fiscal and monetary policies but also determined ownership through the sale of Japanese property inherited from the colonial period. In addition, the government distributed foreign aid and foreign capital, and adjusted the heavy and chemical industries.

In particular, Amsden (1989) drew attention to the 'institutional approach' to the Korean economy. She has forcibly argued that the Korean government succeeded in fulfilling its goals by deliberately 'getting the price wrong' in order to promote industries that would not otherwise have thrived (Amsden 1989). According to her, since the 1960s the Korean government has continued both fund-raising for industrialisation, and intervening in the market price mechanism.

In fact, the government has selectively intervened in order to affect the allocation of resources among industrial activities by means of subsidies, credit allocation and various kinds of licensing.

Amsden (1989) points out that in late industrialisation, government should distort relative prices intentionally through selective investment based on the order of priority. She goes further to argue that macro-economic stability would be sacrificed in order to promote industries which have a high priority order. According to her,

> whatever the relationship between inflation and investment in theory, in practice inflation did accompany Korea's push into heavy industry under government leadership in the late 1970s ... and the pursuit of fast growth was not restrained in the interests of price stability. (100)

and she supported Korea's emphasis on supporting heavy industries. Park and Wesphal (1986) made a similar argument claiming that during the 1970s Korea promoted heavy and chemical industries by setting strategic targets as well as by providing various financial incentives. In the financial markets, while the role of government was reduced over time, government intervention never stopped in one form or another (Woo 1991; Whang 1991, 1997). Indeed, the allocation of savings has not relied on market function entirely, instead the rate of interest has been restricted and the credit for leading investments has been controlled (Amsden 1989; Castley 1997; Cho 1990, 1997; Park 1990; Kim 1990, 1997).

The developmental-state perspective justifies the role of government by seeing market failure as a general phenomenon (Amsden 1989; Wade 1990; Weiss and Hobson 1995). The government dominated the market, distorted the price system, and accelerated catch up so that Korea could achieve its economic goals. The Korean government weeded out many obstacles to promote selective industries under such circumstances that, if comparative advantage worked, could not have grown. Amsden (1989) considers that the Korean economy was directed towards huge amounts of investment by distorting the price mechanism and that government intervention in the market was intended to ensure that comparative advantage worked in favour of Korea. It can be justified on the ground that the government intervention is needed even under favourable conditions such as cheap labour, which is the greatest advantage in developing countries. This means that an already-effective market function can be accelerated further by government intervention.

In Korea, strong government determined the direction of economic policy and used market violating administrative measures to attain its objectives. Amsden (1989) strongly insisted that there was a high degree of government intervention and also that the NICs did not follow the World Bank's 'market friendly' approach. Johnson (1987) maintains convincingly the role of government and the characteristic of the state in the process of rapid economic development in East Asia during the 1980s. For example, Korea's economic success has been attained neither by comparative advantage nor by the invisible hand. Rather, he argues that it has been achieved by successful government-directed industrialisation. In other words, government based on plan rationality rather than market rationality intervened in that market to achieve the targets set in the economic development plan (Johnson 1984). He pointed out that the Korean government has vigorously intervened in the market in order to protect the principle of the market.

According to the developmental-state view, government is regarded as the only independent variable and others, such as enterprises and the structure of the division of international labour are regarded as dependent variables. Amsden (1989) suggests that Korea is a model for late industrialising countries. In particular, the characteristics of industrialisation in Korea, according to her, are represented by government intervention in the market by means of relative price distortion to stimulate economic activities. In this view, government intervention is the main explanation of the remarkable development of the Korean economy.

The Dependency Perspective

The dependency[7] perspective, deeply rooted in historical view and structural methodology, accounts for external barriers to development within a socialist framework. This perspective centres on the political economy of capitalism on the basis of experience in developing countries. Many writers on dependency theory seek support for much of their argument in historical processes[8] (Griffin 1969; Wallerstein 1974; Kim 1988). Also, dependency theory takes on a means of socio-political analysis rather than explaining dynamic economic performance systematically (Ahn 1988). It starts from the viewpoint that the international system determines the behaviour of the social stratum in a country. Basically, it

---

7   There is a difference between dependency and dependence. According to the traditional view, a dependency was in use in colonial period that colonial powers affected the colonies with the major economic, political, or military decisions whereas dependence meant there was little or no participation by indigenous people. Also, some argue that dependency has the meaning of political and economic dominance, on the contrary, dependence is mainly used in economic relation but less political. However, although the term is so controversial that no agreement is seen on forms and meaning among scholars, it is best described by Santos (1969). According to him, dependence is a conditioning situation in which the economies of one group of countries are conditioned by the development and expansion of others. Also, it is based upon an international division of labour which allows industrial development to take place in some countries while restructuring it in others, whose growth is conditioned by and subjected to the power centres of the world. Also, the conception of dependency can be applied to the different interest groups and class in a country. In this regard, dependency means the complex concept containing political, economic and social sides and of course, an historical dimension. In addition, the difference between dependency and dependence, according to Caparaso (1978), varies according to whether the state placed in an asymmetric power relation existing in two countries has state autonomy or not.

8   For more details, see Palmer (1978); Baran (1957); dos Santos (1970); Galtung (1971); Frank (1967); Amin (1974); Cardoso (1977); Singer (1950); Myrdal (1957).

comes up against modernisation theory in substance and denies external influences on economic development strategy (Palmer 1978).

Dependency theory was the result of studies of development in Latin America. It was informed by the failure of the export-oriented policy of the 1920s and the import-substitution policy of the 1960s. Dependency theory was designed to explain the reasons for underdevelopment and stagnation in Latin America in the mid-1960s; and to find remedies for the problems. It was critical of import-substitution, which was a dominant development policy at that time.

Development theory in Latin America was based on export-oriented industrialisation policy until the Great Depression in 1929. This is the theory that introduces foreign capital to developing countries in the name of economic aid and then sets out to industrialise them in the form of capitalisation. Eventually, the level of development is stepped up by an ever-increasing volume of exports. However, in the 1920s, Latin American countries had to change their export-oriented policies due to the Great Depression in 1929 (Griffin 1969). Export-oriented industrialisation policy in Latin American countries had been to export primary goods, such as agricultural products and raw materials to the core, and then to import consumer, intermediate and capital goods from the core, in particular the US (Frank 1979; Amin 1974). However, the volume of primary goods, which were the major exports of Latin American countries was blocked because of the Depression so that Latin American countries could not import in return. The poor economic performance of Latin American countries resulted in an increase in unemployment, income disparity, absolute poverty and malnutrition, leading to political and economic crisis. Therefore, Latin American countries abandoned export-oriented policy and instead adopted import substitution industrialisation policy in order to overcome political and economic crises as well as to transform themselves into self-supporting economies. According to Griffin (1969) and Furtado (1976), countries in Latin America believed that import-substitution industrialisation not only improves dependent trade structure and surmounts economic stagnation, but also clears up dominant-dependent relationships. However, this policy required a growing amount of imports of intermediate and capital goods and in turn, it increased the need for more foreign capital. That is, the 'vicious circle' that typically plagues developing countries. It deepened the dependency of Latin American countries on the core. As a result, the dependency economists associated the causes of stagnation and underdevelopment in Latin America with external factors such as foreign aid, trade structure, technology and foreign direct investment (FDI) rather than with internal factors (Frank 1979; Galtung 1971). Myrdal (1957) argued that developing countries can remain in a situation of underdevelopment if they take part in international trade and introduce foreign direct investment.

Amin (1974) pointed out the reason for the dependency of Latin American countries on the core, especially the US: first of all, Latin American countries heavily depended on imports of intermediate and capital goods for import substitution industrialisation; secondly, industrialisation, was initiated by multinationals; thirdly, land reform, which was a prerequisite for self-reliant industrialisation was not thoroughly carried out; and lastly, indigenous enterprises in the process of industrialisation had gradually lost their entrepreneurship. In other words, the structure resulted in exploitation by the core as Latin American countries were deeply incorporated into world capitalism. Thus, it is clear that economic development from traditional society to modernisation does not take place by way of capital movement and technology transfer. More interestingly, as import substitution develops, even higher levels of intermediate and capital goods are imported. According to them, the way to stand their own feet is to weaken their ties to their core or break away from the core.

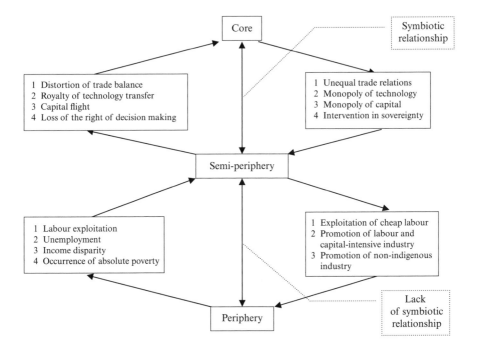

Figure 2.2 The structure of dependency theory

Figure 2.2 shows the structure of dependency theory in the world capitalist system, which consists of three groups: the core, semi-periphery, and periphery (Wallerstein 1974). The periphery is subdivided into semi-periphery and periphery. The core (the advanced) always dominates the semi-periphery (middle income countries) and periphery (the underdeveloped). The semi-periphery not only maintains a close relationship with the core, but also dominates the periphery. The core centres on manufacturing industry based on strong authority and high wages, while the periphery provides primary industry based on weak authority and cheap labour. Accordingly, the periphery with its weak basis of manufacturing industry is forced to import raw materials, intermediate and capital goods from the core. According to Frank (1967), each periphery (semi-periphery) serves as an instrument to suck capital or economic surplus out of its own peripheries and to channel part of this surplus to the core, of which all are peripheries. In addition, multinationals have appeared since the late 1950s. The periphery was forced to import the advanced technology because the technology was embedded into intermediate and capital goods. As a result, as shown in Figure 2.2, dominance and exploitation of the core over the periphery have been deepened.

According to dependency theory, economic dependency can be explained in the frame of an asymmetric economic relation of developing countries with advanced countries. The theory is deeply incorporated into the system of the international division of labour. Figure 2.3 shows dualistic international economic relations of dependency theory presented by Prebisch (1965), Frank (1979) and Galtung (1971).

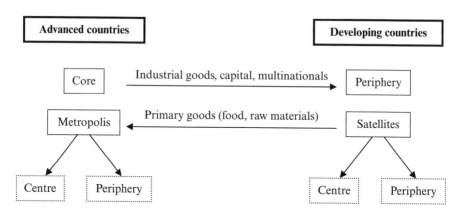

Figure 2.3   Dualistic international economic relations of dependency theory

The international economy is divided into the core and the periphery and each core and periphery is subdivided into a centre and a periphery. The core that consists of the advanced countries exports industrial goods and capital (including FDI) to the periphery and in contrast, the periphery exports food and raw materials to the core. Prebisch (1965) pointed out that orthodox economics based on comparative advantage cannot be applied to developing countries in general. According to comparative advantage theory, trade is beneficial even if a country does not have an absolute advantage in the production of a good. This principle explains why countries specialise in producing and exporting products based on their endowment of resources. Also, it is unnecessary for a country specialising in primary goods to attempt industrialisation because the benefits are naturally distributed by trade and if the country tries to industrialise, the country can lose even the benefits attained by international division of labour due to low production efficiency, according to comparative advantage theory. However, Prebisch (1965) refuted comparative advantage theory by arguing that the benefits of technical innovation were historically concentrated on the core industrial countries. Furthermore, prices for primary goods per unit had stayed constant or even had gone down, while prices for industrial goods per unit had risen due to high income elasticity of demand. Accordingly, developing countries had to export more primary goods than before in order to import the same amount of industrial goods. As a result, terms of trade in primary goods compared to industrial ones have become worse as income in the international economy increased.

Figure 2.3 shows that there is a dual structure between the centre in the centre nation and periphery in the centre nation, and between centre in the periphery nation and the periphery in the periphery nation. Galtung (1971) systemised unequal relationships between the domestic and international systems. According to him, there is disharmony of interest between the centre and the periphery and this encourages the periphery in the periphery nations to take part in international vertical division of labour, engendering further poverty.

Amin (1974) represented the process of underdevelopment in the world economy. Figure 2.4 explains the unequal exchange system between the core and the periphery. Exports from core to periphery are high quality, high in price and high in wage, while those from periphery to core are low quality, low in price and low in wage. According to Amin (1974), unequal international specialisation forms not only 'high in wages' in the core but also 'low in wages' in the periphery and this increases the vast capital accumulation in the core by causing outflow of wealth from the periphery to the core. Thus, capital accumulation in the core, in fact leads to the process of unequal development deepening as well as expanding 'development of underdevelopment' in the periphery.

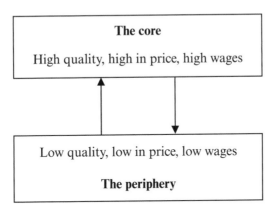

Figure 2.4   The structure of dependency relationship between the core and the periphery

Prebisch (1950) pointed out that unequal exchange brought about unequal growth between the core and the periphery. According to him, the unequal exchange system caused the core to be well-off but the periphery to be badly-off. Lim (1987) argued that the ultimate reason why the periphery is exploited by the core is that the periphery can not produce high added value products.

Application to the Korean Economy

The dependency economists applied the process of Korean economic development to their paradigm by arguing that successful economic development in Korea was achieved by heavy dependence on foreign capital, technology and trade (Castley 1997; Park 1990; Frank 1991) and thus would lead, as it always did, to stagnation and underdevelopment (Park 1991). They have claimed that during the 1960s and 1970s, Latin American countries had a dependency relationship with the US which brought about unequal economic relationships; similarly Korea also fits into the dependency framework on the grounds that she was a Japanese colony and received a huge amount of US aid (Frank 1991).

Technology transfer from Japan to Korea accounted for 52 per cent of total imported technology between 1962 and 1995 (MOST 1996) and 61 per cent between 1962-1978. Also, the number of other means of technology transfer such as joint-ventures, licensing, management contracts and subcontracting have increased rapidly (Dahlman and Kim 1992) leading to upgraded technologies and skills in manufacturing industry.

Moreover, capital shortage is one of the biggest bottlenecks to development in developing countries and thus, the essential condition for economic development is to increase the amount of savings and investment. Korea's capital formation was mostly provided by foreign capital during the 1960s and 1970s. Japan accounted for more than 50 per cent of the total foreign capital (MOF 1985).

On the other hand, Korea adopted an export-led industrialisation policy in spite of the fact that parts, intermediate goods, machinery and equipment and technology were lacking. A trade structure that assembles and processes final goods by using machinery and equipment imported from foreign countries can not be avoided under export-led industrialisation. This structure caused heavy dependence on production goods from advanced countries, in particular Japan.

Quality control and a marketing network for exports will be needed. American consumers' tastes were familiar with Japanese goods and thus Korea needed to produce at least similar quality as that of Japan's in order to penetrate the US market. With poor technology and capital shortage Korea had to import high quality intermediate and capital goods (Watanabe 1981, 1990). However, Japan not only supplied capital, production goods and technology needed for exports but also helped to distribute Korea's exports to other countries. Japan was the source of supply for industrial goods and at the same time the absorber of and a distributor for Korean exports.

The strong dependence for these goods on Japan reflects that Japan is deeply embedded in the Korean production system. Korea created a strong development mechanism through dependence on Japan.

Some Critical Perspectives on the Three Major Approaches

The arguments on the Korean economy from the viewpoint of the neoclassical and the developmental state have generally centred on where to draw a line between the role of market and government. The former has been supported by the neoclassical school and the latter by the developmental state. While the neoclassical school emphasises the importance of the market in the allocation of resources and the need for outward looking strategies, the developmental state theorists stress the Korean government's role in determining the direction of economic policies and then achieve its economic goal. The common factor in both approaches is the importance they place on internal factors, in particular whether or not the government has followed the principle of the market. Therefore, as pointed out by Castley (1997), the two main schools neglected external factors by focusing too much on internal factors (see Table 2.2).

Table 2.2   Different views on developmental factors among three schools

	Neoclassical view	**Developmental state view**	**Dependency view**
Role of market	O	<	<
Role of government	<	O	<
External factor	<	<	O

Note: O indicates a strong support; < indicates less importance or indifference.

On the other hand, during the 1970s, trade dependence on GDP in Korea accounted for just below 80 per cent and now it accounts for approximately 60 per cent of GDP, representing a heavy dependence on trade. It is odd to stress the supply side as the contributory factor for the success story of the Korean economy in the sense that economic development requires a balance between supply and demand. The truth, however, is that the economy is achieved by the interaction between internal and external factors. In general, the role of government as an internal factor can be considered in explaining the Korean economy. However, capital and technology have been introduced mainly from Japan and the Korean economy has been revitalised throughout trade. As an external factor, Japan's role has been crucial in the Korean economy.

Many of those economists who emphasise Korean economic success have a tendency to ignore a long historical process as well as external factors. Especially, growth in Korea has been stimulated and conditioned by a number of international, social, political and cultural factors, all deeply grounded in Korean history. Although the most visible and striking aspects of Korean economic development occurred after 1965, the post-1965 period of rapid and sustained growth can be fully understood only in the context of a long historical process that began after World War II.

The developmental-state view emphasised the role of government as the visible hand at the expense of other factors such as the role of private firms, the structure of international division of labour and favourable international environments. Kim (1998) argues that overemphasis on the role of government has reflected a certain political stance so that it has been capitalised on as a political tool domestically and internationally. Nam (1994) also points out that much of the propaganda in favour of the government' role in economic development was made to persuade Koreans to accept authoritarian power for several decades.

The developmental-state view focuses on the successful aspects of government policy while the less effective aspects are often neglected or treated as less important factors (Moon 1988; Rhee 1994; Green 1994). The notion of the 'strong state' is supported by the development state view but it is difficult to accept as an explanatory variable. State strength and state autonomy are relative as well as situational concepts and Shafer (1990) pointed out that it is too simple to regard a government which is 'strong' today as necessarily strong forever. Government-led policies can change over time and may become weaker in the process of rapid industrialisation. More generally Rhee (1994) pointed out that government policy cannot be accepted as the main or more significant factor affecting economic performance.

In East Asia, the production cycle of the international economy and its timing played a crucial role in achieving Korean economic development (Eckert 1990; Koo 1987; Cummings 1987; Castley 1997). During the 1960s and early 1970s, the world economy was growing significantly. Some countries were investing actively and interest rates were relatively low. There were few trade barriers in the Third World and among these countries, there were few that could compete with Korea. Cummings (1987) maintained that US hegemony after World War Two promoted developmental and authoritarian states in East Asia. Referring to the production cycle, he considered that economic development in Japan, Korea and Taiwan began in the early twentieth century and that it should be regarded as a regional phenomenon, with its own hierarchy of core, and semi-periphery, that was gradually recreated after World War II.

The debate on the role of government in economic development centres on market failure and government failure. However, the two are not necessarily 'opposites': market failure can result from the failure of economic institutions, which can be due to a failure on the part of government. Government regulation and preferential treatments (for example of certain industries) have been major causes of market failure.

Two questions derive from dependency theory: universalisation and appropriateness. 'Universalisation' is about whether dependency theory can be applied to developing countries in general: 'appropriateness' asks if the theory can be applied, in particular, Korean economic development. 'Dependency' itself is an ambiguous concept and it is inappropriate to say that dependency is a cause of underdevelopment.

Since the 1960s, dependency theory has provided a widely-accepted explanation for Korean economic development, in the sense that Korea's success has been achieved partly through dependence on others: for example export markets abroad. However, the appropriateness of the theory to Korea can be questioned in a number of ways. First, Korea's history is very different to that of Latin America: its economic development took off around 300 years later than that of Latin America. Second, the presence of multinationals in Korea is much lower than in Latin America; manufactured goods account for a much higher proportion of Korean exports; and Korea has a much fairer income distribution. Finally, a theory that recognises underdevelopment or stagnation as a consequence of the outflow of surplus value cannot explain Korea's capital accumulation and rapid industrialisation.

It is irrelevant to apply the so-called 'state-led industrialisation through import substitution' model (Fishlow 1990) to the Korean economy. In the initial stage of import substitution, consumer goods are substituted and in second stage, production goods such as machinery and equipment are substituted by domestic production. These stages do not describe the Korean experience. Moreover, the base of manufacturing industry in Latin America (the 'model' for the dependency theory) is weak and agricultural products account for the majority of exports. Accordingly, imports of manufactured goods always surpass exports of agricultural products, so that trade deficit results in current account deficit, leading to the further introduction of foreign capital.

Of course, the Korean 'success' story includes a certain element of dependency but in the Korean case, the interplay of internal and external factors has characterised the process of economic development. Korea can be regarded as the country that broke away from dependency on the core, thus achieving rapid and sustained economic growth and an advanced stage of industrialisation.

In contrast to the import substitution policy of Latin America, Korea adopted an export-led industrialisation policy. Labour-intensive export industries were promoted to obtain foreign capital, create employment and improve income distribution. Throughout the 1980s and the much of 1990s, manufactured goods accounted for 90 per cent of all exports from Korea, compared with less than 2 per cent from agriculture. On the other hand, Korea like Latin America, depended on foreign technology, giving rise to imports of embedded intermediate and capital goods. This is not the result, however, of a dependent economic structure but rather the result of rapid economic progress. Thus, the Korean economy is maintained not only by export-led industrialisation but also by a self-supporting economic structure that grew out of dependence.

According to the dependency theorists, Korea could have experienced underdevelopment because of its reliance on the world trading system. However, per capita GNP increased at an annual average of 8.5 per cent between 1970 and 1997 (*The Economist* 1998), in contrast to the pessimistic predictions of dependency economists.

Korea has not relied upon direct foreign investment as a source of foreign technologies. Korea has borrowed technology but has not encouraged foreign ownership. Together with modern capital goods that Korea has imported in such large quantities has come the know-how to operate them. These goods have been used manufacture exports to advanced countries, especially the US and Japan. Thus, Korea's rapid growth has been achieved by the expansion of trade with the core.

Concluding Comments

The argument on Korean economic development has been contentious. The debates on dependent development have been more popular at home than abroad, while those on government intervention have been more fashionable abroad than at home. There are different views as to whether government intervention in the market process has played a positive role in the phenomenal economic growth of Korea; and whether the notion of dependent development, subordinate to advanced countries, can be applied in the case of Korea.

Radlet and Sacks (1997) argued that there is no need for a special theory to explain economic growth in East Asia. According to them, these countries already had the potential to catch up and trends in the world economy worked in their favour. For example, the Korean economy advanced in overseas markets in the early 1960s when a long-term economic boom in the world economy was at its height. By observing the outstanding growth of Japan, centred on exports, Korea recognised the need to join the world economy through export promotion based on labour-intensive manufacturing industry. At the same time, the growth in demand in advanced countries could absorb the labour-intensive light industrial goods produced by Korea, while capital accumulation in advanced countries enabled Korea to acquire the capital it required.

It could be easy to conclude that the reason for economic success in Korea is because of the 'right' policies, such as export-led industrialisation, were followed, in contrast to Latin American countries, which favoured the 'wrong' policies, notably import substitution industrialisation. But this is to ignore the other factors contributing to economic outcomes. In particular, the interplay between internal and external factors is thought to be crucial in explaining the varying degrees of economic 'success'. So, too, is the role of the various institutions that develop and evolve as a country progresses.

Government and institutions maintain complementary relations and become competitive over time. These relationships can provide a favourable environment for economic growth. For that reason, an understanding is needed of the evolution of key institutions by exploring the interaction over time between internal and external factors. This is the purpose of the following chapters.

Chapter 3

An Evolutionary Analysis of the Economic System

In the previous chapter, critical comments were made on the neoclassical view, the developmental-state view and the dependency view. The former two views see government and market as alternative mechanisms for the allocation of resources, while the latter focuses on the cut-off of an unequal exchange relationship from the core as an alternative way for breaking away from dependency. The neoclassical view expects that most of the incompleteness of the market can be resolved by private institutions (World Bank 1993), whereas the developmental-state view considers government intervention as the solution for market failures (Amsden 1989; Wade 1990). As Aoki, Murdock and Okuno-Fujiwara (1997) argue, these two views see the role of government and that of the market as substitutes, with competing roles in solving market failures. On the other hand, dependency theory explains the imbalanced economic relationship between the core and the periphery. The dependency view regards the international division of labour and economic diffusion as the main factors of underdevelopment. According to this view, outward-looking industrialisation works unfavourably for economic development so that developing countries can suffer from low growth, a low level of industrial structure and economic penetration by multinationals (Frank 1967; Amin 1974; Evans 1979; Lim 1985). For that reason, the dependency view favours inward-looking industrialisation requiring strong government intervention to break away from the dependency relationship brought about by an unequal exchange system. However, all views of economic development focus on how to maximise the effective role of market and government.[1]

---

1   In particular, according to the neoclassical and developmental-state views, government role and market function are alternative mechanisms in solving the negative direction of the allocation of resources. So, there is little fundamental difference between the two views in the sense that government intervention and market failure are substitutes for each other. Kim and Ma (1997) argue that it is hard to draw a clear dividing line between the two since the difference comes from the difference of cognition as to where market failure is pervasive or not. Indeed, most of the Korean scholars and economists have shared similar views to the developmental state view. This view has been particularly emphasised by those who work at the government-sponsored research institutes. Similarly, they do not neglect to stress the fact that Korean economic success has been achieved by the market-based economy. Some Korean scholars have focused much on the dependency view that Korean economic development is attributable to the role of outsiders, especially the US in politics and Japan in market economy. However, what they have neglected is

As noted previously, there is no generally accepted theory to explain the success story of the Korean economy. Each of the theories examined was of some relevance to Korea but none significantly encompasses the special characteristics of the Korean experience.

The most striking feature of Korean economic development is the synergy between internal factors, for example the role of government, and external factors, such as the role of foreign capital and technology. To analyse this, it is proposed to adopt a framework that combines appropriate aspects of all three theories. This chapter explores a middle ground drawing on all three views but with the developmental-state view as the most useful starting point.

Positive and Negative Aspects of Internal and External Factors

Internal Factors[2]

The role of internal factors has been explained by the two main schools of economic development: the neoclassical and the developmental state schools. Both emphasise endogenous growth factors focusing on the importance of a favourable climate for economic enterprise and the role of government while placing less emphasis on external factors such as the roles of foreign capital, multinationals and foreign technology. The neoclassical school stresses the importance of the allocation of resources corresponding to market forces and outward-looking strategies. The developmental state school emphasises the role of government in determining the direction of economic policies by providing the private sector with various incentives (North 1990; Aoki and Dore 1994).

The argument in the two schools on how to draw a line between the role of market and government has over-stressed the importance of internal factors. This is seen in comparing policy aims and policy outcomes, which are often not the same. Rhee (1994) argued that investment adjustment and the allocation of resources by the Korean government have frequently had poor results.[3] Thus, the role of government as a main internal factor can be divided into two: positive

---

that they do not see a dependent position as a progress of development, as emphasised by Watanabe (1982). For more details, see Kim and Ma (1997) and Cho and Yoo (1988).

2   In this study we confine internal factors mainly to the economic field. This study cannot cover all the factors that affect economic development. For the purpose of clear analysis, a classification of the more predominant factors for economic development is needed. Thus, dealing with social factors such as class structure and other less tangible forms of influence such as business culture and working attitudes are beyond the scope of this study. In particular, we place importance on the analysis of the role of government and private institutions, which have comparative advantage vis-à-vis government as internal factors.

3   Planned growth by the Korean government and actual economic performance have been never met through the entire economic development period. Also, in the process of heavy and chemical industrialisation, distorted resource distributions were predominant. Until recently, resources have often been allocated along political rather market lines.

and negative factors. Positive factors help market functions work favourably for economic development whilst negative factors are unfavourable for economic development. However, the definition of positive and negative factors can vary according to place and time. In particular, judgement is inevitably *ex post facto*. For example, no policy maker probably imagines that the policy they adopt will turn out to be negative. At the outset, they hope that policy will solve market imperfections and help to achieve economic progress. But in reality, some policies will have positive outcomes while others may be negative. For example, the active promotion in Korea of heavy and chemical industry (HCI) led to rapid growth in the 1970s but caused an unbalanced economic structure because of distortion in the distribution of resources. The promotion of HCI has been criticised as a cause of the ups and downs of economic performance. However, it is suggested by others that HCI investment in the 1970s contributed significantly to Korea's rapid economic growth in the mid-1980s to mid-1990s.[4]

Economic development cannot be attributed, however, to single policies but rather to a mix of policies that are linked and which have a changing relationship with each other over time. This is different from what most developmental statists argue. For example, Amsden (1989) and others[5] hint at the unchanging role of government yet Kim's (1997) view is that the role of government *must* change in the course of successful economic development. Kim concluded that the Korean government moved from a 'comprehensive' to a 'limited' role that focuses on enabling policy goals to be pursued rather than on planning industrial policy as a whole. The 'comprehensive government' provides integrated economic plans and long-term goals for the economy by focusing on economic development as a principal goal of the state (Mason et al. 1980) and for this, according to Kim, investment in human resources is required. However, as the economy progresses, various institutions, presenting different demands emerge. Thus, as Kim (1997) and Fukagawa (1997) argued, government has to negotiate with these institutions, whereas in the past, the inclination might have been to suppress or, at best, to ignore them. The 'limited' role adopted by government is one that recognises the range of skills needed to secure development and understands that these skills are available in many other institutions besides government itself.

A strong role for government can be justified in most developing countries since markets there do not work properly in effectively allocating resources, according to the developmental state view. Thus, government intervention is needed to mobilise capital and to distribute resources in order to accelerate the rate of growth. In developing countries, economic development is the result of active government intervention. However, government in these circumstances has limited capacity

---

4　Most literature is positive regarding the contribution of HCI policies to recent economic development in Korea. However, the World Bank Report (1993) concluded that the costs of the strong promotion of HCI were much greater than generally known. In fact, economic development in the early 1980s was damaged partly as a result of excess investment in heavy and chemical industries. Many firms in Korea went bankrupt or downsized their business.

5　For more details, see the writings of Johnson (1982) for Japan and Wade (1990) for Taiwan.

to adjust the economy both internally and externally. As Stiglitz (1989) and Lee (1992) explained, there are various bottlenecks which are difficult to overcome in both developing and advanced countries.

In time, private sector institutions emerge in the economy to supplement what government can do and to strengthen the market for goods and services. The neoclassical view is that private sector institutions develop to substitute for market failure or market weakness. Both neoclassical and development-state views see a more zero-sum than a complementary relationship between government and the market yet it is surely important to distinguish between the substitute and the complementary role. The former envisages a trade-off, where an increase in the role of government reduces the role of the market and *vice-versa*. The latter implies a mutual relationship where both government and market are committed to making up for any weak points in the functioning of the market. Successful economic development tends to be determined by a complementary, rather than a substitute role.

In developing countries especially, neither government nor private sector institutions alone can solve important market imperfections (Jwa 1999). Thus, government may have a role in improving the capabilities of the private sector and in encouraging the formation of new private sector institutions. The private sector, in turn, may help government: for example, by attracting foreign capital and technology.

External Factors

The role of external factors is as important as the role of government. External factors too, have both positive and negative aspects.[6] For example, a country with positive internal factors, say, a strong government approach to industrialisation, will not be successful unless external factors also (say, a willingness to import) are working in its favour. In the modern world, no country can stand on its own feet without exposure to others.

The dependency view tends to regard external factors as negative and unfavourable to economic development (dos Santos 1970; Frank 1967). The investment of foreign capital is seen not only to impede long-term, self-sustaining economic growth but also to engender inequality in developing countries. Foreign technology deepens further dependence on the core creating a lopsided economic relationship (Galtung 1971; Amin 1974). In other words, the end of one kind of dependence is seen as the beginning of another.

In general, in developing countries where capital is in short supply, foreign investment supplements local capital in the process of industrialisation. Industrialisation requires a huge amount of capital for investment as well as for infrastructure. Moreover, as Castley (1997) argues, investment is not 'one-shot' expenditure in fixed capital but a continuous process, since initial development needs further investment as industrialisation proceeds.

---

6   This is emphasised by dependency scholars as mentioned in the previous chapter.

Like the role of government and other internal factors, the role of external factors is complex and changes over time. Some factors are more significant than others; some are important at one stage and less important at others; and some are so important that they determine the direction and pace of development.

In the case of Korea, a unique external factor in economic development is Japan. Castley (1997, 1998) argues that economic growth in Korea has been caused not primarily by the government but by foreign interests, particularly those arising from the restructuring of Japanese industry. He argues that Japanese multinationals played an important role in investing in Korea during the period of rapid economic development in the 1960s and 1970s and even into the 1980s. However, the relationship between Japan and Korea is not static and as this thesis will show, Japan's role in Korean economic development has gradually changed from a vertical to horizontal relationship as the Korean economy progressed. These developments and changes over time, however, were not achieved independently: in fact, the story of Korea's economic development shows clearly the inter-relationships within and between internal and external factors.

The Interplay of Internal and External Factors

As noted already, the explanation of Korean economic development has been dominated by three major perspectives. The neoclassical and the developmental state scholars have focused on the role of the market and government, while the dependency scholars have emphasised outside influences. In a word, the former two have focused on internal factors, the supply-side of the economy and the latter on external factors, the demand-side of the economy. However, as Castley (1997) argued, economic development in a country cannot be attained either by external or by internal factors alone. Every textbook of economics explains that economic development can be attained only by balancing supply and demand. Indeed improved productivity, raised quality and well-developed enterprises will be to no avail if there is not sufficient demand for goods from overseas markets. Internal factors are neither a sufficient condition for economic development in general nor, in particular, for a country with a small domestic market. Similarly, external factors such as capital and technology will not move in or, if they do, will not be effective unless the receiving country is ready for, or can adapt to them.[7] As pointed out by Enos and Park (1988), it is essential that a developing country should have a basic level of indigenous technological capability in order to absorb imported technologies. Unlike the period when the economies of today's advanced countries began to take off, it is not possible now for underdeveloped countries to develop independently. There must be contract and trade with other countries, especially advanced countries. Interaction between internal and external factors is essential.

Clearly, economic development brought about by the interplay of both internal and external factors is not a simple process caused either by internal or external factors but by the synergy between them. However, the combination

---

7   This is explained by aid programme to the Third World. It can hardly be said that the aid programmes to the Third World turned out to have positive results.

of internal and external factors alone may fail to create a positive direction for economic development. As dependency economists have argued, the combination of negative factors in internal and external factors may cause the so-called 'development of underdevelopment'.

A positive linkage between internal and external factors can create a new pattern of development while a negative linkage can engender the development of underdevelopment. Industrialisation is not determined by external factors only.[8]

The process of industrialisation, leading to economic development, is illustrated diagrammatically in Figure 3.1.

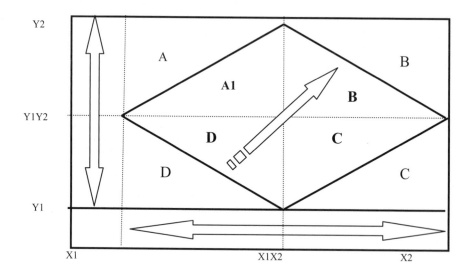

Figure 3.1   Possible economic development path in the process of the interaction between internal and external factors

Note: The diamond represents the possible area for economic development; X1 and Y1 represent negative factors between external and internal factors, whilst X2 and Y2 refer to positive factors between external and internal factors, respectively.

Development takes place when both internal and external factors tend towards the positive, as shown by the diamond shape A1, B1, C1 and D1. Where one set of factors is highly positive (for example external factors in C) while the other is negative, development will be limited. The optimum area for development is in the triangle B1, where both internal and external factors are positive and interacting together in a complementary way.

---

8   For more details, see Castley (1997).

Towards a Formation of the Economic System

This section explains the process by which looking first at internal factors it has been noted already that there are limits to the role of government in overcoming market imperfections as well as failures by government itself. In response, government policy focuses on improving the role of private-sector institutions by providing various incentives. Government does not regard itself as the only player in solving market failures (Amsden 1989; North 1990; Lee 1992; Aoki 1995; Okuno 1996; Aoki et al. 1997; Jwa 1999). Accordingly, various institutions emerge as a result. Complementary relationships are formed and can be successful both in solving market imperfections and government failures; and in fuelling rapid industrialisation. Cho (1997) describes this mechanism as the government's 'risk partnership' with private institutions, i.e., big firms. Under poor capital market environments, banks were controlled by the government and this led to a close relationship between the government, banks and chaebol. According to Cho (1994) and others,[9] the risk partnership in Korea allowed the credit-based economy to become highly leveraged chaebol that not only explore risky investment opportunities but also expand their businesses without the danger of major financial crisis. The risk partnership does not always create positive results but in the case of Korea's rapid and sustained economic development, as Cho (1997), and Cho and Kim (1997) point out, this risk partnership has created quite an effective development strategy. At best, complementary relationships have helped to create prosperity and at worst, the cost of any government failure has been borne partly by government and not all transferred to the private sector.

Aoki and Okuno[10] give a convincing explanation of the evolutionary process between government and private institutions contributing to economic development in a country (1995, 1996, 1997). From a macroeconomic viewpoint, economic capabilities in a country can be attained by internal factors, i.e., the role of government and private institutions. The neoclassical view in a market economy regards government intervention as indirect because it is implemented through taxes and subsidies, and as Balassa (1981) argued, through arm's length regulations. The cost of policy implementation in this view is to collect taxes on appropriate activities by making sure that subsidies are used for pre-planned activities (Lee 1992). This sets the parameters of the market. However, if policy implementation is transacted between government and big private firms, as argued

---

9   For more details, see Y.-J. Cho (1997) and Cho and Kim (1997).

10   Comparative institutional analysis first appeared in 1990. In the late 1990s, Masahiko Aoki, a professor of economics at Stanford University opened a new programme, a course on 'comparative institutional analysis; it presented a new analytical framework based on the experience of economic development in Japan. It is not, therefore, a universally applicable model, not even widely accepted in economic circles, since Japanese economic development is regarded by many as unique—the nature of a different process of industrialisation from that of western countries. But an analysis of interaction which reflects the complexity of various economic systems is needed since the analysis of the western market system has shown its limits, particularly in the age of competition. See also North (1990).

by Lee (1992), they do not have to rely solely on changes in market parameters and this reduces the cost of implementation. As Aoki, Murdock and Okuno-Fujiwara (1997) pointed out, private-sector institutions have important advantages compared with government, in particular in their ability to provide appropriate incentives and to process locally available information. In fact, a direct and continuous relationship between the government and big private firms enables them to share information so that they can face unforeseen contingencies. Thus, with various incentives and better information the government can see if private firms implement its policies effectively or not.

On the other hand, as argued by some neoclassical scholars, private-sector institutions do not solve all important market imperfections and this is particularly true for economies in less developed countries where the capabilities of the private sector are limited. The role of government here is to facilitate the development of private-sector institutions that can overcome market failures and government is not regarded as the only player (Aoki et al. 1997). As Lee (1992) pointed out, the government is an influential factor working in favour of the political economy of its institutions. North (1990) argues that the evolution of institutions brings about a favourable environment for cooperative solutions, thus promoting economic growth. Thus, in an economic system there is a complementarity that develops the economic system over time, brought about by interactions between government and various institutions.

As Fukagawa (1997) argued, in contrast to Amsden's bipolar (government-chaebol) model (1989), the Aoki-Okuno model[11] is about to adopt other independent variables influencing economic development. Yet, Amsden's bipolar model explaining the course of Korean economic development is significant because it goes beyond the viewpoint of a zero-sum relationship between government and market. It shows that economic development can be attained through a 'positive sum game' between government and private institutions. As Amsden (1989) argued, government intervention in Korea was not necessarily antithetical to market function. Rather, she showed in her explanation of the Korean economy, that government, quite contrary to the neoclassical view, is able to accelerate market function through artificial distortion of the price mechanism, the so called 'get the price wrong' policy.

However, Amsden overlooked changing economic environments. As North (1990) argued, institutional change reflects the way that societies evolve through time. It is important not to forget the argument that the effectiveness of government intervention depends on the stage of industrialisation (Cho 1994, 1997; Whang 1997). Although Amsden's model made the major contribution to understanding the experiences of economic development in Korea, it does not encompass sufficiently the evolution of each institution and thus there are many points to be explored, debated or challenged. According to Amsden (1989), the key players were government and chaebol. Other institutions were seen as subservient to and restrained by the government. This view was supported by Rhee (1994)

---

11 For more details, see Aoki (1995, 1992; Aoki and Dore (1995); Aoki and Okuno (1996); Okuno-Fujiwara (1997).

who said that government indicates and the private sector follows. This may be possible if the size of the economy is within the range that government is able to control. However, a top-down approach can seldom explain the process of capital accumulation, while the analysis of policy shows that policies do not necessarily bring about intended or even positive results. As note already, Kim (1997) pointed out that economic development leads to and requires a change in the role of government, whereas Amsden (1989) can be criticised for not dealing adequately with changes in the relative roles of government and emerging institutions.

This is an important criticism, since it is argued here that an economic system is internally formed by the relationship between government and private-sector institutions and that they interact to overcome various market imperfections.

For example, government promotes industrialisation not only by establishing a sounder, more stable economic environment but also by providing various incentives, and private firms operate within the framework set by government, after implementing government instructions. However, government and private firms need support from external factors. As Castley (1997) reminds us, the task for industrialisation is too big for government and private firms alone. In order to solve internal problems, parts, intermediates, capital goods and technology are imported. In general, imports of capital goods bring about imports of advanced technology since technology is embedded in capital goods. Moreover, capital goods give rise to the creation of a production system in a country and intermediate goods are essential for the production system to work. With a limited domestic market, external trade plays an important role in industrial growth. As Sano (1997) pointed out, an expansion in the size of the market can be attained by exports, which enable firms not only to adopt new technological processes but also to finance the requisite imports of capital goods and purchase of technology. Castley (1997; 1998) emphasised the role of external factors by arguing that developing countries desperately need substantial assistance from advanced countries in order to overcome various bottlenecks, which are beyond their capability. Although his argument is inclined to the roles played by external factors, it is in part true that the process of industrialisation in developing countries requires substantial external assistance.

The Economic System[12]

The economic system develops through a process of institutional evolution, influenced by external factors. The term 'institution' refers to an economic agent

---

12 The economic system I argue in this study is different from the system explained by others, including North and Aoki. In this study, the economic system has been shaped by the interaction of internal and external factors dealing with both micro and macro-economic matters. However, the economic system explained by others is mainly focused on internal factors and thus, deals with the microeconomic level. Also, this microeconomic approach is closely related to firm-specific analysis and there is little room to embrace interchangeable roles of internal and external factors shaping certain pattern of economic system.

within a country such as the government, business and finance.[13] An institution may function as a tool that not only participates in market activity; regulates economic behaviour of individual agents and organisations; and enforces formal rule and informal constraint (conventions and code of behaviour).[14] External factors may consist of hardware such as foreign capital, multinationals, foreign technology, trade network and business strategies, and software such as business practice. Over time, these external factors have been steadily embedded into the institutions and in this process, a unique economic system which is geared to the environment in an economy, is created. The role of government is important in influencing the economy but it is not the only factor that determines the economy's direction.

Stiglitz (1989) pointed out that capital markets, even in developed countries do not operate fully since government failure and market malfunction such as the problems of adverse selection and moral hazard exist. These phenomena prevail in developing countries in particular. Accordingly, government needs partners and new players emerge in an economy in response to market mechanisms. Government and new institutional entrants first play as a partnership although their aims are not usually the same. Lee (1992) argued that the intent of government is to affect the decision-making of private firms so that the government's goals are more likely to be attained. Conversely, the intent of the private firms is to maximise profits, reduce risks, and maintain stable growth. Thus, it is argued here, in contrast to the neoclassical view, that institutions are created and evolve towards a certain pattern of the economic system.[15]

---

13 Lee shows how the government-business relationship in Korea contributed to Korea's economic development. He sees the relationship between government and business as hierarchical, but not considering the changing institutional structure between the two. See Lee (1992), Amsden (1989) and Wade (1990).

14 For a distinction made between institutions and organisations, see North (1999).

15 One of the principal reasons for regarding economic institution as a constant exogenous factor is that the neoclassical school assumes a perfect competitive market without transaction costs. Transaction costs refers to all kinds of costs in operating an economic system and they are a comprehensive concept relating to all kinds of business transactions such as negotiation, monitoring, adjustment and enforcement and so on. Unlike the assumption of the neoclassical school, indeed, transaction costs are not free goods and exist between individual agents asymmetrically. They are normal phenomena that occur under imperfect information. In addition, for the neoclassical school the analysis of economic system is out of its scope because of the assumption of zero transaction costs. On the other hand, the neo-institutional school ignores the assumptions of the neoclassical school: (1) assumption of perfect competitive market (provision of perfect information and no transaction costs); (2) assumption of economic system as a constant exogenous factor. The neo-institutional school assumes that economic institution as well as economic system is determined endogenously so that they analyse how an economic system in an economy is created, determined, and evolves. In such analysis, individual agents and organisations play a critical role in changing economic institutions. In this regard, as North (1990) and Eggertsson (1990) argued, the right of ownership is a key to the understanding of economic activity and performance. For example, if there was no rule for the right of ownership, physical power only would decide economic resources so

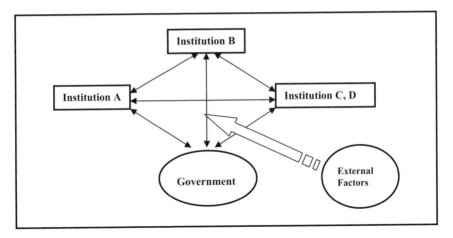

Figure 3.2 Evolutionary relationship between each institution and external factors in the economic system

Figure 3.2 illustrates a formation of the economic system through an evolutionary relationship between a growing number of institutions and external factors. In order to solve problems such as the shortage of capital and technology, government and institution A build a working relationship as strategic partner. Government may provide institution A with incentives to promote the goals of government and both work together as long as mutual benefits are maintained. Institution A can enjoy the benefit of its strategic complementarity that maximises its profits, as long as the institution satisfies the intent of the government.

As the economy develops, other institutions (B and, later, C and D) emerge as further partners, gradually strengthening the economic system and contributing to economic development. Throughout the process, as Figure 3.2 shows, external factors continue to impinge on and interact with the whole system. The way this process in reality in Korea is presented in the following chapters.

---

that transaction costs would be unlimited resulting in the deterioration of the efficient allocation resources. In other words, the higher transaction costs in an economy, the lower economic performance in the country. Accordingly, the sound establishment of the right of ownership provides not only minimum transaction costs but also optimal allocation of resource. In a word, the core of the neo-institutinal schools is to explore the causal relation between the right of ownership and economic development and moreover, to analyse how the right of ownership evolves. Although the neo-institutionalists analyse a process of how an economic system in a country has been formed through time but they clearly tend to neglect a process of how external factors has affected the formation of the economic system in the country. Thus, this study focuses on how the economic system has been formed and evolves by analysing the interplay of internal and external factors in the course of economic development.

Chapter 4

The Korean Economic System

The positive and negative influences of both internal and external factors in shaping the economy of a country have been discussed in earlier chapters and the importance of the interaction between internal and external factors has also been examined. This model of economic development is used in this chapter as basis for the consideration of the formation and development of the Korean economy.

In the first section, the key influences on the Korean economy are outlined. Then the origins and development of the system are presented, and the modern workings of the system are discussed in the final section.

Key Influences on the Economic System of Korea

In 1961, the Korean government's first five-year economic development plan identified two key objectives. First, to attain rapid and sustained economic growth, and second, to develop a self-reliant economy. These objectives, followed in successive five-year plans, have been successful. The Korean economic system was first innovated by the Japanese colonial policy.

Economic growth was achieved largely through internal influences on the economy. The chaebol underpinned rapid economic growth, and a government-led industrialisation policy encouraged political and economic alliance.

Self-reliance of the economy has been attained mainly through the influence of external factors, in particular the influence of the Japanese economic model. Following reconstruction in the 1950s, the development of the Korean economy has continued to emulate the economy of Japan (Amsden 1989; Watanabe 1990; Kuznet 1994). The Korean government adopted not only the Japanese manufacturing-based industrial policy, but also the capitalist economic policy. As the Korean economy has developed, external factors have become deeply embedded in its institutions and these in turn have become integrated into the economic system. For Korea, Japan has continued to be an important source of capital and technology, and also one of the most significant trade partners.

The internal and external factors can each be described in isolation, but it is the interaction between all of these influences that has shaped the Korean economy. The connection between different aspects of the model are illustrated by the interaction between the government and the chaebol which, with the development of the economy, has shifted over time from a complementary to competitive relationship. The strategic dependence of chaebol on Japanese goods and technology illustrates the interplay between internal and external factors, and the more recent emergence of a third internal influence on the economy, the financial institutions, reflects the continuing interaction of these factors in the development of Korea's economy.

The Origins of the Modern Korean Economy

The economic policy enforced on Korea during the Japanese colonial period (1910–1945) was one of the most significant influences in the early development of the contemporary Korean economy and provided a foundation for the rapid growth in the economy since the early 1960s (Mizoguchi 1979; Kohli 1994; McNamara 1990; Eckert; 1990; Suh 1978).[1] Although Korean culture and identity were crushed during the colonisation by Japan, there was significant development of industry and investment in infrastructure during this period.

The relevance of the economic policies of Japanese to the modern Korean economy are debated (Amsden 1989; Jones and Sakong 1980; Kim 1997). Although it has been suggested that the influence of Japanese policies became negligible during the political and socio-economic instability in Korea from 1945 to the early 1960s, the government that was formed in 1961 under Park Chung-Hee implemented economic policies that were strongly influenced by the policies of Japan.

Japanese Colonial Economic Policy: The Strong State

During the Meiji era (1868–1912) in Japan, the Meiji government focused on developing specific key industries that were managed by family-owned conglomerates called zaibatsu. Industrial development was encouraged through

---

1   Most Korean scholars have a negative view on Japan's influence on Korean economic development during the Japanese colonial period (1910–1945). They mainly focus more on the period of hash rule in which Korean culture and Korean identity were crushed and less on the growth of productive capacity and investments in infrastructure that occurred during the colonial years. Some go further to argue that Japan has worked to distort a natural course of the Korean economic development that was already underway in the turn of the 20th century. According to Eckert (1990), such a biased view is deeply tinted with nationalist feeling and laden with presuppositions about the nature of economic development. In fact, most official scholars and economists in Korea have tried to ignore or place less weight on the influence of colonial heritage in terms of the economy for the purpose of informing other countries of the people's excellency when Korea was regarded as a successful economic model for developing countries by the World Bank. In particular, from time to time, overemphasis on self-reliant economic development by the government has been capitalised on as a political propaganda in both domestic and abroad. In contrast, foreign scholars tend to show a more balanced view on the Japanese colonial period, even though they are in accord with the Korean scholars on the character of colonial rule. The foreign scholars mainly emphasise industrial structure laid during the period would contribute to shape a modern Korea after liberation.

government subsidies, tax incentives and government managed distribution of products. Funding for development was provided through increased taxes on agriculture and business taxes. The Meiji also actively sought capital and technology from western countries to support industrialisation.

The strong commitment of the government to the planning and facilitation of zaibatsu enabled rapid industrial growth in Japan. As Japanese colonial influence extended into Korea, the government-zaibatsu[2] coalition was well developed, and the economic system developed in the Meiji era was implemented in Korea.

The system established government-led economic strategies that not only mobilised resources, but also provided knowledge and leadership for business development. On the strength of its growing experience, Japan enforced the zaibatsu system even more vigorously in Korea than it had in Japan. As the Korean economy grew and infrastructure was established, Japan responded by making further investments (Chung 1973) in areas such as health and education.

Development Dependent on the Japanese Economy

During the colonial period, Japan orientated the Korean economy to meet the requirements of its own economy. The economic strategies employed were formulated to provide Japan with an enclave export sector and the industries developed were tailored to the needs of Japan. Korea was established as a market for Japanese products and capital investment, and also a supplier to Japan of food and raw materials.

Substantial investment in infrastructure such as railways, roads, communications, electricity, harbours and irrigation was made in Korea to facilitate an export-oriented economy and productive capacity grew considerably during this time. In addition, many Koreans in both Korea and Japan were exposed to modern technology and organisation and learnt new production and management techniques, leading to institutional change.

By the end of the colonial period in 1945, the trade link between Korea and Japan was firmly established and the Korean economy was intrinsically dependent on the economy of Japan. This was to be of great importance in shaping the later evolution of the Korean economy.

---

2   The government-zaibatsu system not only played a crucial role in accelerating Japan's industrialisation but also contributed to establishing its wartime structure. Zaibatsu remained until they were dissolved by the US Occupation. In particular, chaebol in Korea are similar to zaibatsu. The meaning of the Chinese character in both zaibatsu and chaebol are exactly the same. It seems that chaebol in the Korean language comes from zaibatsu in Japanese, given the strong influences were left by Japanese during the colonial period. In fact, from the early 1930s, the use of the Korean language had been forbidden and Japanese was enforced as the official language.

Characteristics of Economic Development in the Korean Economic System

Growth-Oriented Development Strategy

The government in 1961 recognised the importance of its role in the initial stage
of economic development. In particular, Korea's knowledge of and proximity to
Japan, the historical relationship between the two countries and the spectacular
Japanese economic performance since the mid-1950s strongly influenced the
Korean political and economic leadership in formulating Korea's growth
strategies.[3] With low incomes and a small domestic market, it was essential for
Korea to adopt an outward-looking policy rather than a domestic-oriented policy.
The policy was implemented by chaebol, who were given great privileges by the
government. The privileged position of chaebol remains to the present-day as
does the outward-looking strategy based on 'growth first, redistribution later'.

Export-led growth strategy
Growth through exports needed high quality products and competitive prices.
In the early years, although labour was cheap, the quality of exports could not
be guaranteed. An export-led industrialisation policy was adopted with various
incentives to boost the growth of exports. This remained in force until recently,
although inevitably it heightened Korea's dependence on foreign raw materials,
intermediate and capital goods.

Chaebol-centred growth strategy
Big businesses was seen by government to be in a better position than small firms
is the efficient use of resources and in strengthening competitiveness through
economies of scale. Thus, the government encouraged the big businesses, which
became the chaebol, to invest in strategic industries.

Growth through Dependence

Japan that influenced Korea in the past has remained a model of economic
development for Korea, in particular as Japan began to re-emerge as an
international economic powerhouse after the mid-1950s. Since then, Japan has
had a leading role in the world economy.

---

3   During the Park period (1961–1979), Japan was a model for Korean economic
development. Economic development planning in the Park regime was quite similar to that
of the Meiji period in Japan. Leading entrepreneurs and bureaucrats including President
Park were educated in Japan and disciplined under the Japanese colonial education system.
Park himself graduated from the Japanese military academy (1940–1942) and served in
the army of Manchuria as a Japanese military officer under the Japanese name of Takaki
Masao. Indeed, Park believed that Japanese economic development model in Meiji Japan
was the best for Korean economic development. Industrial policy in the Park regime was
similar to that of Japan such as the allocation of bank credit, the protection of domestic
market, and entry barriers to foreign companies in specific industries.

Table 4.1   **The influence of Japan on the Korean economy in the twentieth century**

Major Japanese economic policies	Influences on Korea (Yes/No)
The policy of economic growth first, redistribution later was a priority and various incentives were given to attain this goal.	Yes
Government worked cooperatively with the business community through an indicative planning process.	Yes
Government intervened in the economy to a greater extent than in most Western countries and this was done at both the macro and micro levels.	Yes
There is large business group, called zaibatsu and later keiretsu driving economic development.	Yes
Foreign technology played a crucial role in the structural change of the economy.	Yes
Package of lifetime employment and seniority wages is maintained.	Yes
Long-term economic programmes for a self-reliant economy were maintained	Yes

Table 4.1 summarises some of the main influences of Japanese economic policy on the economic policy of Korea. During the colonial period, the Japanese government intervened actively in Korea by using strong bureaucrats who planned economic and industrial policy in a top-down way. As a result, a development structure of government plans and big business implementation was created. In addition, as the result of the Japanese export enclave policy during the colonial period, Korea's industrial structure was formed in a similar way to that of Japan. Following Japan's experience during the high growth period of the 1950s to the 1970s, Korea adopted a growth-oriented strategy attracting foreign direct investment and technology. In this process, changes in Japanese investment and technology transfer were particularly crucial and have been gradually incorporated into the Korean economy.

In general, the GNP of a small country pursuing high economic growth is highly dependent on trade. Korea had no comparative advantage in primary goods, and a fragile industrial structure resulting from the damaged social infrastructure after the Korean War of the early 1950s. With a weak and not self-sufficient economy, Korea followed a transitional development pattern that imported parts and capital goods and then exported final goods by assembling and processing the goods that had been imported. Under this pattern, the expansion of exports leads to an increase in imports. In other words, exports need imports to achieve further exports while imports need exports to raise funds for further imports.

Technological progress is essential for the upgrading of the economic structure in a country. Imports of capital goods bring imports of advanced technology since the advanced technology is embedded in the goods and in turn, this promotes productivity. High productivity makes import substitution possible and strengthens export competitiveness in exports. This was what happened in Korea. Korea introduced capital goods and technology and maintained a high degree of trade dependence on Japan. In this process, contrary to the dependency view, Korea created a unique development mechanism, growth through dependence on Japan.

The Korean Economic System in Action

The key relationship in the development of the Korean economic system is that of government and chaebol. This can be seen in Figure 4.1 which represents diagrammatically the Korean economic system.[4] As pointed out by Amsden (1989), the Korean government established successive institutions in order to supplement development strategies, and launched regular economic development plans. As a strategy to consolidate complementarity, the government intervened deeply in private business activity and restricted the role of third parties in promoting targeted industries, except for those in a government-chaebol relationship. Throughout the entire economic development period, the choice of chaebol as strategic partners was efficient in achieving developmental goals.

As Sano (1977) pointed out, capital is the most powerful resource in persuading firms to cooperate with government policies. In Korea, all private banks were nationalised and some specialised banks were established in order to allocate financial resources for certain purposes. They were under the control of the government and used as a carrot and stick, for example, in persuading chaebol to fall in line with government policies; and in punishing (if necessary) those that refused to follow policy, by threatening a withdrawal of policy loans. All banks acted as agents of the government, in allocating and rationing credit in accordance with government guidelines. Thus, banks had little autonomy to influence chaebol's activities and this continued until the advent of financial liberalisation in the early 1980s.

The government controlled commercial loans at first by dominating financial institutions and later controlled financial quotas with artificially low-interest rates, imported technology embedded in production equipment, and the licensing of various technologies. In general, production costs per unit are lower when a smaller number of producers can benefit from the economies of scale that derive from volume production. Without doubt, the government restricted chaebol's entrance in each strategic industry in order to attain its targeted goals.

Funds and materials were allocated by providing various incentives across industries after careful coordination with the EPB (Economic Planning Board), the BOK (the Bank of Korea) and major manufacturing industries, which were mainly led by chaebol. At the same time, as shown by Lee (1992), government forced M&A (Merger and Acquisition) of private firms to maximise economies of

---

4   For the relationships between government and chaebol, see Johns and Sakong (1980), Johnson (1985), Amsden (1989), Lee (1992), Fukagawa (1997) and Kim (1997).

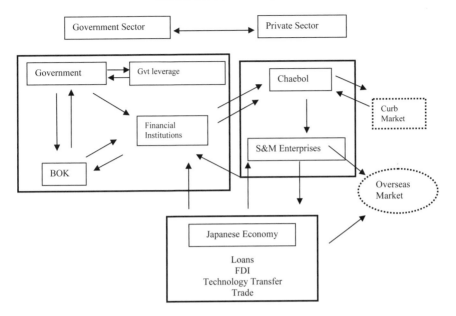

Figure 4.1   The Korean economic system

scale; provided various forms of assistance; and applied administrative guidance in order to achieve maximum intended resource allocations.[5]

Fukagawa (1997) pointed out that government strategy was basically to minimise risks for RandD by making chaebol rely on technology embedded in production equipment and to stimulate chaebol's investment by offering financial credit.[6] Chaebol's businesses were expanded by financial credit, which reduced the risk of bankruptcies and created windfall capital gains by turning the credit into the curb market. Even if a chaebol was to get into difficulty with new businesses, and faced having to dismiss workers, the responsibility would fall to the government. In such circumstances, the government could not help but extend assistance to relieve those firms that were caught in dire situations, since the government was afraid of unemployment and the social and political unrest it might cause. In fact, the government employed various measures to avoid the occurrence of such risks. Often, the government maintained its power by creating permanent jobs, thus minimising the risk of complaints from the labour force. Under the complementary relationship between government and chaebol, further assistance to chaebol was given, and in response, chaebol continued to expand their businesses in order to create jobs.

The government not only controlled domestic prices by direct negotiation with chaebol but also influenced chaebol through strict adjustment of exchange rates, by using financial institutions which were under the government's hand (Yoo and

---

5   See also Amsden (1989) and Johnson (1987).
6   See also Kang (1996), Whang (1997), and Lee (1999).

Lee 1997). In addition, the government intervened in the labour market directly so that chaebol could expand the scale of production with little labour movement and rapid wage increases (Deyo 1987).[7] In the course of economic development, labour was suppressed: wages were kept low and workers rights were severely limited in order to maintain a competitive price mechanism favourable to the chaebol (Kim 1997; Bae 1987). All these measures enabled the government to avoid the pressure of unemployment.

Chaebol expanded and diversified their businesses. Government urged chaebol to attain agreed development goals as quickly as possible, and forced them to achieve outstanding performance, in exchange for government subsidies and other licences in lucrative sectors. In addition, as pointed out by Watanabe (1986), with the launching of export-promotion policy, the government needed to promote more competitive goods for exporting in international markets.[8] There was little support for small and medium-sized firms, so that chaebol depended on the import of overseas industrial goods, mainly from Japan. Accordingly, the SME sector in Korea remains relatively underdeveloped, even today. Indeed, for small and medium sized firms, it is optimal strategy not to expand businesses beyond a critical scale since there is a risk of M&A by chaebol if they expand their business too far.

The Park government that took over power from the military in 1961 had no connections with the previous regime and this enabled a shift from import-substitution policy to export-promotion policy with little resistance from vested interests. The introduction of Letters of Credit (L/C)[9] to stimulate exports encouraged the emergence of new entrepreneurs, and learning from the Japanese economy was one of the major conditions for a business's success (Taniura 1989).

By the 1970s the leading sector for industrialisation was shifting from labour-intensive to capital-intensive industry and in this process, as Yoo and Lee (1997) explain, the curb market supplemented support of outward-looking industrialisation. The government intentionally adopted a low-interest rate policy and thus inflation was allowed. In this process, the allocation of resources for foreign loans was substantial. Cho (1997) argues that the resource allocation lowered the risk of uncertainties in overseas business and enabled chaebol's big investment projects to shoot up one after another. However, small and medium sized firms that were excluded by the government from the allocation of foreign loans by the government and had problems in approaching the organised financial

----

7   See also Bae (1987) and for the change of business-labour relationship in the 1990s see Nam and Kim (1997).

8   See also Watanabe and Kim (1997).

9   Between the early 1960s and the mid-1980s, a Letter of Credit was the most important export promotion policy. With this letter, exporters could borrow from any bank as much the L/C indicated. A L/C, which they contracted with an importer, enabled them to finance up to 90 per cent of the total amount of exports. The L/C gave entrepreneurs a crucial opportunity that allowed them to expand their businesses and to set up new projects. The L/C itself was a goose that lays a golden egg.

market were a major customer of the curb market, that carried high interest rates.[10]

The existence of a complementary financial system between organised and curb markets enabled the government and chaebol to invest in heavy and chemical industries from the beginning. Chaebol introduced modern equipment and expanded production levels by acquiring foreign loans and financial privilege from the government.[11] This caused business growth and led to the expansion of the curb market.

As the economy grew, the concentration of the economic strength of chaebol began to influence substantially the entire industrial sector from the late 1970s.[12] In the boom period, the government used industrial policy to restrict the growth of chaebol. However, economic policies oscillated between stabilisation of chaebol (i.e., regulation), which was unfavourable to them and growth (special financial assistance), which worked in their favour.

Outward-looking industrialisation has been inseparable from foreign trade. However, capital was always in short supply. Domestic savings were limited since, as argued by Sano (1977), the traditional agriculture sector cannot produce a sufficient surplus to underpin industrialisation. By inviting foreign firms, mainly Japanese firms to invest, the Korean partners, mainly chaebol, not only economised on their initial investment but also were freed relatively from interest payments. In addition, as Kang (1996) argued, the Korean government made it difficult for foreign investors to withdraw their businesses as the amount of investment by foreign partners was specified in law. Management and production technologies were transferred.

---

10 For arguments on unfair competition between chaebol and small and medium companies, see Hong (1998).

11 For more details, see Taniura (1989), Hattori (1988), Cho (1994), Cho (1990; 1997) and Kim (1999). For the period since the late 1980s see Rhu (1997).

12 There has been much written on the chaebol's role in economic development. For the arguments on the negative roles of chaebol, see Park (1997), Hong (1997, 1998), Kim (1999), Choi (1999) and Chang (1999); on the positive roles, see Kang (1996), Kong (1993, 1995), Hattori (1989, 1997) and Jwa (1999); and for general roles, see Cho (1991, 1995, 1997) and Lee (1999).

PART 2

Chapter 5

The State and the Chaebol

This chapter analyses the government-business relationship by focusing on the two main institutions which have played a crucial role in the process of Korea's economic development: the state and the chaebol. These two institutions led and shaped Korea's economy in the course of economic development. In particular, during the 1960s and 1970s, as many developmental statists pointed out, the government played a central role in driving the economy towards the correct direction by enlisting the chaebol's support with various financial incentives. At the same time, the chaebol have been the leading actors in bringing about rapid and sustained economic development and the centrepiece of development strategies. They have gradually played a significant role through time as the implementers of the government's industrial policies and as entrepreneurs who maximised various market incentives.

However, as the Korean economy progressed, the relationship between the government and the chaebol has reflected the changing economic environment. They have moved from a symbiotic to a competitive relationship based on complementarity. This chapter examines the changing relationship between government and the chaebol and the role of the chaebol in the growth of the Korean economy.

State and Industrial Organisation

Evolution of the State in Korea: From Authoritarian Government to Developmental Government[1]

An authoritarian government controls the whole economy and restricts freedom and open criticism of government policy and public affairs. For economic

---

1   Market-based orientation of government is typical in advanced countries. Market-based government is fundamentally different from authoritarian and developmental government. The relations between government and businesses move towards a principle of laissez-faire (Balassa 1983). The neoclassical economists argue that the market and businesses work effectively without active government intervention so that the role of government is limited to supplying public goods and social infrastructure. Furthermore, active government intervention gives rise to negative impact on the efficiency and productivity of the market and thus, it is nothing but to improve various laws and regulations in such a way to meet the realistic market circumstances. Policies aimed at regulating and controlling businesses are developed to intervene in the market only to

development, this type of government exerts strong bargaining power, which forces its preferred policies on the private sector with carrot and stick. The strength of the government, according to Okuno-Fujiwara (1997), stems from the relative bargaining power of the government vis-à-vis the private sector. However, as Kim (1997) pointed out, it is difficult to change this strength in a just and peaceful manner, unless society becomes more mature as a result of economic development (Jung 1998). In other words, social maturity through time caused by economic development may reduce the strength of government. Kim (1997) supports a shift of power in government by arguing that a change of economic environment forces a change in the government's status.

A developmental government, on the other hand, gives priority to economic development as the primary goal of the nation and induces capital to invest in the promising industries selected by the government, as well as in human resources, in order to attain economic development. Basically, such a government does not have confidence in the workings of the market believing that the market knows better than government. Government provides short-term and long-term goals as part of an integrated economic development plan, by making decisions about what, when and how much to produce. As argued by Mason et al. (1980), government also provides capital for investment through domestic and foreign capital loans, capital assistance for R&D, and technology and technological assistance through national and regional research facilities.[2] The government acts as a mediator with multinational corporations for foreign direct investment and technology transfers, establishes trade offices for expertise on exports and imports, provides tax holidays and tariff exemptions, and loosens regulations (Jones and Sakong 1980; Krueger 1994).

Under developmental policies, government provides incentives for businesses to attract capital for government-selected industries. In particular, government is capable of leading those businessmen who are reluctant to invest in the selected industries because of high transaction costs, even if the goals of businessmen are not always in accord with those of government. Both, however, eager for the economy to flourish and to create prosperity. Accordingly, the relationship generated between government and businesses is often a cooperative one.

In practice, there is little to distinguish between the authoritarian and the developmental state in the sense that the long-term aims of both are similar. A government which is both authoritarian and developmental in its approach will

---

prevent market malfunctions (Corbo 1992). These policies tend to put government in an antagonistic relationship with businesses, as the former tries to monitor and control the latter, while the latter are trying to attain their goal of profit maximisation (Beardshow 1998). Indeed, the goals of government and businesses are different, and quite often this difference provides the seeds of conflict and tension in government-business relations.

In fact, a relative laissez-faire government was to a limited extent established in Korea in 1948 by the Rhee government. However, it was not sustained for long and in the late 1950s it disappeared when the Rhee regime began to show signs of authoritarian governance toward the end of his term, in order to establish a prolonged one-man rule.

2   See also Jones and Sakong (1980).

seek to intervene in the market and to control the private sector by carrot and stick. Often, as argued by the developmental statists, underdevelopment of the private sector and a poorly functioning market can provide the justification for an 'authoritarian developmental' government.

Mizoguchi (1979) pointed out that during the Japanese colonial period, the Koreans had experienced authoritarian governance as the Japanese colonial government had increasingly controlled Korea. Seung-Man Rhee (1948–1960) who was the first President to be democratically elected in Korea also adopted a limited authoritarian approach in the sense that, as Kim (1997) pointed out, he began by entrusting various institutions to market discipline, but became more inclined to authoritarian governance towards the end of his term. With the legacy of an authoritarian government during the Japanese colonial period, the Park regime, which took power by military coup in 1961, legitimised the establishment of an authoritarian government by promising political stability as a means of attaining economic development. Some organisations, including the Economic Planning Board (EPB), were founded to help implement Park's goal for economic development. Kim (1997) argued that the founding of the EPB and other government offices geared toward economic development, the creation of successive five-year economic development plans, and the nationalisation of banks all increased the power of the government under Park. Indeed, Park saw political instability as a major cause of the poverty and rampant corruption of the past (Kim 1997). He believed that political instability and social unrest were caused by freedom of expression and freedom of the press and that democracy should be suspended for some time in the interests of national security.[3] Indeed, as Kim (1997) argued, it was hardly possible for opponents to mobilise against the suspension of democracy because of the nationalistic feeling and patriotic ideology that prevailed at the time (McNamara 1990).

However, the 'temporary' suspension of political rights and limitations on civil liberty was sustained throughout the Park regime (1961–1979), and was later described as a 'Korean-style' of democracy.[4] During this time, according to Ogle (1990), the police and the Korean Central Intelligence Agency were ordered to monitor and report labour activities, and extensive force was used to prevent and control labour strikes under the pretext that this would increase competitiveness and help to induce foreign capital.[5] The 'Korean-style democracy' existed until democratisation was proclaimed in 1987.

In Korea, the government was 'authoritarian developmental' during the 1960s and 1970s (Kim 1997). Economic development plans were promoted in an authoritarian manner by forcibly intervening in the market, and by designating economic plans in a developmental manner. In this sense, as emphasised by the developmental statists, the hand of the government was omnipresent in the

---

3   He even saw democracy as an indirect cause of the Korean War.

4   Some argue that this 'suspended democracy' promoted economic development, while economic development led to a growing demand for 'real' democracy.

5   During the 1960 and 1970s, there were several prominent cases in which underground labour leaders were prosecuted.

market, to attain a growth-oriented strategy. Okuno-Fujiwara (1997) argues that several proponents of the authoritarian government view have stressed that a strong government, which relies heavily upon direct state intervention over the use of a competitive market mechanism, may have an advantage in industrialising a developing country, possibly at the cost of repressing democracy. Obviously, as stressed by Kim (1997), the Korean government used its authoritarian power over the private sector to enforce its economic policies. Amsden (1989) pointed out that the government tamed the chaebol by using discipline and punishment in attaining economic development. She further argued that this prevented the Korean government and the chaebol from becoming corrupt. In the early 1960s the government dominated the chaebol, but as development progressed over the entire economic development period, the relationship between government and the chaebol became gradually complementary and then competitive.

Type of Industrial Organisation and the Evolution of the Korean Chaebol

Zaibatsu

Zaibatsu refers to a business group that dominated the Japanese economy until the end of World War II.[6] Zaibatsu emerged in the course of modernisation during the Meiji era and grew rapidly under the patronage of government. Zaibatsu played a leading role in the earlier Japanese industrialisation and from 1931 they contributed to the Japanese war effort in cooperation with the military government (Miyashita and Russell 1994).[7] As a result, with the Japanese defeat by the allied forces in 1945 the zaibatsu were in the end dissolved as part of the resolution of war crimes between 1945 and 1947.

Each zaibatsu centred on its founder and his successors in the same family. The head office was a holding company, which established directly controlled firms under its influence. The directly controlled firms established subsidiaries (Argy and Stein 1997). The structure was that of a pyramid. Each zaibatsu dominated vertically the business management of its affiliated firms and their subsidiaries, through the holding company (see Figure 5.1). The holding company owned most of the stock of the directly affiliated companies and financed them through its own bank (Ito 1992). The general trading companies called sogoshosha, acted as proxy for manufacturers in zaibatsu by purchasing raw materials and by selling products. Other goals, such as parts and components for manufacturing, were provided by the subsidiary companies in the zaibatsu or by their subcontractors (Flath 2000).

6　The four big zaibatsu, i.e., Mitsui, Mitsubishi, Sumitomo and Yasuda were involved in such key industries as steel, international trading, and banking in prewar Japan. The big four zaibatsu consisted of 17 affiliated firms accounting for 25 per cent of the total paid-up corporate capital at the end of the war (Ito 1992; Cho 1997; Lee 1999). In addition, the share of industrial production in the prewar period by the top 15 zaibatsu was 51 per cent of coal, 69 per cent of aluminum, 69 per cent of steam locomotives, 50 per cent of raw silk, 49 per cent of chemical dyes, 30 per cent of gunpowder and 50 per cent of paper and pulp (Lee 1999).

7　See also Ito 1994.

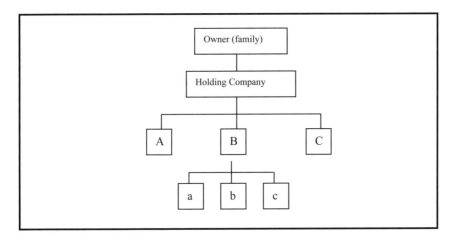

Figure 5.1   The structure of Zaibatsu

Note: Large capitals represent directly affiliated companies. Small capitals represent subsidiary companies.

Each zaibatsu usually included financial institutions such as a bank, trust company, and insurance companies (Ito 1992) and zaibatsu-owned financial institutions played the role of capital pipeline for each affiliated firm. Each zaibatsu formed a large-scale business group through diversification and by investing in any businesses that carry profits. In short, the zaibatsu were large family-owned conglomerates. Flath (2000) argued that zaibatsu enjoyed a monopolistic position through their overwhelming capital mobilisation and organisation. Zaibatsu had a close relationship with government since they grew in a climate of government-led industrialisation.

Keiretsu

Despite the forced dissolution of the zaibatsu in 1945–1947, three of the famous names—Mitsui, Mitsubishi and Sumitomo—have survived and are now known as keiretsu.[8] Basically, the keiretsu form interlocked associations, which are either horizontal or vertical and cover most Japanese companies. The horizontal keiretsu are essentially similar to the zaibatsu, consisting of a group of large firms in different industries with common ties to a powerful bank, united by shared stockholdings, and trading relations (Miyashita and Russell 1994). The vertical keiretsu are a set of suppliers and distributors linked by long-term contracts

8   In Japan the Big Six keiretsu are Mitsui, Mitsubishi, Sumitomo, Fuyo, Sanwa and Daiichi Kangin, of which Fuyo, Sanwa and Daiichi Kangin emerged after the World War II.

and made up of one very large company and hundreds or thousands of small companies subcontracted to it (Flath 2000).

Horizontal keiretsu   At the centre of a horizontal keiretsu there is always a main bank[9] and a GTC (General Trading Company), and they are equivalent in influence. There may also be a second firm, a giant manufacturer. Around these two or three giants circle the core members, usually three financial firms—a life insurance company, a non-life insurance company, and a trust company—and one or two very large manufacturers. According to Miyashita and Russell (1994), together the financial firms, the trading company, and the group's key manufacturers give the keiretsu its identity (see Figure 5.2).

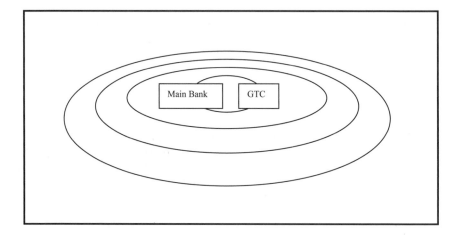

Figure 5.2   The structure of a horizontal keiretsu

Although each of the keiretsu includes hundreds of firms in its extended group, only a few dozen are considered members of the club. According to Miyashita and Russell (1994), this is explained by the group's inner sanctum, a body of the biggest and most important firms whose top executives meet regularly in a presidential council, where they discuss matters of concern to the group as a whole.

There are certain elements that are common to all large horizontal keiretsu: the main bank and the general trading company (Ito 1992). The GTC is obviously concerned with commerce, and in a horizontal keiretsu it has the vital role of

---

9   A main bank is a financial institution that controls and distributes money flowing to a group of industrial concerns. The bank can provide a useful information service for group companies and my act as a coordinator for group activities. If necessary, it will provide management assistance because it holds equity in most of the major companies, and scrutinises the performance of the group. In particular, the bank exerts an absolute power in adjusting an ailing company by despatching a specialist management team from the bank's executives.

coordinating trade, not only within the group, but among different groups and even with foreign customers. The GTC also holds equity in many of the group firms, provide financing through in different ways than the banks, and like the banks, it sends directors to oversee member companies' management (Cho 1997). By combining the information gained from the GTC, which deals with many group members on a daily basis, with that gained from the main bank which examines the firm's accounts, the nucleus of the keiretsu can form an amazingly detailed and accurate picture of what is happening inside each company in the group (Morikawa 1992).

Vertical keiretsu   Vertical keiretsu are large and more common in manufacturing industries. They are particularly prominent in the electronics and automobile industries, although almost every other field has its own vertical keiretsu, including advertising, publishing, broadcasting, and other non-manufacturing businesses (Morikawa 1992). Horizontal and vertical keiretsu overlap to a large extent. Many of the biggest vertical keiretsu lie inside the Big Six.

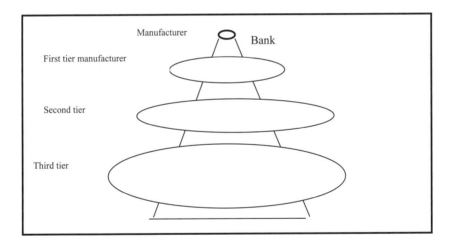

Figure 5.3   The structure of a vertical keiretsu

At the top of the pyramid, there is a large manufacturer and in orbit around, there is a key bank more or less equal in status with the manufacturer (see Figure 5.3). Each pyramid descends from a single powerful company (Miyashita and Russell 1994). Beneath the top, there are many subsidiaries. In the case of manufacturing industry, these are usually the first-tier factories producing goods for the 'parent' company up above. According to Morishita (1992), beneath these companies there are at least a few hundred smaller ones in each vertical keiretsu, and they are arranged hierachically.

The parent company at the apex of the manufacturing pyramid is responsible for coordinating the vast, complex system of design, development, manufacture, and assembly inside the pyramid, then advertising the finished products and delivering them to the market (Flath 2000). The first-tier subcontractors handle many of the final steps in the production process and also play an important role in coordinating the second- and third-tier subcontractors.

Chaebol[10]

There are various definitions of chaebol and the definition varies subtly according to both scholars and other points of view (see Table 5.1).

Chaebol represents a transitional stage in the growth of firms, compared with western-style business groups. As can be seen from the above definitions, most chaebol are owned and managed by founders and their families. In general, the major chaebol developed in two generations. Samsung and LG are the largest of the first generation, which began their businesses during the colonial period.[11] The second generation began in the 1960s under the Park regime: Hyundai and Daewoo are its largest members.

Hattori (1987; 1989) argues that in the chaebol the ties are personal, and transfers of managerial and financial resources among firms are common. Chaebol are characterised by family ownership control, interlocking ownership, heavy-debt financing, and aggressive diversification. Song (1996) notes that interlocking ownership and debt-financing allow them to control chaebol-related companies with very little equity of their own. They are also diversified, creating an enormous power base for chaebol families.

Figure 5.4 illustrates the interlocking (cross-shareholding) structure, in which a chaebol family owns a core company and/or an intermediary such as a cultural foundation, which in turn has interlocking ownership with member companies (Chung 1997). The Samsung group is an example of this structure (Hattori 1989; Kong 1995; Chung 1997). Importantly, as chaebol develops, the pattern moves from Stage I to Stage II, Stage III and then Stage IV. For the purposes of this study, a chaebol can be described as a business organisation which is run and controlled by an individual or family; which consists of diverse businesses; and which has evolved into a structure suited to the present Korean economic environment.

The comparison of zaibatsu, keiretsu, and chaebol

Although the Korean government forced chaebol to raise finance capital through the stock market, most of the affiliated firms in chaebol are dominated by the founding families, even through their stock capital accounts for less than a third of the total assets of the affiliated firms. Most of the stock held outside the family is owned by financial institutions, but they, too, are controlled by the dominant

---

10 The Chinese characters for zaibatsu and chaebol are identical, both translating into 'money group' or 'financial clique.'

11 A number of very large firms originated in the Japanese colonial period, for example, Samsung, LG, Hyundai, Hyosung, Sunkyung and Doosan.

Table 5.1   Various definitions of chaebol

	Definition	Characteristics
Byun, H.-Y. 1975)	Monopoly capital comprising large scale business group run by single system, which has general finance, labour relations and business management.	Each firm in big firms is formally independent but in fact, interdependent.
Jones and Sakong 1980)	A system of highly centralised family control through holding companies.	1) Firm's group run by owner and family through business diversification; 2) excessive dependence on external capital; 3) growth through export promotion and government-business collusion.
Lee, K.-O. and S.-S. Lee (1985)	A system controlled, and owned by an individual or family, consisting of a large-scale monopolistic firm in business management.	
Joo, C.-H. (1985)	A business group that is a holding company, controlled by the family that also controls many affiliated firms.	
Hattori, T. (1988)	A diversified business group that occurs by a natural process of late-comer's industrialisation. It is characterised by closed ownership held by family or relatives, and diversified business sectors.	1) Quantitative growth through diversification of unrelated fields; 2) monopolistic position in market; 3) government-business collusion; 4) centralised top-down decision-making structure; 5) flexible lifetime employment; 6) paternalistic guidance
Jung, K.-H. (1987)	A family-controlled group that runs various unrelated businesses.	1) Management of unrelated industries; 2) dependence on external capital but not the retained capital; 3) centralised control; 4) run by paternalistic business philosophy; 5) owned by a specific family; 6) dependence on overseas business resources.
Yoo and Lee (1987)	A large-scale business group that run and owned by family and relatives in diversified business field.	1) Ownership by family and relatives; 2) diversified business.
Kuk, M.-H. (1988)	A large business organisation that is controlled by owner and his family, or by one or families which dominate large private enterprises.	1) A large-scale business group that can exert economic power; 2) diversified business in unrelated field; 3) a strong fiduciary atmosphere of inner group based on family ownership and control, in particular at the initial stage of growth.

Table 5.1 cont'd

	Definition	Characteristics
Cho, D.-S. (1990, 1997)	A large-scale business group grew under the umbrella of government's assistance that is controlled by family and relatives. A business group controlled and managed by an individual and their family.	1) A large-scale business group in structure; 2) control by family and relatives in form; 3) unusual growth process and capital accumulation in environment.
Kang, Choi and Chang (1991)	A big business group that is controlled, and owned by a specific individual or family and which enters unrelated business fields.	1) Independence in form; 2) not simple big business group but controlled by family and relatives.
Fields (1991)	A legal group consisting of two or more independent business groups that creates goods and services in various production sectors.	1) Owned and controlled by a clan; 2) completely independent with clear firm's form; 3) diversification of industry and products; 4) dependence on external capital due to non-control of major financial institutions; 5) cosy relationship with government.
Kong, B.-H. (1995)	Firms with a strong family-controlled character seeking advances in various business fields.	1) Family-controlled character in ownership and structure; 2) diversified business fields in management structure; 3) catching-up with advanced countries in development.
Kim, I.-Y. (1997)	A large and diversified conglomerate that is controlled by one or two families.	1) Concentration of stock by owner and family; 2) separation of management and ownership; 3) similar structure as zaibatsu, except for bank system.
Fair Trade Committee (1993)	Groups in which the total assets of the affiliated firms based on financial statements exceed 400 billion won.	
BOK	Firms' group with total bank credits including loans and payment guarantees, in excess of 150 billion won.	

family.[12] Accordingly, management independence from the dominant family is negligible compared with that of Japan.

Although chaebol are and zaibatsu were both big business groups dominated by their founding family, ownership and management were separated in Japan. According to Hattori (1987), the families of the Mitsui and Sumitomo zaibatsu

---

12 In particular, the strong influence of the dominant family in management is reflected in the process of highly centralised decision making. With the authority derived directly from ownership, the founder and his or her family intervened in all major decision making as well as on detailed matters.

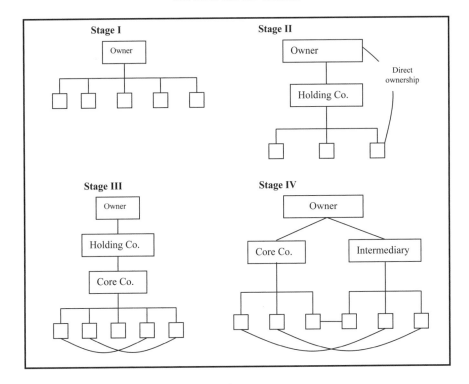

Figure 5.4   The evolutionary structure of chaebol: from Stages I to IV

Source: Adapted from Hattori (1989), pp. 81–2; Kong (1995), pp. 150–54.

did not participate actively in business management, which was entrusted to professional managers. The separation of ownership from management has continued in the present-day keiretsu. In both zaibatsu and keiretsu, all decision making rests with the professional managers rather than the stock owners, and in particular the dominant families (Hattori 1987, 1997). However, unlike the zaibatsu and keiretsu, ownership and management are not separate in the Korean chaebol.

In Japan, one GTC and one main bank play central roles in both zaibatsu and keiretsu. In Korea, although chaebol have GTCs, they are not as strong as those of the zaibatsu and keiretsu. Cho (1990, 1997) says that the GTC of chaebol in Korea are in charge of 'simple functions', rather like an export company. This is not the same as in Japan. More recently, however, as the Korean economy has developed, the GTC has taken a more central role in planning, for example as a strategy unit reporting directly to the chairman of the chaebol.

Financial institutions in chaebol are usually restricted to providing capital to affiliated firms in the group since the stock of the financial institutions are owned by the dominant family. Unlike Japan, where keiretsu have had their own banks to provide financial assistance to affiliated firms, in Korea the chaebol are heavily dependent for bank loans on the commercial banks which are under the government control. Accordingly, the chaebol of Korea have close relationships with government in terms of fund raising for business expansion. The growth pattern of chaebol relies on business opportunity provided by policy-makers (Cho 1997), and thus, the priority in raising funds between chaebol becomes significant. Chaebol have close links with bureaucrats and have received special privileges in the course of their growth (Jung 1987). Such an embedded relationship between government and chaebol has made it difficult to accept a changing economic environment. The dominant and dependent relationships between government and chaebol that are referred to by some scholars can be understood in this regard. However, since the middle of the 1980s, these relationships have been loosened as chaebol have become independent in their fund-raising and acquisition of information.

On the other hand, as Ito (1992) pointed out, the keiretsu of Japan have not such strong relationships with government compared with the chaebol of Korea. Although the relationships between the MITI (Ministry of International Trade and Industry) and the keiretsu are close, the keiretsu are relatively free from the forced authority of agreement.

In many ways, chaebol are more like the zaibatsu than the keiretsu, particularly in the sense that zaibatsu had a very close relationship with the Japanese government. Like the keiretsu, chaebol are technically groups of companies rather than a single conglomerate. But all companies in the group are entirely owned by a single family, thus making them more like zaibatsu. The major difference between chaebol and both the Japanese forms is that the latter had or have main banks at their bases, whereas that is not the case for chaebol (see Table 5.2). For many years all the banks in Korea were state owned, making chaebol dependent on credit from state institutions.

Song (1996) notes that the horizontal relationships between the affiliates in keiretsu are flexible, whereas the vertical relationships between parent firms and their subsidiaries are highly rigid. Thus, flexibility and rigidity coexist in the keiretsu. But in Korea, as Song (1996) says, vertical rigidity is much stronger than in the keiretsu and horizontal flexibility is weaker. All the member firms of the keiretsu are very large and highly competitive in global markets so that they tend to be independent. By contrast, most of the firms in a chaebol are relatively small and not highly competitive in the global market thus allowing for and requiring more cooperation with each other than in the case for firms in keiretsu.

The Evolution of the State-Chaebol Relationship

The Relationship between Government and Business

As argued by the neoclassical school, the role of government in a market economy can be divided into two: the role of judgement that executes and interprets the rules for the market economy; and the role of partner engaging directly in the market economy. The former includes the protection of patent rights, the

Table 5.2   Organisational characteristics of business groups in zaibatsu, keiretsu, and chaebol

	Zaibatsu	Keiretsu	Chaebol
Ownership types	Family groups, strict hierachical top-down structure	Shareholding of group firms	Family groups, strict hierachical top-down structure
Intra-group network	Strict top-down	Cross-shareholding mutual dominance	Strict top-down
Inter-group network	Direct control, loans	Cross-shareholding, loans, joint-ventures	Coordination through banks and government
Subcontract relation	Structured or semi-informal	Structured or semi-informal	Insignificant
Investment pattern	Mostly vertical	Vertical and horizontal integration	Vertical and horizontal
Growth pattern	Bank-financed group activities	Bank-financed group activities	State-financed sector growth

establishment of fair trade by regulating monopoly, the prevention of pollution and the enactment of laws and regulations. In addition, government acts as a coordinator between economic agents. In its role as partner, government is both producer and supplier through its involvement in social infrastructure. In Korea, as argued by the developmental-statists, the government has acted as a producer and a player, rather than an adjudicator.

Government and business interact in various ways (see Figure 5.5). Government acts as regulator of the enterprise, assistant, competitor, consumer, and supplier of capital. As Jung (1989) pointed out, of the many different government roles, those of regulator and assistant tend to affect the relationship between government and business. At one extreme, government maintains a non-interventionist laissez-faire policy by minimising its role of regulator and assistant. Hong Kong is often cited an example of this approach.

At the other extreme, that of the centrally planned economy, government controls prices, owns the enterprises and distributes resources and thus plays a commanding role in the economy.

However, no economy exists at either of these two extremes. All economies can be categorised somewhere between the laissez-faire and the centrally planned economy. When the relationship between government and enterprise is characterised by laissez faire, as the neoclassical school pointed out, there is a distance between government and enterprise. In contrast, the more planned the economy, the stronger control and price distortions exist.

As Cho (1997) pointed out, the relationship between government and business has a structural attribute that changes over time, and this has been the case in Korea. During the 1950s, the relationship between government and chaebol was much closer to the characteristics of a laissez-faire economy. The government denationalised all banks and introduced a much freer market system in many ways. However, when the Park government took power in 1961, the relationship

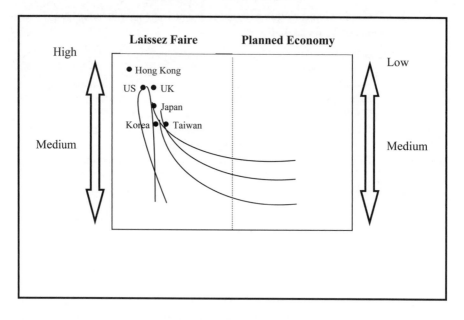

Figure 5.5   Interaction of government and enterprise

Note: Hong Kong since the 1950s; UK since the early 1800s; US since the early 1900s;
         Japan since the late 1800s; Taiwan since the early 1950s; Korea since the 1960s.
         Axes on both the left and right represents strength of market.

Table 5.3   Business-government interactions in Korea*

Areas of interactions	Means used by government
1 Resource allocation	Controlling investment resources and requiring investment rates
2 Direct ownership	Public enterprise
3 Investment choices	Entry permit and exit regulation
4 Corporate mergers	Antitrust and fair trade acts
5 Managerial intervention	Price and wage control curbing labour movement
6 Business subsidies	Tax and financial incentives; Information services
7 Income distribution	Tax administration; pseudo-tax imposition

*   Government intervention in advanced countries can be seen in areas 1) and 3).

Source: Jung (1989): 13. Reproduced with permission of Greenwood Publishing Group
          Inc. Westport, CT.

was abruptly changed closer to the planned economy based on the Japanese economic structure in the Meiji period.

Table 5.3 summarised from Jung (1989) shows various means of government involvement in marketplaces and business activity. In Korea, the government was deeply involved in resource allocation, through controlling the amount of investment funds under its budget, and by allocating various credits through government-controlled commercial and development banks (Jung 1989). In addition, the government controlled the number of firms in selected business fields. In the early 1980s, for example, some companies were compelled by the government to leave certain sectors such as the machinery and automobile industries. According to Jung (1989), the regulation of entry and exit has been one of the most powerful tools for both coercing and courting private businesses. The government intervened in many areas of company operation and regulated both prices and wages in private firms until the early 1980s. Labour unions were suppressed before the announcement of democratisation in 1987 in order to support the competitiveness of private firms in increasing their exports to overseas markets. Furthermore, various financial incentives, including tax concessions, were given to private businesses in selected industries.

However, Jung's explanation of the strong government intervention (1989) does not fully reflect the changing relationship between government and business through the entire economic development period. Indeed, as argued by some,[13] even in the high growth period of the mid-1960s and the 1970s, which is often cited as a typical government intervention period, the government enlisted the support of businessmen and the timing of its entry into targeted industries was often decided by the business reports of chaebol and close negotiation with influential businessmen.[14]

Government strength as emphasised by the developmental-state view is not fixed but varies through time. As Shafer (1990) argued, state strength is a relative as well as a situational concept and thus, it is too simple to say that strong government is strong forever. It is reasonable to argue that economic development gradually brings about a power shift between government and business, regardless of the degree of economic development. Indeed, as the economy has progressed, relationships have become more characteristic of a laissez faire approach, reflecting the rise of the business sector and a less interventionist approach by government.[15]

---

13 For more details, see (1986), Kim (1998) and Samsung (1998).

14 According to Samsung (1998), even during the Park regime, which was the most authoritarian developmental period, Byung-Chul Lee, the founder of Samsung, initiated and advised on some major government policies.

15 Of course, this does not mean that the relationships between the two are approaching the degree of laissez faire typified by the relationships between government and enterprises in the US.

The State-Chaebol Relationship in Korea[16]

The phase of chaos and reconstruction: 1945–1961

In this period, from 1945–1960, Korea experienced the first market economic system run by its own hand in the history of the country. The period provided a framework for Korean economic development incorporating it into the sphere of American economic influence by terminating the Japanese style of economic system. However, separation from the Japanese economy and social unrest after the liberation brought about a sharp collapse in manufacturing which was declined by 40–75 per cent since the end of 1930s, when the Japanese colonial influences was at its peak (BOK 1985). Furthermore, the Korean War destroyed physical infrastructure and reconstruction was essential. These events damaged the market structure and showed the difficulties of economic management.

Rhee (1948–1960), the first democratically elected president of South Korea, gave priority to the reunification of South and North Korea over economic development and economic policies. Economic policies aimed at establishing a self-reliant economy were oriented at import substitution industrialisation. However, economic growth did not live up to the expectations of the Korean government. According to Kim (1997), growth was hindered by a lack of managerial and economic expertise in the government as well as by cosy relations between politicians, government officials, and businessmen.

At the time of liberation in 1945, the Japanese left over 166,300 items of property, including more than 3,000 operating industrial assets and business enterprises, as well as infrastructure inventories, real assets, and land that had been taken into public ownership, amounting to 15 per cent of the nation's land area (Jones and Sakong 1980; Jung 1987; McNamara 1990). By 1957, most of the industrial assets that could be operated immediately had been distributed by the US occupying forces and the Rhee government. It was the first chance for Korean businessmen to accumulate capital by taking over industrial assets left behind by the Japanese during the colonial period. As Cho (1997) pointed out, such an environment provided the basis for business growth and the formation of chaebol.

Industrial assets distributed to friends and political allies of Rhee were sold at from 30 to 90 per cent below their actual value with only a 10 per cent down payment being required (Kim 1998). The balance was to be paid in interest-free instalments over 10–15 years (Orru et al. 1997). The sale price for this property represented a windfall profit, considering the hyper-inflationary situation[17] during the late 1940s and 1950s caused by social unrest and the Korean War (Chung et

---

16 Part of this section has been published in *Current Politics and Economics of Asia*, Vol. 16, Issue 1, 'The Structural Weakness of Korean Economic Development Model: A Historical Overview', 2007, Moosung Lee and Jae-Seung Shim Chin, reprinted with permission from Nova Science Publishers, Inc.

17 Inflation was estimated at 1,600 per cent between August and December 1945, and had risen by another 1,800 per cent by 1949. See Kim and Roemer (1979: 27) for more details.

al. 1997). Moreover, as Jones and Sakong (1980) pointed out, the sale of vested property was accompanied by preferential treatment such as cheap bank loans, the allocation of import licenses for raw materials and the distribution of foreign exchange. It also guaranteed monopoly and oligopoly in the domestic market. Indeed, of Korea's the top ten chaebol in 1961, seven attributed their origins to the purchase of Japan's colonial assets.[18]

Table 5.4   The top ten chaebol groups in 1961

Chaebol	No. of affiliates	Major businesses	Acquisition of the vested property (Yes or No)	Quota of aid capital (Yes or No)
Samsung	13	Import, food, textile, bank	Yes	Yes
Samho	7	Import, textile, bank	Yes	Yes
Gaepung	9	Import, cement, bank	No	Yes
Daihan	5	Import, food, textile	Yes	Yes
Lucky	4	Import, chemical products	No	Yes
Dongyang	4	Cement, food	Yes	Yes
Kugdong	4	Import, glass	Yes	Yes
Korea Glass	2	Import, glass	No	Yes
Dongrip	2	Food	Yes	Yes
Taechang	2	Import, food	Yes	Yes

Source: Kim (1987), p. 57, quoted in Kim (1998), p. 85.

As McNamara (1990) pointed out, most of the Japanese colonial assets were sold to private individuals, with the exception of commercial banks and some public utilities. Mainly, former employees or those who had prior connection with the enterprises reaped windfall capital gains. As Table 5.4 shows, by 1961 seven out of the ten largest chaebol had received vested property and all had received aid capital from the government. These chaebol had either the benefits of the sale of the vested property or American aid accompanying various privileges from the government. Most of them were either members, or relatives of members of Rhee's Liberal Party. Many emerged as influential businessmen and have become leaders in the Korean business community.

Jones and Sakong (1980) explained how capital accumulation occurred through the sales of the vested property. According to them (ibid.), once a businessman

---

18 In fact, of the 50 largest chaebol as of 1983, 40 had been established after World War II and of those, 19 had been established during the 1950s. However, the origin of firms and the year of establishment do not always correspond. For example, Hyundai and LG started their business careers as small firms during the colonial period but the official data of the firms' establishment is recorded as being after the end of the Japanese colonial period.

acquired Japanese property, he also received working capital and loans for reconstruction, as well as the foreign exchange needed for imports of equipment and raw materials. When the businessman began to produce, the import of foreign goods was restricted in the name of protecting domestic industry and at the same time, tax privileges were given. It can be said that a business's success in this period depended on close personal ties to government officials and politicians.

As McNamara (1990) explained, it is true that in the process of selling the Japanese properties a few chaebol were created with the help of the government. In a sense, it can be said that the 1950s were a preparation period of chaebol's rapid growth for the next and subsequent decades.

In the 1950s, the priorities of the Korean government were to maintain a minimum level of consumption and to reconstruct the social infrastructure destroyed by the Korean War. The government budgets depended on the American aid programme and aid was the principal capital source. It financed the demand for various imports, social overhead investment and investment for selected import substitution industries (Kong 1993). During this period, the Korean government was eager to acquire as much US aid as possible for imports of industrial and consumer goods. However, as Cho (1994) pointed out, US aid was not assumed in the long-term programme since it needed an agreement from the Senate of the US each year. Cho (ibid.) argued that this made it difficult for the Rhee government to plan a long-term economic strategy. The influence of the US aid programme on industrialisation in the 1950s must be recognised.

Table 5.5   US economic and military aid to Korea: 1945–1976 ($m)

Period	Economic aid	Military aid	Total
1945–52	666.8	12.3	679.1
1953–61	2,579.2	1,560.7	4,139.9
1962–69	1,658.2	2,501.3	4,139.9
1970–76	963.6	2,794.4	3,761.0
Total	5,745.4	6,847.3	12,592.7

Source: US Government Agency for International Development (1976), quoted in Kim (1998): 91.

The US government aid agency intended and the Rhee government used the aid to finance import substitution industrialisation in Korea. From 1945 to 1948, over 90 per cent of $40 millions of US economic aid were used for food, fertiliser, clothing, fuel, and other industrial goods, and only 10 per cent for economic reconstruction (Kim 1998). The aid was used both to make up the financial deficits of the Korean government, and to import consumer goods. Form 1953–1962, US aid accounted for 80 per cent of total fixed capital, representing 70 per cent of Korea's total national income (ibid.). This large amount of capital was used to reconstruct basic industries such as glass, cement, mining, fertiliser and electric

Table 5.6   Trends of overvaluation of the won to the dollar (1953–1971)

	Official rxchange rate/market exchange rate	Actual amount of payment to importer (won)	Capital gain for importer (won)	Actual Income (won)
1953	0.40	137.1	208.3	345.4
1954	0.45	108.8	134.5	243.3
1955	0.43	147.7	193.7	341.4
1956	0.56	218.0	168.1	386.1
1957	0.49	216.8	225.4	442.2
1958	0.54	202.5	175.7	378.2
1959	0.64	194.5	109.3	303.8
1960	0.74	254.3	89.2	343.5
1961	0.97	307.8	8.3	316.1
1962	0.88	369.3	52.5	421.8
1963	0.72	405.7	154.6	560.3
1964	0.90	362.7	41.7	404.4
1965	1.00	463.4	0	463.4
1966	0.94	670.2	46.2	716.4
1967	0.84	840.0	156.2	996.2
1968	0.79	1,131.4	331.5	1,462.9
1969	0.78	1,425.8	397.8	1,823.6
1970	0.77	1,525.0	459.0	1,984.0
1971	0.78	1,873.5	520.8	2,394.3
Total		10,854.5	3,472.8	14,327.3
Average	0.72	571.3	182.7	754.1
1953–60	0.531	185.0	163.0	348.0
1961–71	0.852	852.3	197.1	1,049.4

Source: Jung (1987): 70.

power supply as well as import substitution industries such as textiles, sugar manufacturing and the milling industry. Foreign capital mainly from aid, which was controlled by the Korean government and counterpart funds, which were raised by selling imports to domestic producers, were the sources of investment for equipment (Sakong 1993).

With the cut-off of official trade with Japan, the so-called 'Macao Trade' played a substitution role for Japan in providing Korea with consumer goods. As Jung (1987) showed, trade brought windfall capital gains for importers since they paid in Korean won, which, for imports, were overvalued in relation to the dollar (see Table 5.6).

As Table 5.6 shows, between 1953 and 1958, the market value of the won to the dollar was overvalued at more than double the official value, giving a large windfall gain to importers. Eight out of the ten largest chaebol in this period were concentrating on trade including Samsung Trading Co. (see also Table 5.4).

Trading companies obtained the import licences needed for consumer goods, raw materials and spare parts for machinery and equipment, and were given foreign exchange by the government. These enabled importers to accumulate capital and thus to become leaders in Korean economic development. Kong (1993) said that one of the most important sources for capital accumulation by chaebol was through the cronyism that prevailed between the government, politicians and businessmen. However, despite criticisms of the government-business relationship in the 1950s, the chaebol were also successful in developing entrepreneurship and competition between themselves in making the most of the resources available to them.

Jones and Sakong (1980) see the growth of the chaebol during the 1950s as the result of zero-sum transfers[19] little related to the accumulated wealth in the sense that the growth was attained by non-competitive allocation of import quotas and import licenses, bargain price acquisition of former Japanese properties, the selective allocation of aid funds and materials, and privileged access to cheap bank loans. According to Shin (1984), the chaebol in Korea are speculative, shallow, commercial and dependent organisations due to these reasons. In other words, it may be concluded that non-productive and non-economic activities through rent-seeking were the source of chaebol's growth.

However, North's (1990:67) conclusion explaining the relationship between the right of ownership and economic organisations, provides a different perspective on the above conclusions:

> Firms come into existence to take advantage of profitable opportunities, which will be defined by the existing set of constraints. With insecure property rights, poorly enforced laws, barriers to entry, and monopolistic restrictions, the profit-maximising firms will tend to have short time horizons and little fixed capital, and will tend to be small scale. The most profitable businesses may be in trade, redistributive activities, or the black market. Large firms with substantial fixed capital will exist only under

---

19 Jones and Sakong explained the accumulation process in this period by using the term 'zero-sum' and 'positive-sum' (Leibenstein 1963). According to traditional microeconomic theory, all voluntary exchange and production result in mutual gains (or at least no loss) for all parties, meaning 'positive-sum.' However, in the real economy 'zero-sum' activity exists when entrepreneurs are involved in activities that add little or nothing to the productive capacity of the economy, according to Leibenstein (1963). These activities are: non-trading activities such as the pursuit of a monopolistic position, increased political power, more prestige, and so on and trading activities which do not increase aggregate resources or aggregate income, although they believe their activities will contribute to economic growth. For more details, see Jones and Sakong (1980) and Leibenstein (1963).

the umbrella of government protection with subsidies, tariff protection, and payoffs to the policy – a mixture hardly conducive to productive efficiency.

Thus, even the rent-seeking itself can be justified as an efficient economic activity in terms of transaction costs, as pointed out by North (ibid.). Indeed, Koo and Kim's argument (1992) supports North's explanation saying that it is more profitable for firms to utilise various rent-seeking than to actively engage in productive activities, which use the retained profits and efficient business administration, especially when the government exposes its inability to monitor corrupt or unfair business practices.

In the 1950s the number of employees in the manufacturing industry continued to rise and employment growth between 1954 and 1959 was well over 15 per cent (Kang 1993). During the same period, GNP grew at an annual average of 3 per cent more than that of the world economy as a whole (BOK 1985). These indicators suggest that although chaebol in this period pursued rent-seeking they also made profitable investments and expanded their businesses significantly.

However, the 1950s began to highlight the conflict of interest in the relationship between the government and chaebol, in terms of industrialisation. Chang (1994) argued that the growth of chaebol did not result in the growth of the entire economy, reflecting the failure of the transformation from commercial capital to industrial capital. Much commercial capital had been accumulated by a handful of chaebol with the help of the government and the main beneficiaries were the chaebol themselves.

The phase of government-led industrialisation: 1961–1979

Political economy of government-led industrialisation In post-war Korea, access to the government-controlled distribution of Japanese properties, low interest loan for traders, the allocation of import licences and foreign aid increasingly involved corruption and favouritism. According to Song (1990, 1996), business success depended to a large extent on obtaining such government favours, resulting in corrupt dealings between the government and businessmen. The military government which came to power in 1961 forced chaebol to cooperate with government development plans by threatening to confiscate the properties allegedly illegally accumulated in the 1950s.

In the 1960s, the South Korean economy was in a difficult situation. It was lagging behind North Korea in terms of per capita income, industrial production capacity and technological level, as well as in military strength. Accordingly, industrial promotion took precedence over politics and democracy. Jung (1998) pointed out that the regime headed by President Park (1961–1979) embraced the private sector by using an effective mix of carrot and stick in order not only to justify the legitimacy of the military coup that had brought it to power in 1961, but also to attain a self-reliant economy.

Since the late 1950s, the so-called three white industries (sugar, flour and cotton yarn) had been flourishing so that employment had gradually increased. However, unemployment levels remained high and at the beginning of the 1960s, the unemployment rate was more than 15 per cent (BOK 1995). Political stability could not be expected without significant job creation.

In addition, a decline in US aid caused a shortage of foreign capital and forced the government to consider alternatives (Kim 1997). To address the problems of unemployment and international balance of payments, an export-promotion policy was adopted. To promote exports, international competitiveness is essential. Cutting costs supports competitiveness in terms of price. High unemployment enabled labour costs to be contained, thus increasing competitiveness. Attaining economies of scale also contributed to the reduction of costs. The search for economies of scale favoured the growth of chaebol and the formation of small and medium enterprises was neglected.

Traditionally, regimes in Korea have been administered by the civil service and thus, the civil service had superiority over the military service (Yoo 1999). Politics had been in the hand of civil officials, but not in the hand of military officials (Yoo 1999) and thus the military officials were not so respected. Accordingly, the government sought to justify and to gain support for its military origins by promoting economic development and bringing about an improvement in living standards. The Park regime adopted military-based efficiency to achieve economic development (McNamara 1990) and thus created an 'authoritarian developmental' government.

Growth-led economic development   A change in government-business relations took place in 1961 when Park took power through a military coup. The Park regime exerted its power over the private sector by using the special law passed by the previous government. The law sought to check the illicit accumulation of wealth.[20] All banks were nationalised in 1961 by a Special Law of Financial Institutions and thus, the main ingredient for business development fell into the hands of government. This strengthened the control of government over the private sector and allowed it to carry out its plans much more strongly than the previous regime did. As Kim (1997) pointed out, this not only forced compliance from the private sector but also demonstrated to the public the government resolve to eliminate corruption. The special law was strengthened and convictions were treated as criminal offences.[21]

Sanctions against business were strongly resented. Critics in the private sector argued that tax evasion during the 1950s was inevitable when tax rates were

---

20 Because of corruption in government-business relation in the 1950s, an anti-chaebol movement developed. The short-lived Chang government in 1960 passed a Special Law for dealing with Illicit Wealth Accumulation, aimed at punishing those who accumulated wealth illicitly by taking advantage of their positions and power. Twenty-four businessmen and 46 enterprises were convicted under this law but the businessmen were not imprisoned because of their strong protests against the law. However, this marked a turning point in the government-chaebol relationship; from cooperation to conflict. For more details, see Jones and Sakong (1980) and Park (1990).

21 For further information on illicit wealth accumulation, see Jones and Sakong (1980): 281.

Table 5.7   Convictions by the Park Regime for illicit wealth accumulation (million hwan*)

Founder and name of chaebol group	Amount of fine		Reasons for fine (hwan)			
	Planned (hwan)	Adjusted (hwan)	Tax evasion	Kickback	Property-related scandal	Others
Lee (Samsung)	2,400	800	736	64	–	–
Chung (Samho)	1,000	361	349	102	66	–
Lee (Gaepung)	550	387	125	153	108	–
Seol (Daehan)	330	481	272	39	62	108
Lee (Tongyang)	170	128	–	40	–	88
Kim (Goldstar)	240	143	119	23	–	–
Park (Hwashin)	97	10	–	10	–	–
Koo (Lucky)	–	96	96	–	–	–
Kim (Samyang)	–	36	36	–	–	–
Lee (Dong-A)	400	211	201	10	–	–
Other 20 people	3,125	1,575				
Total	8,312	4,228				

*   Currency unit used between 1953 and 1962.

Source: Asia Economic Research Institute (1967): 35.

higher than business profits (Lee 1987). Tax reforms were demanded and after lengthy negotiations between the government and the prosecuted businessmen, an understanding was reached that those convicted of illicit wealth accumulation should be fined, rather than have their property confiscated or serve a custodial sentence (Lee 1986; Samsung 1998; see also Table 5.7).

In 1962, the government launched a five-year economic development plan centred on manufacturing industries, requiring a vast amount of capital. The government needed the cooperation of the private sector to invest the huge amount of fines from illicit wealth accumulation in selected manufacturing industries. The fines were turned into the establishment of plants. Chaebol who followed the directives of the government were given incentives such as low bank loans and priority in the allocation of foreign capital (Cho 1997). As Park (1990) and Kim (1998) pointed out, the government provided a momentum that transformed commercial capital to industrial capital. To some extent chaebol, which had enjoyed the benefits of rent-seeking for their own purposes, were driven into a situation where they had to use their capital to invest in the selected industries.

In order to catch up with and out-perform the North and to escape from poverty, growth at any cost was the priority, driven by the expansion of exports and investment (Song 1996). The export targets agreed between the government and private firms were implemented with various incentives provided by the government. However, it was true that, as Song (1996) pointed out, firms which failed to satisfy their export targets without a plausible excuse ran the risk of heavy administrative sanctions by the government.

These measures resulted in a rapid increase in production and export capacity since business success for firms depended to a large extent on their export performance. Chaebol were in a much better position than small firms in benefiting from economies of scale as well as in expanding production capacity. The government, too, favoured a small number of large firms over a large number of small firms, since it was convenient for them to focus government attention in this way (Song 1996). Moreover, in allocating loans, banks preferred chaebol to small firms.

As a result of the nationalisation of the banks, chaebol had only limited access to funds in Korea. Foreign capital, therefore, provided an important source of funding for the chaebol. In addition, the government used various ways to support chaebol, including the amendment of the law of foreign capital, providing favourable terms for investors (Lee 1994).

Accordingly, with the strong back-up of the government, chaebol came to contribute to the rapid industrialisation of the 1960s by transforming their business from import substitution industrialisation centred on consumer goods, to export-led industrialisation including part of the heavy and chemical industry. Affiliated firms in the chaebol drew on foreign capital, in particular Japanese capital, and chaebol grew rapidly in the late 1960s, as a result of the inducement of foreign capital and export-led industrialisation policy.

Chaebol supported by the government were able to borrow huge amounts of long-term loans including foreign loans at low interest rates. They were not dependent on equity capital to expand their business (see Table 5.8).

Table 5.8   Composition of capital management of large business in chaebol groups in the 1960s (%)

	Equity capital	Borrowed capital	Total
1962	8.9	91.1	100.0
1963	12.3	87.3	100.0
1964	14.2	85.8	100.0
1965	24.8	75.2	100.0
1966	22.5	77.5	100.0
1967	20.4	79.6	100.0
1968	16.2	83.8	100.0
1969	19.0	81.0	100.0
Average	17.3	82.7	100.0

Note: 'Large business' refers to a manufacturing firm that employs more than 200 people.

Source: Bank of Korea (various years).

Such business environments enabled chaebol to deepen dependence on foreign capital and many chaebol based on foreign capital grew in size one after another (Kim 1987; Euh 1987; Kang 1998). Since the late 1960s, competition between chaebol for market share at home has become significant. Some chaebol, which grew rapidly in the 1950s disappeared since they lagged behind in coping with the industrial policy of the government (Kong 1993).

Chaebol which were mainly financed by foreign capital and their affiliated firms looked for capital in the curb market, and were willing to pay the high interest rates including the premium rate required by the government as the prerequisite for the introduction of foreign capital.

In the 1960s, chaebol could invest in manufacturing industries under the direct guidance of the government. The capital needed for industrialisation mostly came from borrowed capital (foreign capital + private loans) and chaebol tended to convert the retained capital by accumulating commercial capital through investment in the curb market and in land speculation.

Some chaebol with poor capital had depended for their working capital on foreign capital (Euh 1987). The lax allocation of foreign capital by the government heightened the chaebol' dependence on borrowed capital so that the chaebol' idle capital caused by the loose allocation of foreign capital was invested in the curb market, resulting in high capital gains brought about by the large difference between the official interest rate and the curb market rate. In this respect, the problem of deteriorating business conditions in the late 1960s and early 1970s showed the extent to which industrialisation was limited by depending on borrowed capital.

Because the measure of success for firms was their export capabilities, firms tended to increase their production and export capacity (Song 1996). This forced expansion of output and exports resulted in a high debt-equity ratio, and distorted the firms' internal decision making.

In the 1960s, oligopoly and monopoly increased and entry barriers into industries were gradually raised (Jung 1987). The government restricted entry by most firms into selected industries such as petrochemicals, chemical fertiliser, synthetic fibre, cement and textile but enterprises chosen to work in the selected industries were given many financial privileges by the government.

During this period, chaebol grew in size with the help of external capital. Bank loans and foreign capital were the sources of the growth of chaebol (Hattori 1989). In particular, the normalisation treaty of 1965 with Japan boosted foreign capital-led growth (Castley 1997). Bank interest rate in Korea remained at about 25–30 per cent in the 1960s, compared with foreign loans at 5–6 per cent (Cho 1994; Cho 1997). During this period, the allocation of foreign loans was concentrated on chaebol and this contributed to the capital accumulation of chaebol. In the process, the dependence of Korea on the Japanese economy became deeper while the matter of government-business collusion emerged again as an issue.

Even bank loans made in Korea contributed to the growth of chaebol because the annual rate of interest in the curb market reached 40–50 per cent, at least twice as high as the official rate, instigating a surge into the borrowed capital for business management (Bae, 1994; Cho, 1997).

Industrialisation became more dependent on foreign capital, and exports became even more important. By the late 1960s, the process of rapid import substitution meant that the government faced the redemption of capital borrowed from overseas countries, and exports were encouraged in order to obtain foreign capital. Incentives such as tax, tariff and bank loans were provided for exporters.

In the 1960s, the number and size of chaebol increased. The core business fields of chaebol had been shifted from sugar, cement and food in the 1950s to textiles, ceramics and chemicals in the 1960s. Chaebol also began to diversify through production expansion and export activities rather than through privileges, speculation, price control and tax evasion (Hong 1981). In other words, chaebol began to escape from expansion dependent on political collusion to a growth in their industrial capital through market activity.

The formation of chaebol in the 1960s was similar to that of the 1950s. Chaebol grew in size by providing the government with political kickbacks in return for various incentives such as the allocation of foreign loans, long-term low interest loans, tax benefits and picking up the winner in selected industries. Meanwhile, the government consolidated its political position with the financial kickbacks.

In the 1970s, the chaebol grew in size and led the rapid economic growth of Korea. The number of chaebol was strikingly increased. The major industries of chaebol in the 1970s were capital-intensive industries, construction and financial business, marking a change from the labour-intensive industries of the 1960s. During this period, chaebol participated competitively in strategic heavy and chemical industries such as automobiles, iron and steel, electronics, oil refining, shipbuilding, machinery, non-ferrous metals and petrochemicals (Hong 1987). These industries required a huge amount of investment and the government focused on a small number of chaebol providing oligopoly or monopoly for the chosen chaebol.

Since the 1960s, industrialisation has been promoted through maximising the use of domestic and foreign capital. The need for foreign capital was substantial (Jung 1994; Kang 1995). Imports of intermediate and capital goods for industrialisation were financed by foreign capital. In 1975, the government encouraged some qualified exporters to establish General Trading Companies (GTCs) in order to encourage exports. The volume of exports by the GTCs increased from 12.4 per cent of all exports in 1975 to 33.9 per cent in 1979 (Cho 1990, 1997). The chaebol took over many small firms in the name of increasing exports and thus created 'department store-style' business management, that produces everything from toys to aeroplanes.

With the nationalisation of banks in the early 1960s, chaebol were unable to encompass the entry of the first-tier financial sector (i.e., commercial banks) so that unlike the kereitsu in Japan, the possibility of financial dominance by chaebol was prevented. Chaebol were allowed, however, to enter the second-tier financial sector such as insurance, securities and short-term capital companies (Bae 1994; Cho 1994; Cho 1997). As the economy progressed, demand for the second-tier financial sector increased. This allowed the chaebol to adjust the flow of liquidity between their affiliated firms and to accommodate fund raising and dispersion of stock ownership (Cho 1997).

The phase of structural adjustment: 1980–1986

In the early 1980s, the changing economic environment at home and abroad forced changes on the chaebol. In 1980, the government enacted the Anti-Trust and Fair Trade Act and in 1981 the Fair Trade Commission supervised by the EPB was established. In 1982, the Consumer's Protection Law was enacted and in 1987, institutional tools to regulate chaebol such as the prohibition of interlocking investment and restriction of the amount of investment were reinforced. In addition, the government introduced import liberalisation and tariff reduction in order not only to improve the structure of chaebol, to face the pressure of opening the Korean market to advanced capitalist countries, but also to raise the competitiveness of the chaebol in the world market (Chang 1998). As a result, chaebol attempted to diversify through expanding business sectors between existing affiliated firms rather than by increasing the number of affiliated firms.

In the 1980s, internal dealings between the affiliated firms contributed to the growing size of the chaebol. For example, if a particular affiliate firm went to get into difficulty, other affiliated firms in the same chaebol would assist, even buying goods at above-market prices to allow time for the firm in difficulty to normalise its business management. By warding off the government's monitoring, chaebol were able to maximise their growth. At this time, the government had confidence in the potential growth of Korea based on the rapid economic growth period experienced in the 1970s (Kang 1998). By witnessing the success of Japan, the government came to judge that Korea too could do it. The future was seen to lie in the promotion of high-tech industry, in order to survive cut throat competition with advanced countries (Park 1998) and this is why the chaebol entered the high-tech sector.

High-tech industry such as semiconductors, precision machinery, chemicals, biotechnology engineering, computer, aerospace and telecommunications needs large-scale investment in R&D. This increased from 87.4 billion won in 1980, to 1.8 trillion won in 1987 and to 10.9 trillion won in 1996 accounting for 2.8 per cent of GNP (MOST 1998).

The diversification of chaebol gave them added prominence in the financial sector. Following financial liberalisation in 1980, the share of chaebol in commercial banks increased and they enlarged their businesses into the so-called second-tier financial sector including insurance, securities and short-term financing companies (Cho 1997; Kim 1998). As a result, the top 30 largest chaebol now have at least one or two financial institutions under their umbrellas.

Capital needed for business expansion was raised partly through mutual payment guarantees between affiliated firms; partly through internal transactions (Cho 1997); partly through borrowing in both the second-tier financial sector owned by the chaebol; and partly from the commercial banks controlled by the government (Shin 1999).

Because of the large amounts of investment needed for high-tech, heavy and chemical industries, chaebol become increasingly dependent on commercial loans and this is one of the main influence on the changing relationship between government and chaebol that began in the 1980s.

In 1981, the MOF began to privatise commercial banks that had been owned by the government for the past two decades. However, in the privatisation process, chaebol were specifically prohibited from acquiring these banks (Cho 1997). Chaebol were not allowed to own more than 8 per cent of any one bank's stocks (Kim 1998; Lee 1999). This was to prevent chaebol from ever becoming as formidable as the pre-World War II zaibatsu of Japan, which owned both financial institutions and industrial enterprises.

In the early 1980s, the EPB[22] significantly reduced policy loans to the private sector. These loans had been used as tools of government intervention: that is, loans with substantially lowered interest rates were provided as an inducement for private enterprises to invest in strategic industries, and loans were withheld from private enterprises that did not comply with government policies (Kim 1997). Policy loans were abundant, accounting for 63 per cent of total bank loans in 1979 (Kim 1987). Between 1977 and 1979, 80 per cent of total investment in manufacturing went to heavy industry in the form of policy loans (Moon 1988). Chaebol had a strong presence in this industry and so were the largest beneficiaries of the loans. However, these loans were gradually abandoned with the drive for economic liberalisation and the fiscal tightening of the 1980s (ibid.).

The phase of democratic reform and globalisation: 1987–1997

Provision of welfare services became a focal point in the 1980s, and the economic development plan shifted from high-growth industrialisation to social wealth creation (Hong 1994). However, by the end of the 1980s when the economy showed a substantial down-turn, chaebol began to urge the government to return to growth-oriented policies and to abandon welfare services (Kim 1997). Between 1987–1990, President Roh announced revisions in the Sixth Five-Year Economic and Social Development Plan, which included slowing down the provision of welfare services.

The policies of the EPB also changed to become more regulatory than developmental (Kim 1997). Instead of having policy loans to proactively encourage private enterprises to enter certain industries as a development policy, the emergence of chaebol put growing pressure on the government, which preferred to follow an expansionary rather than a regulatory policy as far as the chaebol were concerned.

In the early 1980s, Korea abolished the direct subsidy system for export activities as well as some traditionally managed and controlled trade systems (Sohn et al. 1998). In the 1990s, regulations on chaebol were increasingly strengthened. In 1991 a specialisation policy for industry was promoted to prevent octopus-

---

22 The EPB was incorporated into the MOF in 1996 to form the new Department of Finance and Economy reflecting the changing economic environments in Korea.

like diversification of chaebol and to raise international competitiveness through large scale production.

On the other hand, the government encouraged the chaebol by providing various incentives such as lifting restrictions on the total amount of their investment, allocating favourable industrial sites and special support for R&D. However, the specialisation policy was not very effective because of limited participation by the chaebol, reflecting their independence from the government as well as a weakening of the government's will to impose its policies on business.

In the past, the government strongly regulated trade unions and their recognition (Hong 1994). However, in 1993 the organisation of plural labour unions was allowed. This has given a great voice to working people and the chaebol have found it difficult to adapt to this change. The increasing overseas investment by chaebol has contributed to globalisation. Since the mid-1980s, the democracy movement and conflicts between labour and capital have sharply increased and these factors have transformed Korea to a high wage economy, affecting both productivity and competitiveness (Fukagawa 1997). In the same way as Japan used Korea in the past, declining industries in Korea are being relocated in developing countries to reduce costs and prices. In particular, with the results of diversification into, for example, the heavy and chemical industry, and high-tech and financial services, the major focus in chaebol changed over time from light industries such as trading, textiles and shoes to high-tech, and heavy and chemical industries such as semiconductors, shipbuilding, automobile, petrochemicals and plant.

Since the late 1980s, the relationship between government and chaebol has changed. During the rapid economic growth period, the government continued to promote chaebol. However, as chaebol grew, the government moved from a chaebol-centred economic policy to one of regulation of the chaebol, using carrot and stick to try to achieve government objectives. However, it was not very effective because chaebol have been increasingly released from government restraints. They have deviated gradually from chaebolisation through government favouritism to self-growth through market discipline. At the same time, the government limited the amount of payment guarantees between affiliated firms, which had enabled the chaebol to expand in the past.[23] A vulnerable structure in which an insolvent affiliate firm could view bankrupt the whole group had become institutionalised and, in the government's view, needed to be changed.

The phase of recovery after the 1997 financial crisis

The relationship between the Korean government and Chaebol has drastically changed since the 1997 financial crisis. Unlike the past, the deregulation of chaebol was associated with the improvement of management structures, transparency in business activities. During the 1980s when chaebol could gain tight control of

---

23 The amount of mutual payment guarantees between the affiliated firms has been reduced up to 300 per cent of equity capital. The regulation is confined to the 30 largest chaebol groups.

their businesses, but the 1990s has seen the increasing control of government in chaebol' business activities. Although there was resistance on the part of chaebol to the control imposed by the government, it was ascribed to the worsening public opinion and deteriorating economic situation that such measures could be made possible. As a result, chaebol which had enjoyed rapid growth under the aegis of the Korean government saw their status and influence decline drastically since the 1997 financial crisis. Before 1997, the government and chaebol relationships were characterized as the former gave favours to the latter, but the Kim Dae-Jung government, which took office since the crisis, has changed the government and chaebol relationship by differentiating between winners and losers: while the winners got all the benefits expected from the government, the losers would not gain any (Lee 1999).

In addition, since the financial crisis in 1997, the government has assisted venture companies in the way that she did for chaebol in the past. As an alternative player for economic development, venture companies during the Kim Dae-Jung government in particular substituted the chaebol-led economic system (which has directly and indirectly allowed a majority of chaebol to go bankrupt).

However, the general election taking placing on 13 April 2000 changed the relationship between the government and chaebols, as the latter has strongly resisted the heavy involvement of the government. Moreover, as the Kim Dae-Jung regime drew to an end, the voices of chaebol for demanding deregulation have raised, in particular, against the backdrop in which the global economies have shown sings of decline. As a result, chaebol has regained the influence although the Kim Dae-Jung government attempted to have kept them under its control since its inauguration (Shin and Sung 2002).

As a result of the reform measures triggered by the financial crisis, the structure of chaebol has become more sound and healthy. First, both insolvent companies and those which have failed to undertake radical reforms have been liquidated. For example, as the debt to equity ratio of companies has been limited to 200 per cent, the financial structure of insolvent companies have drastically improved. Second, the management of companies, which aims to maximize profits, has been improved. Thus the profits of companies have increased with the restructuring efforts, alongside a number of cost-saving measures.

All in all, although the Kim Dae-Jung regime has attempted to sever years-long relationship between government and chaebol, which has even been called as very crony, the government has not entirely abandoned the chaebol-led growth structure. Instead, what has been witnessed is a rather more competitive and complementary relationships between chaebol, venture companies and the government. In response to the increasing external pressure to restructure the government and chaebol' relations, the very structures of chaebol themselves, which range from management skills, culture to financial transparent, cost-benefit ratio, and the like, as well as their government relationships have changed more complementary.

The Changing Structure of Government-Chaebol Relationship

Growth of the Chaebol in Government-led Economic System

The chaebol' weight in the Korean economy has been gradually increased through time. In particular, the share of chaebol in manufacturing industry is overwhelming. Most of the chaebol in Korea have diversified their businesses by responding actively to government policies such as industrial policy and financial policy. In this way, chaebol could enjoy financial privileges. In contrast, firms without any connection with the government lost influence, especially after the announcement of heavy and chemical industrialisation.

The relationship between government economic policy and its influence on the growth of the top four chaebol, namely, Samsung, Hyungdai, LG and Daewoo, since they were established and during each of economic development plan periods since 1950. The growth of top four chaebol is closely linked to government economic policies over this time. They diversified their businesses in accordance with economic policy. The government designated strategic industries under its long-term economic development plans, and promoted chaebol. At the same the government nurtured them by providing various incentives such as low-interest loans, preferential taxes and acquisition of government properties at below market prices. Some chaebol were especially favoured in the 1970s when the government aggressively promoted heavy and chemical industry with financial privileges, inducing selected chaebol to invest in targeted industries. As a result, chaebol were able to chaebolise themselves through the diversification and establishment of affiliated firms. Indeed, as long as chaebol created jobs and increased exports, there were few restraints on their diversification.

The government provided the big chaebol with preferential treatment and this caused a dampening effect on the availability of funds for small and medium-sized enterprises because access to funding was a critical concern for Korean entrepreneurs throughout the period of economic development.

Selected big chaebol were able to grow in size and influence, thanks largely to the relatively generous provision of funds, as long as they followed and satisfied the intention of the government. Consequently, they greatly increased their weight within the Korean economy. It is certain that chaebol were the leading force of the Korean economy through the entire economic development in general and throughout the 1970s and the 1980s in particular. As already pointed out, chaebol were in an extremely advantageous position in various ways. The government erected entry barriers to key industries and at the same time, provided almost unlimited financial assistance to selected chaebol to prevent the risk of bankruptcy. As long as the chaebol complied with the government's industrial policy, they enjoyed benefits by way of export financing, equipment funds and protection against bankruptcy.

Chaebol are few in number. They had to engage in sharp competition to enter new promising business fields, supported by the government. The establishment of the affiliated firms of chaebol began in the early 1970s, with the launching of policy on the heavy and chemical industry. From the mid-1970s, competition

Table 5.9   Core business of the top four chaebol

Chaebol groups	Core businesses	Major firms
	Electric, electronics, and information	SS Electronics
Samsung	Machinery equipment	SS Heavy Industry and SS Aerospace
	Chemicals	SS Chemicals and SS Petro-chemicals
	Car and transportation equipment	HD Motor and HD Motor Services
Hyundai	Electric, electronics and information	HD Electronics
	Energy resources	HD Refine and Seill Petroleum
	Electric, electronics and information	Goldstar and Goldstar Electronics
LG	Chemicals	Honam Refine and Sebang Petroleum
	Energy resources	Lucky Petro-Chemicals
	Car and transportation equipment	DW Motor
Daewoo	Machinery equipment	DW Shipbuilding and DW Heavy Industry
	Distribution, transportation, warehouse	DW Corporation

Note: SS = Samsung; HD = Hyundai; DW = Daewoo.

Source: Department of Commerce, Trade and Industry.

often brought about excess investment, however, and as argued by the neoclassical economists, government intervention failed to produce favourable consequences.[24] In particular, when huge production plans in the second half of the 1970s were drawn up, chaebol hurried to make inroads into the automobile, engine, and heavy electrical machinery industries, bringing about excess competition and investment. In the 1980s, the government intervened in these industries in a readjustment of its policies.[25]

In the 1990s, the government proposed a 'core business policy,' that would force chaebol to specialise in one business field. The policy failed, however, because of resistance from the chaebol. Table 5.9 shows how the top four chaebol overlap and therefore compete in their core businesses: The success of the chaebol in

---

24 For more details, see Chapter 2

25 For instance, the Kia group was burdened with heavy losses and was forced to withdraw from passenger-car production.

resisting government's wishes is evidence of the chaebol growing independence from government influence and control.

Samsung shows a typical example of the most successful capital accumulation representing the whole Korean chaebol by responding to economic development programmes. The process of Samsung's growth corresponds to the trend of Korean economic growth. Samsung acted as the main promoter of economic growth sharing its fortunes with the course of Korean economic development.

According to the annual report published by Samsung, which shows the share of each of the sectors which the Samsung Group possesses (Samsung 1989, various issues), it can be seen the ways in which the growth of Samsung's major businesses has followed trends in government policies from 1966 to 1996. The strategic industries of Samsung, which have played a leading role in its growth, have followed the major economic and industrial priorities of the government. Samsung helped to alleviate the difficult economic situation in the 1940s and 1950s and played an important part in the reconstruction of Korea, in particular after the Korean War. In the 1960s, the main businesses of Sumsung were such labour-intensive industries as textiles and sugar yet the company did not hesitate later to enter new key industries such as electronics, and to built up an industrial base that helped the group to grow through exports. In the 1970s, with a robust big push on heavy equipment, petrochemicals, precision machinery, construction, and shipbuilding, all of which were emphasised by the government, became the main lines of business and evolved towards semiconductors in the 1980s and other high-tech industries such as electronics, computers, aerospace, information and telecommunications in the 1990s. These features have mostly been kept intact even after the crisis. As shown in Figure 5.1, Samsung's business has grown and developed in concert with Korean economic development.

In the process of rapid economic development in Korea, in particular, in the period of rapid increase in GNP, diversification guaranteed the growth of chaebol. Samsung began to diversify in unrelated business lines, often doing so one step earlier than others and making timely investments in new businesses. Diversification in unrelated fields was encouraged by government as the best way for chaebol to diversify their businesses in avoiding risks, accelerating growth, and maximising profits.[26] In other words, it can be said that Samsung has evolved into a fitter form as economic environments have changed. In addition, before 1960, most of Samsung's business was focused on the domestic market. For instance, Samsung's share of the total exports of Korea accounted for only 0.08 per cent in 1956, as shown in Table 5.10.

With the launching of the export-promotion policy by the government in the early 1960s, Samsung's contribution began to increase, so that by 1986 it accounted for 24 per cent (by value) of all Korean exports and for nearly 27 per cent by 1996. Although the share of Samsung in terms of Korea's total exports had slightly decreased in 2002 due to the adjustment of foreign exchange rates and the volume of total exports since the financial crisis, Samsung had still accounted for a significant share of Korea's exports.

---

26 For more detailed argument, see next chapter.

Table 5.10 Share of Samsung's export in total exports of Korea: 1956–2002 ($m)

	Total Korean exports	Samsung's share (%)
1956	24.6	0.02 (0.08)
1966	250.3	6.53 (2.6)
1976	7,715.3	449.78 (5.9)
1986	34,714.5	8,367.00 (24)
1996	129,715.1	34,381.00 (26.5)
2002	162,410.5	31,200.00 (19.2)

Sources: Office of Samsung Executive Staff (1998); National Statistical Office (1985, 1999); Korean National Statistical Office, various years.

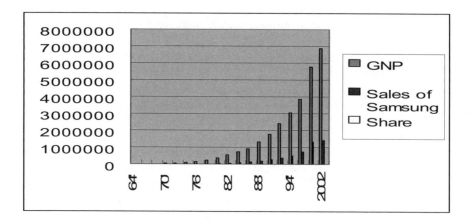

Figure 5.6 The share of Samsung's total sales to GNP: 1964-2002 (unit: 100 million won, %)

Source: Samsung (1998); Korean National Statistical Office (1985, 1999).

As shown in Figure 5.6, Samsung's total sales as a proportion of GNP rose gradually in the early 1970s along with the industrial policy of the government and continued to do so in the 1980s and 1990s.[27] In 1996, the total sales of Samsung amounted to 74,640 billion won accounting for 19.3 per cent of GNP. Even after

---

27 Annual average growth rates of total sales as a proportion of GNP between 1986 and 1996 for the top five,ten and 30 chaebol groups were 17.2, 17.9 and 17.4, respectively.

the 1997 financial crisis, the influence of Samsung has remained unchanged, as its total sales as a proportion of GNP has accounted for around 20 per cent of the Korean economy. Obviously, the Korean economy as a whole is greatly affected by the success or otherwise of Samsung, illustrating the power shift from government to chaebol that has been mentioned earlier.

The Changing Structure of Chaebol

Chaebol continued to expand and dominate the Korean economy, even after government subsidies were drastically cut in the early 1980s. As chaebol gained prosperity and some independence from the government, their relationship with the government became more competitive. Importantly, chaebol were able to show that they could function and prosper without the government's support. Quite contrary to the perspective of the developmental-statists on Korean economic development, government is no longer omnipotent in relation to the private sector.

However, as pointed by Kim (1997) and Lee (1999), the nation's economy has become so dependent on chaebol that their collapse would jeopardise the entire economy, at least in the short run. The view that a 'big company will never die' has been instilled into the government and chaebol, and even the people. Yet, the logic of the chaebol growing independence from government is that their survival is dependent on the market rather than on the hand of government implying that even the largest chaebol, even if supported by the government, could collapse.

Table 5.11 The number of second tier financial institutions owned by chaebol (2001)

Chaebol	Total no. of affiliated firms	Financial institution				
		Securities	Insurance	Short-term finance co.	Credit card co.	Subtotal
Top 5	203	5	4	16	1	16
Top 10	310	6	6	24	1	37
Top 30	624	11	12	51	2	76

Note: Compiled from materials based on parliamentary inspection of the administration.

Source: Office of Bank Supervision and Examination (OBSE) (2001).

In the 1980s, the most marked trend among the top four chaebol was the growth in financial services. According to Kim (1997), by the mid-1980s, eight of the top ten chaebol owned at least one non-banking financial institution—e.g., insurance, securities, and short-term finance companies. In 1987, the number of non-bank financial institutions owned by the top ten and top 50 was 21 and 38, respectively (OBSE 1996). However, as Table 5.11 shows, the number owned in 2001 by the top 10 and top 30 had increased to 37 and 76 respectively. Non-banking financial institutions were very lucrative business and were critical for chaebol in their efforts to become less dependent on the domestic banks and the government (Cho 1994; Cho 1997). Bae (1994) noted that these institutions, developed specifically to get around the nationalised banking system, allowed chaebol flexibility with day-to-day cash-flow problems and with lending within chaebol. Such growth was contrary to the government's directive to prohibit ownership of private banks, which was intended to keep chaebol from becoming too powerful by owning both industrial manufacturing and the banking sectors. Chaebol' investment in financial services also highlights a direct competition occurring between the government and chaebol for the provision of such services. Moreover, chaebol' increased investment in non-banking financial institutions is an indication that chaebol wished to become more independent from the government.

Changes in market structure

As the industrial development of the 1960s and 1970s sowed the seeds of competition, economic growth in the 1980s was accompanied by important changes in Korea's industrial organisation.

The growth-first strategy centred on chaebol was implemented for decades as a policy by which government selected target industries to promote. In a rapidly growing economy, many new markets developed which guaranteed high rates of return on investments, especially when the markets were protected from both foreign and domestic competition (Cho 1997). The capital accumulated in the early phase of success, combined with a preferential supply of loans from the government-controlled credit market, could then be channelled into a new activity. In this process, managerial know-how and technological capabilities grew, with beneficial synergies. Thus, as Yoo and Lee (1997) pointed out, chaebol diversification reflects the process of rapid industrial restructuring in Korea. Even when participating in a new market was unprofitable, there still existed other important incentives to diversify: operating a financial company reduced the risk to business when the financial sector suffered from market imperfections; owning a newspaper or broadcasting company were in some cases a key element of business success; the capital gains from holding the real estate of a new subsidiary by far exceeded any losses from business when real estate prices soared (Cho 1997; Jwa 1999). These factors served as a profitability incentive to diversify.

Regulations to curb 'octopus-like' diversification of chaebol have constituted the core of chaebol policy in Korea. Investment regulations based upon the credit control system have turned the banks into regulators of industrial firms, resulting in a distorted relationship between banks and their customers (Cho 1997). Korean firms have grown through debt financing rather than equity financing (Euh 1994). The desire of owner-managers to maintain a high share of ownership, coupled with debt financing, has resulted in ownership concentration.

Indeed, as Hattori (1989) pointed out, during the 1960s and 1970s, chaebol increased the number of their affiliates in many ways: they either acquired failing firms, state-owned enterprises that were privatised, small-and medium-sized firms, or established new firms to diversify into businesses (see also Yoo and Lee

1997). The concentration of economic power by chaebol intensified during the 1960s and 1970s. The economic growth in the 1970s consolidated the economic power into a small number of chaebol, and they remain the largest business conglomerates even today.

Table 5.12 shows indicators of the performance of the top 5, 10 and 30 chaebol from 1985 to 1995. The share of the top 30 largest chaebol in total value added increased from 12.5 per cent in 1985 to 16.2 per cent in 1995. In particular, as shown in Table 5.14, the share of the top 30 chaebol in the economy has been gradually increased.

Table 5.12 Major indicators of the top 5, 10 and 30 chaebol (whole industries), 1985–1995 (%)

	Value added (1)			Sales (2)			Total Assets (3)			Employment (4)		
	Top 5	Top 10	Top 30	Top 5	Top 10	Top 30	Top 5	Top 10	Top 30	Top 5	Top 10	Top 30
1985	6.6	8.8	12.5	30.8	38.6	48.8	23.5	3.3	42.9	2.54	3.06	4.34
1987	6.1	7.9	11.0	31.5	38.7	48.7	25.1	33.8	45.0	2.53	3.09	4.29
1989	7.4	9.8	12.9	30.5	37.5	47.3	25.5	33.7	45.9	2.61	3.29	4.52
1991	7.2	9.6	13.0	27.2	32.8	41.3	24.0	32.5	43.5	2.55	3.30	4.29
1993	7.8	10.2	13.6	27.6	34.1	41.7	24.0	32.6	43.2	2.40	3.20	4.14
1995	10.1	12.8	16.2	30.7	37.8	45.8	25.4	33.8	44.6	2.62	3.48	4.41

Notes
1 Excluding financial business and insurance
2 The share of top 30s value added vis-à-vis GNP
3 The share of top 30s to the whole industry
4 The number of employment in top 30 to the total employment.

Source: Fair Trade Commission (1996).

The concentration by chaebol was especially noticeable in the manufacturing sector, as shown in Table 5.13. The concentration of economic power by chaebol was one of the legacies of industrial development in the 1960s and 1970s (Jwa 1999). The value added in manufacturing industry to gross industrial products accounts for 29.92 per cent. The share of the value added of the top 30 chaebol by sector accounts for 33.55 per cent in manufacturing, 11.71 per cent in transportation, warehouse and telecommunications, and 11.27 per cent in construction. On the other hand, the value added of the top 30 largest chaebol in agriculture, forestry and fishery accounts for 0.05 per cent and electricity and water-supply for 1.03 per cent. The low percentage is because most of these utilities are owned by the government. It does not indicate lack of interest in these sectors by chaebol. Clearly, chaebol have the great impacts on the domestic economy and manufacturing industry is dominated by them.

Table 5.13   The value added of chaebol to total industry by sector (in 1995, billion won)

	Total industry (A)	Top 30 (B)	(B/A) %
Agriculture, forestry and fishery	23,068 (7,30)	12	0.05
Mining	1,109 (0.35)	53	4.78
Manufacturing	94,485 (29.92)	31,704	33.55
Electricity, gas, and water-supply	7,893 (2.49)	103	1.03
Construction	49,636 (15.71)	5,596	11.27
Retail, wholesale, food, accommodation	40,085 (12.69)	2,580	6.44
Transportation, warehouse, telecom.	25,945 (8.21)	3,039	11.71
Financial insurance, real estate, service	59,268 (18.76)	2,328	3.93
Social and private service	14,298 (4.52)	–	–
Financial-related service	12,861 (4.07)	–	–
Gross industrial products (C)	315,787 (100%)	46,415	14.70
GNP (D)	348,284	–	–
C/D × 100 (%)	90.7	–	–

Note: Financial business is excluded.

Source: Kyoyoungup (1996).

Table 5.14   Share of top chaebol in manufacturing industry (%)

Year	Value added			Amount of sales			Total assets			Employment		
	1985	1990	1995	1985	1990	1995	1985	1990	1995	1985	1990	1995
Top 1–4	11.7	17.0	27.2	21.9	23.4	27.3	23.6	26.0	28.0	6.5	6.9	8.1
Top 5–10	4.8	5.8	7.1	11.6	9.2	9.9	9.7	10.5	11.5	1.7	2.1	2.6
Top 11–30	5.7	6.2	6.7	9.6	8.0	7.6	12.3	10.2	10.7	3.4	2.7	2.5
Total	22.2	29.0	41.0	43.1	40.6	44.9	45.6	46.8	50.2	11.6	11.7	13.1

Source: BOK, various years.

Table 5.14 shows, for the period from 1985 and 1995, the changing share of the top 30 largest chaebol in manufacturing industry. Their combined share of the added value in manufacturing industry increased from 22.2 per cent in 1985 to 41.0 per cent in 1995.

The emerging political influence of the chaebol

Up to the early 1970s, the fate of chaebol was largely extent determined by the hand of the government. However, since the late 1970s, with the results of rapid growth of chaebol the government has gradually begun to lose its power to control chaebol. Instead, as chaebol gained prominence in the economy, they began to compete with the government for more influence. As it become evident that many policies simply could not be developed and implemented without cooperation from chaebol, the government invited leading chaebol owners for their support on important policies

(Kim 1997). Despite these gestures by the government, several large chaebol openly rejected the government' policies. Furthermore, instead of taking a reactive position to the government's policies, chaebol as a group began proactively to exert collective power demanding important policy changes and reforms.[28]

In particular, since the 1980s, some groups in the government that try to understand the business circle have emerged, as some businessmen were appointed to the post of the Vice President, the Ministry of Finance and other important posts in the government (Lee 1999).[29] At last, in 1992, the chairman of a chaebol came to run as a presidential candidate. As the relationship between the business circle and the government changes, the influence of the chaebol on society has become increasingly significant and the chairman of the top chaebol has been recognised as the 'President of the Korean Economy.'

The Changing Relationship between the Government and Chaebol

As explained in Chapter 3, in the process of interplay between internal and external factors, an economy develops, with the relationship between the two factors being complementary and evolutionary through time.

As Table 5.15 shows, up to 1960, the government in Korea was relatively passive on the issue of economic development and business activities and the framework of the government-chaebol relationship had not been built yet, due to social chaos and political instability. The role of government in this period can be defined as a rule maker. Since 1961, the relationship between the government and chaebol has become significant. In the initial stage of economic development, the government intervened deeply in private business activity and the government restricted the role of third parties intentionally, except for the government-chaebol relationship. As Amsden (1989) pointed out, between the early 1960s and the late 1970s, the government indicated and chaebol followed, while improving various laws and regulations in such a way as to meet the realistic needs of the national economy. The relationship between the government and chaebol was indicative and direct: the government was the planner and chaebol were the implementers. In a sense, the relationship between government and chaebol was static during this period, as the developmental-statists argued. However, their arguments on Korean economic

---

28 In the early 1980s, there was a discussion about the reorganisation of the heavy and chemical industries. Daewoo was supposed to participate in plans for reorganising the electricity generating industry. Kim, Woo-Joong, the chairman of Daewoo rejected the government's first attempt at reorganisation indicating that he could not implement the government's plan because the plan would require large amount of capital and instead, he requested financial support from the government. In the end, the plan failed and a state-run firm was established for electricity generation. Yet, up to the end of 1970s, it would have been unimaginable for chaebol to reject government's proposal.

29 Since the late 1980s, the role of chaebol has been extended to the political arena. In 1988, Chung, Mong-Joon, president of Hyundai Heavy Industries successfully ran for the National Assembly and he is still a member of the National Assembly. Other leaders have also been elected to the National Assembly.

Table 5.15 The changing relationship between the government and chaebol

	Rhee regime (1948–1960)	Park regime (1961–1979)	Chun regime (1980–1987)	Roh regime (1988–1992)	Kim regime (1993–1997)	Kim regime (1997–2002)
Government policies	Laissez-faire Preferential assistance	Government-led Foreign capital introduction, import substitution, export-led	Export-led rapid industrialisation, direct investment, assistance and regulation	Price stabilisation, import liberalisation, fair trade	Economic liberalisation, deregulation	Neoliberalims Free market economy
Government-chaebol relationship	Rulemaker-implementer	Rule maker, indicator-follower, implementer	Indicator, assistance-implementer	Assistance, regulator-implementer	Regulator-implementer	Regulator-implementer
Government assistance	President-private firm	Government-private firm	Negotiation of government and private firms	Public tender	Abolished in principle	Reforms in financial sector, xhaebol
Preferential privilege	Allocation of aid, vested properties and foreign capital, import quotas	Commercial loan, industrial policy	Policy loan, adjustment of insolvent firms	Regulations related to real estates	Part regulation	Strengthening management power and shareholders
Bank ownership	Privatisation	Nationalisation	Privatisation, reinforcement of control	Privatisation, deregulation	Privatisation, deregulation	Liberalisation of financial markets
Development pattern of chaebol	Financial chaebolisation	National capitalistic development/ transformation to industrial capital	Business restructuring/ reinforcement of R&D	Restructuring of organisation/ business opening	International-isation/mix of financial sector	Transparency and reform of finance in chaebol

Table 5.15 cont'd

	Rhee regime (1948–1960)	Park regime (1961–1979)	Chun regime (1980–1987)	Roh regime (1988–1992)	Kim regime (1993–1997)	Kim regime (1997–2002)
Institutional Evolution	Denationalisation of banks	Export promotion meeting; nationalisation of banks; chaebol	National investment fund	Fair trade commission; second-tier financial sector; labour union	Independent of central bank and its functional reinforcement	Free competition
Evolution of the chaebol	Emergence and formation of chaebol, derailed capital accumulation, deepening overseas dependence, bipolar system	Formation of chaebol groups, establishment of GTC/expansion of organisation by cross-funding, emergence of professional manager quantitative expansion	Reinforcement of R&D/FDI/ Organisation of subcontracting Company.	Diversification, challenge to the government, progressive independent from government dependence	Overseas network/ organisation of industrial cluster/ M&A, multi-polar system	Liberalisation of foreign investment Balanced growth of chaebol and small and medium-sized firms

development gave insufficient attention to the changing relations of institutions as the economy became more mature

The primary objective of the Park government (1961–1979) was to building up a small number of selected chaebol with financial institutions controlled by the government. All banks were nationalised so that they became an agent of the government and thus, the role of the financial market in controlling firms' activities was very limited (Cho 1994). In addition, chaebol expanded their businesses through diversification enabling themselves to become stronger.

The Chun government (1980–1987) denationalised the banks, adjusted policy on HCI, and passed the Act of Fair Trade (Park 1994). As a result, the relationship between the government and chaebol gradually changed. It became less direct and was often influenced by legal considerations and bank lending decisions. Through their history, the chaebol have been both assisted, monitored by the government.

Chaebol evolved as the major player in the course of economic development by diversifying their business lines. From the early 1970s, the Park government promoted chaebol by centring on the achievement of efficiency. However, in the 1980s, the adverse features of economic concentration leading to income disparity became apparent, so that the Chun government shifted its policy from growth-orientation to wealth-orientation (Jung 1987, 1994). This policy was reinforced by adopting direct and indirect regulation of chaebol through the enactment of fair trade, import liberalisation, and promotion of small and medium companies; and by reducing export finance and financial privileges for chaebol.

In the late 1980s, as a result of the great influence of the chaebol on the economy, the Rho government (1988–1992) was forced to implement strong regulation on chaebol, threatening their existence by cutting new loans to them, and by preventing growing chaebolisation (Lee 1999). From 1995, the Kim government (1993–1997) implemented the real name accounting system for the first time in Korean financial history (Jung 1998). In both the Rho and Kim regimes, deregulation and globalisation intensified. Although the government continued to control chaebol, financial privileges were so indirect that direct privileges were reduced. Such a trend has further been accelerated in the Kim government (1998–2002), as both economic policies and corresponding reform of chaebol's business activities haven been undertaken by the logic of neoliberalism, which emphasizes free and open competition.

The relationship between the government and chaebol has been dynamic over time, but both have always shared their fortune with each other. Although government intervention has been reduced over time, writers such as Cho (1998) believe that the ill-effects of government-led economic policies have been accumulated. For example, in the 1990s, financial markets were vulnerable to changing market conditions and labour market were too rigid (ibid.).

In sum, in Korea, institutions have changed as the economy has grown in size and complexity and the reinforcement of internal complementarity centred on chaebol has been affected not only by the government and the financial institution but also by the changing economic environments. The role of government in steering the economy was important to begin with but became less efficient in the 1970s when the HCI period brought about excess capacity, resulting in an increase in the number of unsound firms in the 1980s and 1990s. Both government and chaebol have faced a pluralistic and complex society, which has not existed in the past. The government in becoming one of the many stakeholders in the economy, has gradually given up the strict control of chaebol, and has changed from courting and threatening them to regulating them.

Government-Chaebol in the Korean Economic System

From the viewpoint of the neoclassical school, government-led economic policy does not mean that government participates in economic activity as an economic agent but takes part in the market as an endogenous variable. However, as presented by the developmental-statists, economic activity in Korea has been determined by a government that restrains the decision-making of private economic agents and determines in advance what the result of economic activity should be. On a macroeconomic level, government preferred direct control to indirect control. But on a microeconomic level, it decided that the chaebol would be the winner in economic activity and provided the support needed to achieve this outcome.

Because of this, the concentration of economic power in the chaebol began to influence the entire economy substantially from the late 1970s. This forced the industrial policies of the government to restrict the growth of chaebol. However, the government could not abandon the two basic goals: attainment of high-growth and a self-reliant economy, so that economic policies had to return to a chaebol-oriented approach. The government promoted chaebol by erecting entry barriers and at the same time, provided almost unlimited financial assistance to prevent the social and economic problems that might be caused if any chaebol were to become bankrupt. Accordingly, chaebol rushed into unrelated businesses in order to grasp new opportunities, without regard to economic efficiency and the economic linkage effects. Chaebol not only maximised their profits but pursued 'survival of the fittest' strategy in pursuit of their own self-development. The pattern and behaviour of chaebol have been developed in the unique Korean economic environment. As a result, they have grown so quickly that they have been instrumental in restricting the role of government.

This should not be regarded, however, as a 'failure' by government but rather as a recognition that the role of government is bound to change as an economy evolves and develops. In a relatively small economy and a 'simple' economic environment, government can exert control, as the Korean government did until the 1980s. But with a large and complicated economy, as Korea now is, the omnipotent government role is no longer applicable. A new understanding between government and chaebol, recognising the role of the market, has emerged in the Korean economic system.

Chapter 6

The State and Financial Institutions

The previous chapter explained the evolutionary relationship between the Korean government and chaebol. The Korean government did not see itself as the only player in economic development and needed partnerships to minimise the risk of market failures and to strengthen its strategic alliances. As the economy has become mature, other players have been required and financial institutions emerged as a response.

From the beginning, financial institutions were put under the control of the government and were used as carrot and stick not only in drawing chaebol's attention to the targeted industries but also in threatening their activities by withdrawing policy loans provided through various channels. Thus, the relationship between government, chaebol and the financial institutions is a nexus for understanding Korean economic development, in particular, how the financial institutions have been used as an instrument for the allocation of resources. In the process of economic growth, financial institutions under heavy government intervention and regulation, have continued to grow and have emerged as a determining influence on the direction of Korean economic development. This chapter examines the evolutionary relationship between the financial institutions and the government, and discusses how the financial institutions have emerged as an independent variable.

Financial Institutions and Economic Development

The Role of Financial Institutions

Capital plays a crucial role in the process of economic development and the funds required capital for industrialisation are raised through the accumulation of capital (Sano 1977). Capital needs to be accumulated through the efforts of many generations. At the initial stage of economic development, most countries suffer from a lack of fund-raising for economic development. In general, the shortage of retained capital is supplemented by foreign capital. Foreign capital enables a recipient to consider an alternative development pattern, widening development choices for economic development.

Small domestic income makes full use of investment capital impossible and at the same time, circulation of industrial capital has been insufficient due to long-term gestation period including high risks. Credit and information play an important role in the financial market. Like industrial capital, both credit and information need long-term accumulation as well. Accordingly, at the initial stage of economic development, the capital available to firms through direct investment is insufficient. To maximise long-term capital mobilisation by firms, financial institutions play a crucial role.[1] Historically, financial institutions develop with a view to raising the required funds for industrialisation as efficiently as possible.

Britain relied less on the financial institutions for long-term capital in the course of economic development because domestic capital was to some extent accumulated when industrialisation took off (Cain and Hopkins 1993). In contrast, capital was much scarcer and more fragmented in late-comers in Europe such as France and Germany and it was riskier to invest in industries because of long-term returns (Gerschenkron 1962). In addition, late-comers needed larger equipment investment and better technology than Britain did at the initial stage of industrialisation.

With such different economic environments, various financial institutions were developed in Europe and industrial capital was raised through them (ibid.). In France, Credit Mobilier (CM) emerged as a new type of bank. Unlike the commercial banks, the CM provided long-term industrial capital by participating in rail construction.[2] In Germany, the universal banking (UB) system played an intermediate role in providing long-term industrial capital. This was the system that combined the role of the commercial bank mainly engaged in short-term capital with that of the CM. The UB kept close to firms, and maintained a partnership with them from their establishment onwards. The relationship enabled the UB to get information for firms' investment. Moreover, the UB had dominance over firms through its supervisory board. The dominance went beyond finance, to include managerial and entrepreneurial decision-making. It was argued that this helped to maximise the efficient use of industrial capital.

Japan, by contrast, had a segmented and fragmented financial system. In particular, unlike most of the advanced countries, the Japanese government played an active role in raising industrial capital (Sakakibara 1993). The government provided various privileges for firms through commercial and credit banks. Low interest rates were set and firms shouldered huge debts (Ito 1992). Capital was raised through a high savings rate and the accumulation of financial assets. Government intervention caused rent-seeking that prevails in the process of resource allocation. However, the government could maximise the efficiency of

---

1　'Finance' refers to the circulation of capital. However, in order to provide capital, information between the supplier (individual saving), who has excess capital and the demander (investor), who is short of capital is necessary. Financial transaction becomes real when demand and supply are met. A financial institution is a kind of company that creates the required information between demand and supply and transfers that information to both sides.

2　Traditionally, commercial banks provide short-term capital for firms while investment banks supply long-term capital. In addition, venture capital is the main supplier for small and medium-sized companies, particularly newly established small and medium-sized companies.

resource allocation by maintaining close co-operation with the private sector, and by depending for industrial policy on private firms, the keiretsu.[3]

In the course of industrialisation, the development of financial institutions contributes to raising industrial capital. Financial institutions not only mobilise capital, but minimise risk caused by the provision of capital over the long-term. Through the financial institutions, capital is effectively mobilised and directed to productive sectors.

Understanding of Government Intervention in Financial Institutions

Gerschenkron (1962) argues that a developing country can develop much faster than an advanced country by taking advantage of the backlog of technological innovation developed and improved in the more advanced country. This enables the developing country to heighten the speed of industrialisation.[4] In addition, the normal process of economic growth can be shortened by watching and by mimicking other development strategies. In other words, the developing country can establish its industrial structure more effectively than advanced countries by following the lessons of successful economic growth in advanced countries (Cho 1994; Watanabe 1982).

In general, developing countries tend to establish larger factories than advanced countries, mainly in manufacturing industries. However, the bigger the factory with more advanced technology, the more capital it needs. As stated earlier, firms in advanced countries raise the required funds for business expansion on their own but in developing countries, government raises the required funds and then distributes them through financial institutions. The government is the fund-raiser for the business expansion of firms, leading to industrialisation. Gerschenkron (ibid.) pointed out that the higher the degree of backwardness, the deeper will be the degree of the government's role; and the stronger the role of government, the more discontinuous development is likely to be. Indeed, the often feverish degree of government intervention in financial institutions can be explained by the attempt to catch up with advanced countries.

In Korea, government-led industrialisation policy was adopted to develop the economy. The government attempted to condense the process of economic development by cultivating the sources of intensive growth by improving technological capability and industrial relations (Ohkawa 1970; Cho 1991, 1994; Watanabe 1982). For this, the government put the financial institutions under its control and allocated financial resources to targeted industries as well as selected

---

3 Unlike other advanced countries, Japan has a unique financial system, the so-called main bank system in which the business relationship between banks and firms is long-term oriented and sustainable. The main bank is the largest single lender to firms and holds a significant equity interest in the firms. In addition, it has special powers to manage the firms' affairs in times of financial distress.

4 In the case of Korea, this pattern is indeed called a 'condensed economic development' or a benefit of late-comers. For more details, see Watanabe (1982 and Cho (1994). For the Japanese economy, see Ohkawa (1970).

firms. That is, bureaucrats decide the priorities for economic development and government tells financial institutions which firms and which industries will receive financial credit and how much they will be given. In addition, government intervenes in the internal management of financial institutions, for example, in personnel and budget planning in order to monitor whether its directives are being carried out. In such circumstances, the independent role of financial institutions is weak.

Evolution of Financial Institutions in Korea

Legacy of Financial Institutions

After liberation in 1945, some financial institutions and modern banking businesses were inherited from Japan and thus, Korea could reduce the initial instalment costs needed for establishment of modern financial institutions.[5] However, it is hardly possible to expect efficient currency management when government controls most of the financial institutions. After liberation Korea experienced rapid and high inflation. From 1936 to 1947 the amount of issue increased by 158.5 times, and RPI (Retail Price Index) and WI (Wage Index) rose by 770 and 158 times, respectively (see Table 6.1). Unstable and insistent currency management, and high inflation shrank the economy and the financial institutions did not expand.

After World War II, the financial stocks that were owned by the Japanese during the colonial period were passed over to the US military occupation and later to the Korean government and in the process, where the responsibility for them lay became ambiguous. This caused inefficient bank management. Specialised banks that provide long-term capital such as savings and trust banks were allowed to deal with short-term capital. Furthermore, as Kim (1997) and Cho (1994) pointed out, Chosun Bank, the central bank (now the Bank of Korea) competed with commercial banks by providing general banking services, which meant that it could not carry out the role of bank supervision. This blurred the distinction between the commercial and the specialised banks.

The central bank was not independent from the government, which could require the bank to supply the necessary currency needed for policy implementation. By issuing notes in this way, the value of the currency became unstable, impeding the development of the capital market (Lee 1999). Currency instability caused underdevelopment of the long-term capital market, resulting in the growth of the curb market. Moreover, banking was not managed effectively because most of the financial institutions were owned by the government.

---

5   For literature on Japan's colonial influences on Korea, see Ahn and Nakmura (1989, 1993), Eckert (1990), Grajdanzv (1944), Kohli (1994) and Mizoguchi (1975, 1979).

Table 6.1   Amount of issue, prices and wages indices (1936–1947)

Year	Amount of circulation issued by Chosun Bank (won)	RPI	WI
1936	210,654 (100)	100	100
1937	279,502 (132)	109	120
1938	321,978 (152)	131	131
1939	443,987 (210)	153	140
1940	580,534 (275)	169	146
1941	741,607 (352)	174	168
1942	908,646 (431)	183	183
1943	1,466,777 (696)	202	200
1944	3,135,692 (1,4888)	226	224
1945	8,763,341 (3,791)	9,606	2,560
1946	17,710,623 (8,407)	21,619	10,837
1947	33,388,164 (15,849)	76,998	15,801

Notes
RPI refers to Retail Price Index based on the necessary goods purchased by Seoul residents.
WI refers to Wage Index based on average wages earned by workingmen in Seoul.
1936 = 100.

Source: Chosun Economic Statistics (1949).

Establishment of Financial Institutions: 1945–1960

In the late 1940s, efforts were made to establish new financial institutions, to arrest rampant inflation and to encourage production. As pointed out by Park (1990), it is necessary to establish a financial system to provide long-term industrial capital. Thus, the Bank of Korea Act (BOK) and the General Banking Act (GBA) were enacted to stabilise the value of currency through strict currency management; to carry out commercial banking; and to strengthen the supervisory role.[6]

In the 1950s, both the central bank and the commercial banks failed fully to perform their roles. Cho (1994) pointed out that the BOK was unable to take important policy instruments for market stabilisation except for the adjustment of the money supply or of interest rates, which were the typical policy instruments used by the Japanese colonial government. In addition, commercial banks were not used to exercising autonomy since they were accustomed to government

---

6   On paper, the BOK became independent of the government, having the authority to carry out its financial policy. With the enactment of the GBA, commercial banking was given to the existing financial institutions.

ownership. This did not change until government-owned bonds were transferred to them in the late 1950s.[7]

In the 1950s, the government did not have a comprehensive economic development strategy, and did not have a clear and independent vision or set of policy goals, because economic policy came under strong US influence, as pointed out by Cho (1994). In the late 1950s, price stability and increases in interest rates motivated the denationalisation of banks both to distribute various financial goods through a market mechanism and to boost the efficiency of market function in the financial market (Lee 1999). Importantly, a relatively independent central bank was established and private owners came to control the commercial banks. The new financial system, based on the denationalisation of banks, laid the foundation for economic growth and a development bank was established to supply industrial capital. However, this does not mean that banks were freed from the government's hand. Rather, the government continued to intervene in the allocation of resources and in particular, most of the supply of industrial capital through the industrial development bank depended on government borrowing and this caused rent-seeking such as corruption and lobbying activities for bank loans.[8]

As pointed out by Cho (1994) and Park (1990), the bank privatisation of the late 1950s stimulated the growth of the financial market, and stabilised the value of the currency as well. However, interest rates were regulated and this made capital accumulation by private savings insufficient so that most of private investors could not help but turn to the curb market, with its high costs incurred (Cho 1997). In addition, government intervention in distributing industrial capital caused inefficiency. Chung (1991) says that most of industrial capital was provided by money borrowed from the government, which accounted for over 90 per cent of total loans between 1955 and 1961. This was raised by bank notes issued by the BOK, and the counterpart funds were created by grants (ibid.).

Between 1957 and 1960, the financial institution were reformed and rampant inflation began to be stabilised because of the privatisation of banks and the strengthened authority of the BOK.

As shown in Table 6.2, between 1954 and 1960 the amount of annual increase in the money in circulation and in price inflation had been rapidly reduced and these provided the foundation for the development of a financial market. However, government intervention through regulation of interest rates brought about distortion of resource allocation.

---

7   Between 1954 and 1957 bonds of commercial banks owned by the government began to be handed over to the private sector.

8   The government adopted import restriction policy because of the shortage of foreign exchange. Mainly in the process of the allocation of import quotas that accompanied foreign exchange allocation, rent-seeking occurred. As a result, windfall gains fell into the hand of importers, leading to inefficient allocation of resources.

Table 6.2   Major indicators of the Korean economy between 1954–1960 (%)

Year	Increase rates of currency against previous year	Increase rates of prices*	Economic growth rates
1954	93.3	37.3	5.5
1955	62.1	68.0	5.4
1956	28.7	22.5	0.4
1957	19.8	23.1	7.7
1958	33.1	-3.1	5.2
1959	20.7	4.3	3.9
1960	-2.6	8.3	1.9

*   Consumer Price Index, purchases by Seoul residents.

Sources: BOK (1990); National Statistics Office (1970).

Extensive Growth of Financial Institutions: 1961–1979

In 1960, political instability and incremental inflation led to sluggish economic growth. The government established by military coup in 1961 favoured the Japanese approach to financial systems. As in Japan, the new government in Korea took control of the financial system, intervened in financial institutions, and encouraged market segmentation through the creation of specialised banks. So, the small and medium-sized industrial bank was established to assist small and medium-sized firms. The introduction of foreign capital and loans guaranteed by government were allowed. Capital accumulation was accelerated through the Korea Development Bank. In late 1962, in order to manage a small amount of finance, small-scale mutual financial companies were incorporated into the Citizens National Bank. Fisheries cooperatives were established to promote credit for and the sale of marine products. These specialised banks, which were established to allocate capital for special purposes were not controlled by the BOK.[9]

The government's ownership and control of the central bank and other financial institutions were strengthened. Commercial banks were under tight government control, for example, through confiscation of any illegal property acquisition (Amsden 1989; Lee 1999). The voting rights of private share holders were limited to 10 per cent in order to control personnel and business management. The BOK was supervised by the Ministry of Finance and a right of re-examination

9   This does not mean that they were completely from free from government. Correctly speaking, they were relatively freer than other commercial banks. As in many countries, executives were appointed by the government and the budget was supervised by the government.

regarding monetary policies was given to the Minister of Finance (Cho 1994; Cho 1997). As a result, competence and the responsibility for monetary policy fell into the government's hand.

Between 1961 and 1962, these changes to the financial system brought about a rapid increase in bank loans and the BOK could not control a sharp increase in the volume of currency (Kim 1990, 1997). The government introduced currency reform both to absorb money, and to take control of inflation. However, as pointed out by many,[10] currency reform shrank business activities, and accelerated economic instability. In particular, a shortage of funds squeezed the business activities of small and medium-sized firms and the freezing of funds had to be lifted. Currency reform damaged the reputation of the financial institutions and many people preferred to invest in goods and property, reducing the funds available, making it difficult for firms to raise funds for business.

Park (1990) believes that money supply was used deliberately by the government as the means to attain development throughout the entire economic development period. The government intervened in the financial market. Under its development plan, the total amount of money supply and the use of capital were decided by the government. The central bank lost control over the value of currency and this affected business transactions. Meanwhile, government intervention in the financial market heightened inefficient economic activities, causing firms to protect the existing value of their assets, and thus avoid capital losses caused by high inflation (Kim 1997; Cho and Kim 1997).

A flourishing curb market resulted from government intervention (Park 1985). Instability of currency value, political instability and regulation of interest rates weakened the growth of the financial market, instead, resulting in a prosperous curb market based on short-term capital carrying high interest rates. However, even the curb market was affected by direct government intervention.

Table 6.3   Investment and saving rates as a proportion of GNP: 1960–1964 (%)

Year	Investment	Domestic savings	Foreign saving
1960	10.86	0.82	8.57
1961	13.16	2.86	8.60
1962	12.80	3.26	10.69
1963	18.11	8.69	10.42
1964	14.04	8.74	6.85

Source: BOK (1970).

With the establishment of various specialised banks, the supply of domestic funds increased. As shown in Table 6.3, domestic savings rates increased from 0.82 per cent of GNP in 1960 to over 8.7 per cent in 1964. However, it is hardly

10 Particularly, see Cho (1990, 1997), Cho (1994) and Ro (1994) for more details.

possible to expect efficient resource allocation when resources are distributed by government. Park and Cole and Park (1984) pointed out that every year the government allocated 50–70 per cent of loans as policy loans to selected industries and the remaining funds also were controlled. According to Jwa (1999), government should have a better knowledge of and information about the functioning of the economy than all other participants in economic activities if government is to create positive results in resource allocation. The neoclassical school argues that the market is more efficient than government in distributing resources. In resource allocation by government, efficiency can be neglected.[11]

The military government planned to ignite economic development and to attain a self-reliant economy by mobilising domestic capital (Cho 1996). Some argue that domestic fund-raising for industrialisation in developing countries does not go smoothly because it is generated within national boundaries through the efforts of many generations (see Cho 1994; Bae 1994; Cho 1990). This was certainly true in the case of Korea. Low domestic saving rates caused by low incomes made it difficult for firms to mobilise long-term capital. The government raised funds through the financial institutions, which were under government control. Thus, as Park (1994) noted, the improvement of domestic savings and the introduction of foreign capital were accelerated as a means of mobilising capital in different ways. The government saw financial institutions, mainly commercial banks, as a distribution outlet for savings to be raised by appealing to the patriotism of the people that savings lead to national strength (Kim 1987). The role of financial institutions was to allocate financial credit indicated by the government to the selected firms or targeted industries.

The capital market developed rapidly because of an increase in savings and this created different patterns of capital mobilisation from those in the past. Up to the mid-1960s, the financial institutions depended for capital mobilisation on loans from the BOK and the government. However, from the mid-1960s, fund raising through deposits increased sharply (see Table 6.4).

As shown in Table 6.4, the share of bank deposits as a proportion of GNP increased from 10 per cent in 1965 to 33 per cent in 1972. During this period, bank deposits increased sharply. In addition, banks began to play an important role in raising long-term funds for firms. Up to the early 1960s, credit supply by banks was restricted. However, from the mid-1960s, firms increased fund-raising from banks and instead the share of internal capital for firms decreased. Financial reform in 1965 played an important role in raising long-term funds for industrialisation.[12] Cho (1997) stressed the impacts of financial reform in 1965 on

---

11 In the allocation of resources a close relationship between government and firms can reduce inefficient resource allocation. However, banks can maintain closer relationships with firms than can government. Accordingly, resource allocation by government may be efficient but that by banks can be more so.

12 However, Cho (1996) argues that it is misleading that financial reform of 1965 based on real interest rate should be regarded as financial liberalisation. He pointed out that increase in interest rates approaching market rates promoted financial liberalisation. However, the government intervened actively in allocating resources and amending the

Table 6.4   Share of deposits to GNP: 1965–1972 (%)

Year	Bank deposits/GNP	Commercial bank deposits	Special bank deposits
1965	9.7	70.5	29.5
1966	11.7	68.2	31.8
1967	16.0	66.8	33.2
1968	22.5	67.0	33.0
1969	28.7	66.0	34.0
1970	29.5	64.1	35.9
1971	29.8	65.1	34.9
1972	33.1	67.4	32.6

Source: BOK (1975).

the Korean economy by pointing out that the extent of government intervention on the interest rate level was not only substantially lowered, but brought about rapid growth of the financial sector.

Along with the development of the financial sector, in the late 1960s several specialised banks were established. In 1967 the Korea Exchange Bank and the Korea Housing Bank were established. In addition, ten local banks were established for easing the shortage of capital for local firms. Unlike all commercial banks in Seoul, local banks were privately-owned and were less restricted by the government. Moreover, financial companies, which deal with various bonds were established for raising funds directly from the capital market. In 1968, the Law of Capital Market Promotion was enacted to accommodate fund-raising through the capital market so that going public and investment in securities were encouraged with various tax privileges.

In addition, some laws were established for foreign capital introduction. Following the 1965 Normalisation Agreement between Korea and Japan, commercial loans from Japan were sharply increased (Castley 1997). Commercial loans were guaranteed by the government. Firms that wanted to borrow from foreign countries needed to get approval from the Economic Planning Board (EPB) and the EPB needed approval from the National Assembly for the loans. The BOK and the Development Bank issued a letter of guarantee (Hattori 1989). There were no risks for firms in borrowing foreign capital due to the government's guarantee. The Japanese government also guaranteed repayment for Japanese firms that provided capital for Korean firms, and invested in Korean firms as well.

---

banking system. In this sense, Cho argued that government intervention is incompatible with financial liberalisation.

The guarantee procedures were extended to commercial and specialised banks and became an important capital source for Korean firms.[13]

In the 1960s and 1970s, foreign capital accounted for a large part of raising industrial capital in Korea. The government guaranteed reduced transaction costs by smoothing capital flow between domestic firms and foreign investors. In particular, international financial transactions need higher credits and more information than those of domestic transactions. In this sense, the role of government in introducing foreign capital was crucial. However, foreign capital introduction and efficient resource allocation are not necessarily compatible. Fund-raising is one thing and how to use the funds is another. In general, capital productivity can be high in times of relative capital shortage (Krugman 1994). An increase in capital input brings about higher productivity. An efficiency of resource allocation can be higher when the resources are allocated in a productive sector. In general, however, government intervention reduces productive activities because the efficiency of the investment is not clear. Accordingly, resources are distributed in inefficient ways, increases in production brought about by capital input are traded off and this reduces the efficiency of capital transaction. Corruption, political influences and the problems of indebted firms are products of government intervention.

On the other hand, the need for non-bank financial institutions was heightened when fund-raising through banks fell into difficulty because capital mobilisation was limited due to falling interest rates despite the fact that the need for capital mobilisation was increased (Cho 1994; Ro 1994). To achieve this, investment and financial companies, merchant companies, mutual savings and finance companies, and credit unions were established. Cho (1994) argued that tight control on interest rates weakened the ability of banks to raise funds needed for those targeted industries. Fund-raising through firms' credit was needed, rather than resource allocation by the government. After all, development of the capital market was needed to respond to such a request. In 1972, the government vitalised not only a circulation market by making firms that received certain amount of loans go public but also a securities market. In addition, the government encouraged firms to mobilise funds directly through the capital market. In 1977, the Securities Supervisory Board was established to run the securities market effectively as the capital market grew. In addition, laws on accounts and the disclosure of information on accounts, which were needed for effective management of the listed firms, were enacted. The capital market grew rapidly with the results of such policies. The listed firms increased from 66 in 1972 to 352 in 1980 (Kim

---

13 Frieden (1981) pointed out the crucial role of the government and foreign capital for Korean economic development by arguing that private firms accounted for more that half of the total foreign debts and these were generated by the payment guarantee of the government. Indeed, the payment guarantee made Korean firms accumulate higher debts than other firms in the world. In addition, he argued that like other developing countries, the Korean government played an intermediate role in connecting domestic investors with foreign capital. The government took various measures making it easy for private firms to borrow from foreign investors and furthermore distributed foreign capital to domestic firms by borrowing directly from foreign capital suppliers.

1990). In 1972, as a part of 8.3 Act,[14] laws governing mutual credit unions and credit associations were enacted to induce capital from the curb market into the organised financial market (Lee 1999). In addition, a law on short-term capital mobilisation was enacted to regulate the underwriting of short-term loans. In 1976, merchant companies joined with foreign financial institutions to provide foreign capital assistance and medium-to long-term loans for firms.

Table 6.5   The share of credits and deposits in bank and non-bank financial institutions (1972–1980, %)

| | Bank | | Non-bank | |
	Deposits	Credits	Deposits	Credits
1972	81.7	77.4	18.3	22.6
1973	78.6	73.9	21.4	26.1
1974	77.3	75.5	22.7	24.5
1975	78.5	74.6	21.5	25.4
1976	76.1	74.4	23.9	25.6
1977	75.3	68.9	24.7	31.1
1978	74.5	67.8	25.5	32.2
1979	72.2	66.5	27.8	33.5
1980	69.1	63.8	30.9	36.2

Source: BOK (various years).

With the growth of non-bank financial institutions, as shown in Table 6.5, the share of deposits in non-banks increased from 18.3 per cent in 1972 to 30.9 per cent in 1980, while that of banks dropped from 81.7 per cent in 1972 to 69.1 per cent in 1980. Goldsmith (1969) argued that at the initial stage of economic development, banks play an important role. Over time, the relative importance of banks in economic development is reduced as non-bank financial institutions develop. Korea neatly fits his argument. Still, financial institutions remained under government control and the curb market did not disappear.

Nevertheless, inefficiencies in Korea in the allocation of resources were relatively reduced. Above all, capital allocation was related more closely to business

---

14 On 3 August 1973, with the rapid increase in indebted firms the government incorporated capital in the curb market into the financial market. All firms were forced to report their debts and the reported debts were to be repaid in five years, at a monthly interest rate of 1.35 per cent with a three-year grace period. This indeed reduced the burden of debts for firms. The reported amount of debts amounted to 80 per cent of M1. This indicates the size of the curb market and at the same time, the room for developing the financial market. In other words, if the capital market operated more effectively, capital in the curb market would be absorbed in the financial market, thus helping its development.

performance than to the government's discretion. Exports withstood sharp international competition, financial policy on exports could be distributed more efficiently. In addition, foreign capital in general has the effect of heightening a firm's investment portfolio because there is substantial negotiation on investment efficiency between recipients and suppliers.[15] Negotiation became direct between domestic firms and foreign investors and approval by the government was given after the negotiation. This process began to limit the scope of government decisions on foreign loans, which were judged increasingly on economic rather than political grounds. Foreign investors, of course, can be relatively freer from government influences in the country to which they are lending. Pressure for repayment can also reduce political influence in the allocation of resources. If domestic loans are not repaid, a firm's debt can be solved by money supply issued by the BOK with the approval of government (Chung 1991). In the case of foreign capital, government placed emphasis on investment efficiency, reducing political influences in distributing resources due to the burden of repayment. Furthermore, severe competition between firms reduced inefficient resource allocation. Jwa (1999) argued that competition is effective in reducing inefficiency caused by monopoly or oligopoly.

In spite of the fact that various inefficiencies were caused by the government in resource allocation, foreign loans reduced the inefficiency caused by the government, and thus contributed to Korean economic development.[16] Although loans were made in accordance with industrial policy, the increase in investment through mobilisation of industrial capital resulted in rapid and sustained economic growth (Cho and Kim 1997).

Nevertheless, government intervention in the financial market brought about the pressure of increase in money supply. In addition, most of the financial institutions were owned by the government so that business efficiency was not improved. At the same time, government guarantees for foreign loans brought about an underestimation of risks, resulting in excess demand for capital and in the end increasing the indebtedness of firms. Indeed, this is a vicious cycle of government intervention where an increase in indebtedness gives a continued excuse for government intervention while, in turn, government intervention brings about non-performing bonds.

The Phase of Financial Liberalisation: 1980–1997

In the 1970s inefficiency in the allocation of resources caused by the government increased transaction costs, and reform of the financial institutions as a main method for streamlining the entire economy was increasingly needed. In the 1980s, the government liberalised the financial institutions, which were under government control throughout the 1960s and 1970s, giving them autonomy to mobilise and distribute funds, and to set their own prices as well. Accordingly,

---

15 For more detail on negotiations between businessmen, particularly Samsung and the government, see the autobiography of Lee, Byung-Chul, the chairman of Samsung up to 1987.

16 For more details, see Chapter 7.

hundreds of regulations and directives that had suffocated financial institutions, in particular commercial banks, were simplified or abolished. Table 6.6 summarises major financial liberalisation and market opening policies.

In 1980, the government lifted some regulations in the financial market and privatised banks by selling government-owned bonds to the private sector. In 1982, the Banking Law was amended so that orders issued by the Bank Supervisory Board to the management of the financial institutions came to an end. Between 1982 and 1983, for the purposes of absorbing curb market capital into organised financial institutions, two commercial banks, 12 investment and finance companies and 58 mutual savings and finance companies were established; and between 1988 and 1990, a number of investment and finance companies were upgraded to banks or securities companies (Kim 1997; Ro 1994). In addition, the government power to appoint bank executives was weakened. However, despite apparent liberalisation, bank management was still controlled by the government so that inefficiency was being accumulated. Cho (1990) noted that continued government control on all banks after liberalisation left the privately owned banks with highly indebted firms and vulnerable to external factors. Ironically enough, together with struggling industrial restructuring in areas such as shipbuilding and construction, the highly indebted firms have kept giving excuses for government intervention in allocating credit. In fact, as Cho (1994) argued, 'denationalisation' was a transfer of ownership from the government to private owners rather than a whole liberalisation of banking operations.

In 1982, financial privileges on export goods were eliminated by equalising the interest rates on both policy and commercial loans.[17] In 1984 interest rates became market-based, improving the efficiency of the financial markets. It was a significant first step towards the expansion of the financial institutions, although rates ranged narrowly from 10 to 10.5 per cent a year, depending on the terms of the loan.[18] Currency regulation changed from direct to indirect. In 1988, the liberalisation of interest rates on loans by all financial institutions was announced but did not happen immediately. However, with the rapid growth of financial institutions and the opening of the financial market, the government was forced to deregulate, resulting in interest rate liberalisation by stages, beginning in 1991 (see Table 6.7).

Entry barriers to the financial industry were lowered and several new banks, including joint-commercial banks with foreign investors, were established. Investment finance and new non-bank financial institutions were also approved.[19]

---

17 Between 1986 and 1989, Korea recorded trade surpluses for the first time. This provided the justification for reducing subsidies in selected industries, although policy loans were gradually reduced. Importantly, policy loans have not disappeared and still remain at a substantial level.

18 November 1984, the band rate was adjusted between 10 per cent to 11.5 per cent, giving more autonomy than before.

19 The Han-il Bank, Korea First Bank and Seoul Bank and the Chohung Bank were privatised in 1981, 1982 and 1983, respectively. In addition, the specialised banks were transformed to commercial banks and in 1989, Korea Exchange Bank was privatised in 1989.

Table 6.6   Major financial liberalisation and market opening

	Financial market	Capital market	Foreign exchange market
1981	Denationalisation of commercial banks	Allow forward exchange transaction.	
1984	Announcement of financial liberalisatioin	Allow indirect investment in securities by Korea Fund.	
1988		Become IMF Article 8 country.	Abolish overseas investment on selected industries.
1993	Introduce recommended BIS capital adequacy incrementally. Completely liberalise operations of short-term money market. Introduce real-name accounts.	Eliminate ceilings on foreigner's stock investment in companies with over 50% of equity held by foreigners. Allow foreign investment trusts and investment consulting companies to participate in the equity of domestic investment trust firms.	Expand range of daily interbank foreign exchange rate fluctuations from 0.8% to 1.0%. Allow nonresidents to open 'free won accounts.'
1994-5	Introduce ceilings on aggregate rediscounts gradually. Diversify short-term financial products such as greater range of maturities of commercial paper.	Relax requirements for opening branches by foreign securities companies. Raise direct stock investment ceilings (15% to 20%) for foreigners. Allow international organisations won-denominated bonds in the domestic market. Permit establishment of domestic representative office of foreign credit-rating firms. Raise ceilings on equity participation by foreign investment trust investment consulting companies.	Completely lift restrictions on overseas portfolio investment by domestic institutional investors. Raise ceiling on settlement in won for visible transactions. Abolish ceiling on foreign currency deposits exempted from underlying documentation requirements.
1995	Introduce real-name on real estate purchase.		Allow country fund.
1996–7	Complete liberalisation of interest rates excluding demand deposits. Introduce financial products linked to market rates such as MMCs, MMFs. Liberalise commercial foreign loans by small and medium firms.	Permit foreign banks to establish subsidiaries. Lower capital requirements for branches of foreign securities companies.	Progressively permit full settlement in Korean won for visible and invisible transactions.

Note: BIS = Bank for International Settlements; MMC = money market certificates; MMF: money market funds.

Sources: National Statistical Office (1995). After 1995, compiled from Park (1996).

Table 6.7   Trends of interest rate liberalisation

	Year	Contents
Stage I	1991	Focused on items that are less effective under regulation, i.e., short-term loans and credit, long-term credit for 3 years or more
Stage II	1993	Long-term credit for 2 years or more, time and saving deposits for 3 years or more, and all loans except for policy loans
Stage III	1994–96	Credit for 1 year or more, time and saving deposits for 2 year or more Credit for 1 year or less except for demand deposits Enlargement of credit items for short-term market Liberalisation for policy loans assisted by the BOK
Stage IV	1997	Short-term credit and demand deposits not liberalised in earlier stages

Source: Ministry of Finance and Economy (1995, 1997).

Furthermore, the financial market was increasingly opened to foreign capital. Opening of the financial market not only increases the accountability of the financial institutions, but realigns them to international standards as well. This reduced the degree of government intervention and the inefficiency of the financial institutions themselves. Competition between the financial institutions increased their efficiency and benefited consumers. Capital mobilisation was improved by the inflow of foreign capital.[20] And the inefficiency of resource allocation caused by government intervention was reduced since the financial institutions were liberalised. However, it is to some extent true that financial institutions accustomed to the help of the government have tended to resist changes, including the streamlining of their management that requires downsizing and restructuring.

The Phase of Future Financial Liberalisation: 1998–2002

During the Kim Dae-Jung regime, the financial institutions have faced an outright opening according to what the IMF has demanded. Since the 1997 financial crisis, most of commercial banks have been nationalised again by the government. Nevertheless, it should not go unnoticed the tendency that the financial institutions have been completely exposed to global standards so that a very competitive environment has been created, giving less room for the government to control as she did in the past. As a result, the crisis has brought about many structural changes in the Korean economic system.

---

20 Chung, U.-C. (1991) argues that foreign loans are more efficient in resource allocation than openness of capital market. According to him, loans are invested in productive sector and in contrast, there is not guarantee that capital inflows caused by market liberalisation are used in productive sector.

Specifically, as the IMF has demanded Korea to undertake reforms in the financial institutions, the Kim Dea-Jung government has conducted the financial reforms in two ways. First, insolvent banks should be liquidated so as not only to recover the soundness of the financial industry, but to normalize the financial markets. With the crisis hitting Korea, a total of 613 financial institutions were restructured. As a way of dealing with insolvent banks, the government allowed a large number of financial institutions either to be closed or to be sold to foreigners (Hur 2002). In addition, the number of large-sized banks has increased in the process of restructuring. Before the crisis, there were no Korean banks which ranked as top 100 world banks in terms of size, but three Korean banks, namely, Kookmin bank, Shinhan bank and Nonghyup, were included within the top-100-bankslist at the end of 2003 (Park 2004). This move, therefore, has precipitated to normalize financial markets and recover the confidence of financial markets. As a result, at the same time, both the freedom and responsibility of financial institutions have been strengthened.

The second reform was to supervise financial markets by making financial institutions privatized and large-scale players. Together with the reforms of financial institutions, the Korean government's financial policy has also been refurbished. That is, not only was the government-led financial policy gotten ride of, but the effective financial supervisory system was also set up by way of merging a number of financial supervisory institutions.

Last but not least, with the recommendation of the IMF, IBRD and OECD, the Korean government has taken measures to improve transparency in the financial statement and corporate governance index, which indicates whether market regulations and corporate governance are appropriate. Thus, Korea could be included in the first group in terms of transparency in the financial statement and the corporate governance index, along with the UK, the USA, Hong Kong, etc. (Barth 2001). In addition, drastic measures have been taken to liberalize capital market in terms of its transactions, as well as to upgrade the system of foreign exchange market to the level of advanced countries.

The relationship between the Korean government and financial institutions has changed. Although financial institutions in Korea have not entirely been freed from the influence of the Korean government, the reform drives triggered by the IMF conditionality have made a space between the government and financial institutions. Thus it has become possible for financial institutions to operate in accordance with the rules of market.

Policy Action in the Financial Market

Types of Policy Instruments

Stiglitz (1993) emphasised the role of government in developing countries when prominent market failure appeared in the financial sector, arguing that pervasive market failure calls for a role for the state. He further argues that financial institutions in most of the rapidly growing economies in East Asia have been created as a result of government intervention in order to improve the stability of the economy, solvency of the financial institutions as well as growth prospects (ibid.).

In Korea, the financial system, which for many years was strictly controlled by the government was used as an integral part of government-led economic development. By placing the entire financial system under unchallengeable government control, the government believed it could attain its goals, leading to rapid and sustained economic development. To be sure, Korea's financial sector played a significant part not only in mobilising domestic savings for capital formation but also in channelling scarce resources to targeted sectors such as the export industries. Table 6.8 shows policy measures and purposes operated by government in general on the financial market.

Table 6.8   Policy measures and operational aims in financial sector

Policy measures	Operational aims	
	Monetary operation	Ultimate targets
General measures	Short-term and long-term	Price stability
Open market operation	interest rate (CPI, government	Stability of business cycle
Rediscount rate	bond and securities, etc.)	Economic growth
Reserve ratio	Bank Reserve Rate	Balance of international payments
Selected measures	Regulation of credit policy by	Industrial development
Window guidance	industry	Improvement of industrial
Selected regulation	Regulation of interest rates	competitiveness
		Maintenance of rapid and sustained economic growth

Measures of financial policy are divided into general and selected measures. The former consists of open market operation, rediscount rate and reserve rate and the latter of window guidance and selected regulation. General measures apply everywhere, whilst selected measures apply to selected parts of an economy. Korea is in the 'selected' category. The government controlled all financial institutions and had authority to control major private investment, the introduction of foreign capital, and the setting of price ceilings. The intended investment was much higher than saving rates.[21] This caused heavy government intervention to maximise the limited resources available and thus, brought about the government-controlled financial system. Indeed, as Kim (1997) argued, the financial sector in Korea was regarded as a necessary condition for a high-growth strategy because throughout the entire economic development process, economic development came first and financial development later.

------

21 For more details on the difference between saving rates and investment rates, see Chapter 7.

In Korea, until well into the 1980s, as pointed out by many,[22] innovation in the financial system lagged behind other sectors. The most significant aspect of the banks' role during the decades of economic growth was to serve as the major source of government-directed loans to the targeted industries, mainly implemented by chaebol.

Table 6.9   Major instruments of trade and industrial policy of Korea

	Market incentives	**Government control procedures**
Non-discretionary	Special tax measures Financial subsidies and export credit Effective exchange rate Effective rate of interest including preferential interest rate Tariff rate adjustment or exemptions	Administrative support including the revision and improvement of laws and acts Price and wage controls (control of prices of electricity and water for industrial uses. Control of labour unions and wages of industrial workers) Industrial estates development and location policy Provision of infrastructure facilities Tax inspection (automatic audits) Deferment of trade and capital liberalisation measures Export-import link system permitting the use of export earnings for imports
Discretionary	Rationing of credit including the allocation of foreign loans (the amount of borrowing, loan period, and time of renewal, etc) Decisions concerning subsidies	Government persuasion and 'window' guidance of various types Adjustment of controlled prices. Allocation of export targets Tax inspection (selective audits) Coordination of investment in plant and equipment Promotion of scale economies and efficiency by encouraging merger

Source: Song (1996): 100.

Policy instruments have a tendency to change from discretionary to non-discretionary measures, reflecting the power shift between each institution as

22 See Park (1985, 1990); Bae (1994); Cho (1994); Cho (1988, 1997); Cho and Kim (1997); Cho and Hellman (1993); Chung (1991); Cole and Park (1984), Harris (1987), Park and Kim (1994) and Kim (1997).

an economy scales up. Table 6.9 presents the major instruments of trade and industrial policy in Korea. Overall, the government made extensive use of both an incentive system and command procedures, but measures have changed over time. The government did not hesitate to intervene in targeted sectors often on a highly selective and short-run basis. Over time, the sustained and rapid growth of chaebol and the accumulation of experience by both the government and the chaebol needed a different style of policy implementation. In particular, the strength of government intervention began to reflect the changing economic environment brought by the gradual emergence of institutions as a response to market desire. Naturally, since the early 1980s the government has come to depend more on the free market mechanism, an incentive mechanisms and on non-discretionary measures than on discretionary measures and command procedures.

Government Policies in the Financial Market and their Effects on Economic Development

Financial institutions in Korea were tightly controlled by the government from the early 1960s to the 1980s. All banks and non-bank institutions were subject to extensive government intervention and supervision in various ways. Interest rates on deposits and loan rates had ceilings, and even banks' lending portfolios were indicated by the government. Competition among financial institutions was restricted by entry barriers set by the government. Indeed, such entry barriers enabled chaebol to enjoy various benefits. In particular, as Ro (1994) pointed out, for almost two decades, between the early 1960s and the early 1980s, the government did not allow commercial banks to open, giving existing institutions oligopolistic benefits. Major bank management issues, such as budget planning, wage increases, branch opening plans, and dividend payments, needed implicit or explicit government approval. Indeed, the government did not allow banks to experience trouble, so there were no incidents and mishaps brought about by bank failure in Korea until 1997.

Policy loans and credit allocation and its influence on economic development
Policy loans and credit allocation were central to financial policies until financial liberalisation arrived in the early 1980s. The government planned and implemented economic development programmes by strengthening control of the financial market. For this, credit allocation by way of bank loans was used as the most important industrial policy instrument. Bank loans are broadly divided into policy loans and general loans (Cho 1994; Song 1996). Especially, policy loans were made on favourable terms either to investors, particularly exporters earmarked in targeted industries or to achieve industrial policy set by the government. The loans usually provided concessionary terms and interest rates (Park 1985). As shown in Table 6.10, interest rates for policy loans varied widely according to the goal of each loan. Average interest rates on export-related industries during the 1970s were significantly lower than those of general loans. In particular, rates on loans for exports were twice as low as those for general loans.

Table 6.10   Average interest rates on major policy loans during the 1970s

Types of policy loans	Interest rates
Exports	7.5
Exports preparation of agricultural and marine production	7.5
Agricultural development	7.5
Fishery	8.0
Shipbuilding	11.5
Promotion of small and medium companies	15.0
Machinery industry promotion	14.0
General loans*	18.0

*   Loans on other bills with maturity of up to one year.

Source: BOK (various issues).

Policy loans were in place as early as the 1950s to promote exports, although the size of the loans then was not significant. It became considerable when the government launched export-promotion policy by giving privileged treatment to all exporters in the early 1960s. In the promotion of heavy and chemical industries (1973 to 1979), as pointed out by Kim (1997), policy tools became industry-specific as well as firm-specific. In other words, in the diverse categories of policy loans provided in the 1970s, the government allocated more resources to export financing, shipbuilding, small and medium industries, machinery, HCIs, payment of delayed wages, build-up of an industrial complex, and the rationalisation of industry, among others, and these resources were distributed to chaebol for the purpose of maximisation of the scarce resource. Nam's calculation (1989) revealed that the share of policy loans among all specialised banks and commercial banks credits accounted for more than 40 per cent throughout the 1970s, although it was reduced to 35 per cent between 1983 and 1988. In fact, throughout the 1970s almost all bank loans could be categorised as policy loans, in that there was little room for banks to allocate financial resources autonomously. Ro (1994) argued that banks neglected to improve investment or loan analysis techniques or to introduce new types of produce due to entry barriers as well as to protection by the government. Government made chaebol invest in risky projects with various incentives but this led to rent-seeking and moral hazard among chaebol, government officials and financial institutions. By making financial institutions rely on long-term and low interest rates, the capital structure of financial institutions was deteriorated and this resulted in a rapid increase in the share of non-performing loans as a proportion of the total assets of commercial banks.

Government control and intervention made banks less innovative in the financial sector. In allocating credit, chaebol and firms with collateral were favoured by banks as profitable and safe, compared with small and medium-sized firms. The top-down relationship between government and commercial banks created the relationship of master and servant, and the obedient attitude of the commercial banks to the government resulted in a huge amount of non-performing assets from the late 1970s onwards. Government hesitated to allow ailing chaebol to go bankrupt for fear of job losses and that wider economic mishaps might result in political instability. The commercial banks did not stop providing the loaded cartridges to these companies, which were on the verge of bankruptcy and in turn, the BOK, the central bank, supported subsidised loans and discounts to these commercial banks (Cho 1994; Kim 1997). Over time, the accumulation of indebted firms together with the significant size of non-performing assets was considerable.

Long-term government plans, and the annual financial stabilisation programme earmarked funds for selected industries, which were distributed the funds by the banks, in accordance with government instructions. The interest rate for the specific industries was the lowest among bank loans, and required a letter of credit (L/C), without which no access to bank loans for the specific industries was given (Hattori 1988). Policy loans covered certain portions of the production costs for exports, the imports of raw materials and intermediate goods for export, and purchases from local suppliers of export-related goods. Indeed, as pointed out by Cho (1997), policy loans were closely linked to export performance. Exporters had to exceed export targets, which were adjusted annually. If they succeeded, they received more credit. If they failed, future credit was withheld. The government distributed a huge amount of investment to exports centred mostly on manufactured goods by adopting an outward-oriented development policy. Thus, banks preferred exporters. Exporters could access both long-term loans for fixed investment and short-term loans.[23] All loans from commercial banks for export were lower than general loans.

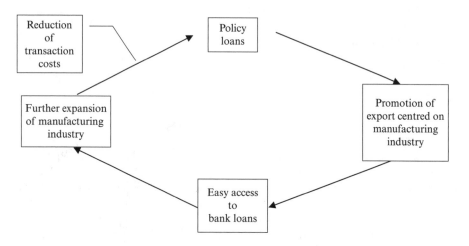

Figure 6.1   A virtuous cycle between policy loans and business expansion

---

23 Short-term loans for up to 30 days from the borrowing date.

There is a virtuous cycle between policy loans and business expansion (see Figure 6.1). Financial privileges to promote exports were a strong incentive because exports gave easy access to bank loans. Policy loans centred on manufacturing industry were automatically approved. They resulted in lower transaction costs for access to bank loans. The automatic access to bank credit promoted investment in export-related industries.

In general, bank credit is critical for firms when official interest rates are lower than the expected earning rates (Ro 1994). In this case, firms ran their businesses with borrowed money that is normally short-term. In such circumstances, bank credit plays a crucial role in holding sway over a firm's destiny. Financial institutions were encouraged to support exporters in various ways. Exporters had priority for loans compared with other manufacturers for the domestic market, since exporters were regarded as more reliable as long as their volume of exports met the criteria set by the government.

HCI and National Investment Fund (NIF) and its influence on economic development

In the 1970s the government promoted heavy and chemical industrialisation. The HCI policy set out to transform industrial structure from labour-intensive to capital intensive. It was driven by both economic and political factors. Politically, there was a security crisis because of debate on a possible withdrawal of the US army from the Korean peninsular; also Vietnam had fallen into the hands of the communists (Doran 1993). A self-reliant defence policy centred on heavy and chemical industries was stressed. As a result, political influences in the allocation of resources were considered as important as economic factors.

In these circumstances, it may seem natural that government intervened in heavy and chemical industries for resource allocation. The HCI needs a long gestation period for investment, and involves high risk. Although chaebol were established and developed throughout the 1960s, most of the chaebol could not raise the required funds for the large-scale industrial transformation that was needed.

Firms could not mobilise funds directly from the poorly developed financial market. In addition, there was not enough foreign capital for investment in the HCI. Thus, the government established the National Investment Fund (NIF) in 1973 with a view to raising domestic funds (Cho 1994). The NIF depended on domestic savings, raised by domestic financial institutions and public organisations. It was forced to purchase certain types of national investment bonds, which included a savings element (Taniura 1989). As shown in Table 6.11, between 1974 and 1981, when HCI was actively promoted, the NIF provided 57 per cent of equipment capital. This reflects the degree of government intervention.

Foreign capital was also utilised for fund-raising. Between 1977 and 1982, over 46 per cent of commercial loans went into the purchase of machinery and equipment related to the HCI. In the 1960s, commercial loans guaranteed by the government accounted for 75 per cent of the total foreign loans. This was introduced in the form of supplier's credit in the process of importing parts, intermediate and capital goods (Castley 1997). In the 1970s, as foreign banks began

Table 6.11   Share of NIF loans to the heavy and chemical industries (%)

	Loans by NIF as a proportion of loans by all financial institutions	Loans for equipment capital provided by NIF as a proportion of loans for equipment capital by all financial institutions
1974-81	18.4	56.8
1982-91	14.4	37.0
1974-91	16.2	45.8

Note: Total financial institutions include banks for deposits and development banks.

Source: Kim (1993): 128.

to establish their branches in Korea, foreign capital was introduced by financial institutions rather than by private firms. Accordingly, as shown by Kim (1993), fund-raising through financial institutions increased gradually, accounting for 32 per cent of total money in circulation between 1977 and 1981.

Government intervention in the HCI proved inefficient in the allocation of resources (World Bank 1993). Excess money supply in the domestic market brought about non-economic activities to maintain the value of assets. The government tightened credit control to contain inflation. However, this did not work because the government allowed firms to invest too much in heavy and chemical industries. The prices for assets rose sharply and price control for goods stimulated the curb market (Yoo and Lee 1997). As a result, productive resources that flew into non-productive activities such as speculation on real estate had a negative impact on economic development. Moreover, the creation of the NIF for long-term capital mobilisation distorted the capital market.[24] Concentration of funding on the selected sectors in heavy and chemical industries reduced capital supply for other industries. Government intervention made it difficult for financial institutions to analyse the efficiency of their lending.

Interest rates and their influence on economic development
The government changed its interest rate policy in 1965 to correct the distorted price mechanism.[25] As shown in Table 6.12, the government raised the nominal interest rate on time and saving deposits for one year from 15 per cent in 1961 to 26.4 per cent (30 per cent on time deposits for more than 18 months) in 1965, and the rate for general loans was raised from 17.5 per cent in 1961 to 26 per cent in 1964. A negative interest rate, in which bank deposit rates are higher than bank loan rates, was adopted to increase bank deposits by inducing the

---

24 In the mid 1970s interest rates for conventional loans were around 18 per cent compared with 9 per cent for loans from NIF.

25 Until 1965, interest rates had remained at a low level, distorting the price mechanism.

inflow of private funds circulating in the curb market, and to allocate them to targeted industries designated by the government, rather than by promoting the autonomous operation of banks. Cho (1994) argued that the change of interest rates in 1965 strengthened government's control over the banking system and its allocation of credit, moving against financial liberalisation.

Table 6.12 Interest rates of banking institutions, 1961–1995 (%)

	1961	1965	1970	1975	1976	1977	1978	1979	1980	1982	1985	1990	1995
Time deposits	15.0	26.4	22.8	15.0	16.2	14.4	18.6	18.6	19.5	10.0	10.0	11.5	11.5
General loans	17.5	26.0	24.0	15.5	18.0	16.0	19.0	19.0	20.0	10.0	10.0	10.0	10.0
Increase rate CPI	8.1	13.6	16.3	24.9	15.4	10.0	14.7	18.5	28.8	7.1	2.4	8.6	4.6

CPI = Consumer Price Index

Sources: BOK (various years); Statistics Office (1985; 1999).

Together with high inflation (see Table 6.12), the negative interest rates brought about excess demand for funds. However, for small and medium-sized firms, which were not favoured by banks, it was difficult to obtain access to bank credit and accordingly, they turned to curb market loans. In addition, the rapid inflow of foreign capital with a low interest rate at below 10 per cent resulted in indebtedness by firms that borrowed excessively from abroad. An Emergency Decree was made in 1972, designed to re-direct private capital from the curb market to the organised capital market, and to reduce transaction costs by removing the burden of borrowing from the curb market.[26] Kim (1990) argued that, despite the intent of government, the effect of the decree was small and the curb market remained in active operation, although a large portion of private savings in the curb market were absorbed into the organised financial market.[27]

Lower interest rates increased the demand for bank credit, contributing to inflation. Ro (1994) pointed out that excess demand for bank credit caused by low interest rates had made Korea suffer from periodical high inflation.

Figure 6.2 shows interest rate differentials between general loans and export loans. Throughout the 1970s, the real interest rates of bank loans and deposits had been close, fluctuating around zero. Provided that policy loans on exports were included, bank loans were significantly negative, bringing about over-borrowing. As Figure 6.1 also indicates, between the mid-1960s and the early 1980s interest rate

---

26 The decree forced both the lenders and borrowers to report the total amount of curb market loans plus outstanding interest to tax offices or financial institutions. The reported curb market loans were converted to long-term loans with a three-year grace period and thereafter a five-year repayment period. Ironically, as a result of the decree, the burden of loans was shared by all taxpayers and other sectors of economy, while the gains from loans went to the specific firms.

27 Curb market loans was indeed closely related to speculation, erupting into major financial scandals in the 1980s.

differentials between government and export loans were prominent, particularly between 1965 and 1972. Indeed, these differentials resulted in severe excess demand for bank credit which in turn, led the government to intervene further in the financial market, through the allocation of financial resources. Cho (1990) argued that financial reform in 1965 strengthened the government's control of financial flow because the reform substantially increased the volume of capital available.

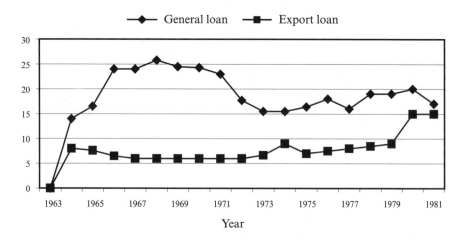

Figure 6.2   Interest rate differentials: 1962–1982 (%)

Note: discounts on commercial bills are for firms with good credit standing.

Source: BOK (various issues).

In 1965, the BOK provided cheap credit to commercial banks, accounting for 20–30 per cent of their total lending in order to sustain the profitability of banks. Cho (1997) described the interest rate reform as financial liberalisation, and pointed out that it reduced dominant pressure by government on the interest rate level, and generated a rapid growth of the financial sector. In the 1970s, the government further tightened its control on credit allocation, moving towards more financial repression as interest rates were lowered. Indeed, throughout the entire economic development period, government policies in the financial market were contradictory: both repressing and assisting.

The curb market interest rate remained surprisingly high throughout the entire economic development period (see Figure 6.3 and Table 6.13). Indeed, the very high interest rates on the curb market induced private savings, accounting for over 70 per cent of total private savings, in particular during the 1970s. Small and medium-sized companies suffered from these high interest rates.

Table 6.13 shows the difference between interest rates on general loans, export loans and curb market loans. As noted previously, export loans were substantially subsidised until the difference between export loans and general loans disappeared

Table 6.13   Comparison of interest rates (%): 1968–1982

	Bank loan rate		Curb market rate (C)	A-B	C-A	C-B
	General loan (A)	Export loan (B)				
1968	25.8	6.0	55.9	30.1	19.8	49.9
1969	24.5	6.0	51.2	18.5	26.7	45.2
1970	24.0	6.0	50.8	18.0	26.8	44.8
1971	23.0	6.0	46.3	17.0	23.3	40.3
1972	17.7	6.0	38.9	11.7	21.2	32.9
1973	15.5	7.0	39.2	8.5	23.7	32.2
1974	15.5	9.0	37.6	6.5	22.1	28.6
1975	15.5	7.0	41.3	8.5	25.8	34.3
1976	18.0	7.5	40.5	11.5	22.5	33.0
1977	16.0	8.0	38.1	8.0	22.1	30.1
1978	19.0	8.5	41.7	11.5	22.7	33.2
1979	19.0	9.0	42.4	10.0	23.4	33.4
1980	20.0	15.0	45.0	5.0	25.0	30.0
1981	17.0	15.0	35.4	2.0	18.4	20.4
1982*	10.0	10.0	33.1	0.0	23.1	23.1

*   Since 1982, the difference between general and export loan rates has disappeared. However, interest rates on the curb market remained very high.

Sources: BOK (various issues); BOK National Accounts, various years; National Statistics Office (various issues).

in 1982. From the mid-1960s and throughout most of the 1970s, interest rates for export loans remained fairly stable, while these for general loans showed a mainly downward trend. Accordingly, the gap between general loans and export loans was smaller towards the end of the period. However, there was a huge difference between the interest rates on general loans and these on the curb market during the same period. Between 1968 and 1982, curb market rates were on average 2.3 times higher than general rates. In particular, the interest rates on the curb market during the same period were on average more than five times higher than these for export loans. Although the gap has reduced over time, it is still substantial. Indeed, these high interest rates on the curb market suffocated many firms, particularly small and medium-sized companies and in contrast, the differentials had given substantial opportunities to those recipients of subsidised loans, especially chaebol. Accordingly, these gaps brought about rent-seeking, heightening transaction costs. Of course, the gaps were filled by the BOK in the form of cheap loans and discounts to commercial banks. Of which, as Ro (1994) argued, discounts to commercial banks were very important measures in controlling money supply because the commercial banks were heavily dependent on borrowing from the BOK.

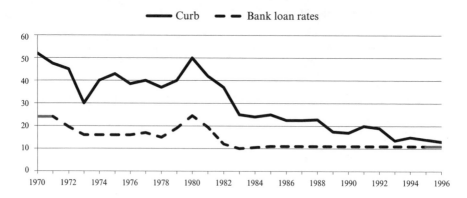

Figure 6.3   Curb and market loan rates, 1970–1996

Source: BOK (1990 1999).

Figure 6.3 presents the difference between the curb market interest rates and these for general loans in the period 1970–1996. Interest rates on the curb market have always been higher and sometimes much higher than general loan rates, which were controlled by the government. Since 1982, the gap has become smaller but still remained in 1996. The government introduced real-name accounts in 1993 and this has marked an important dividing line that induced private savings into the organised financial market. As a result, since 1993 the gap between curb market loan rates and those for general loans has been further reduced. However, the interest differentials were caused by the government policy that preferred chaebol to small and medium-sized firms in order to attain economic goals. Accordingly, there was no alternative for the many firms that were denied access to bank loans and had to turn to the curb market, resulting in further growth of that market.

Manipulation of foreign exchange rates and its influence on economic development
The government manipulated the foreign exchange market in favour of exporters. In the 1950s and early 1960s, the government kept official exchange rates low, accounting for less than 50 per cent of the real value of foreign currencies (Cho 1994). This is quite different from the claim of the neoclassical view on the Korean economy that incentives for domestic and overseas markets are the same. Indeed, the overvalued Korean currency was favourable to imports and hindered exports. With the adoption of the export-promotion strategy, the highly overvalued exchange rates were adjusted to the market value to stimulate exports. In fact, the exchange rate, which was readjusted in 1964, contributed to the gradual growth of Korean exports. Song (1996) argued that rapid expansion of exports and the sustained GNP growth has been maintained through an effective exchange rate system. The neoclassical economists argued that exchange rates for exporters in

Korea were close to those which would have worked under free trade.[28] However, as Chung, Lee and Jung (1997) argued, the official exchange rate was kept low because of high inflation, thus benefiting importers. In this sense, it is reasonable to say that the neoclassical school's argument on the policy of Korea's exchange rates is misleading.

Although the distorted exchange rates discouraged exports, exporters nevertheless benefited because imports were linked to exports. Foreign currencies, up to the amount of export earnings, were made available at favourable exchange rates to exporters who imported the raw materials, capital goods, parts and components required for the production of exports. In addition, various incentives such as taxes, tariffs, and subsidies were given to exporters to promote exports. Exporters enjoyed windfall gains created by government intervention in the exchange market.

Table 6.14 Change of exchange rates system of Korea

Exchange rate system	Period	Characteristics
Fixed exchange rate	10.1945–05 1964	Fixed at 15 hwan to a dollar
Unified, floating exchange rate	05.1964–08.1974	Small floating permitted to dollar
Fixed exchange rate*	08.1974–02.1980	Pegged to dollar
Plural currencies basket exchange rate	02.1980–03.1990	Determined by SDR and exchange rate of five major trading partners
Market average exchange rate	03.1990–12.1997	Controlled by the BOK within floating spread band
Floating exchange rate	12.1997–present	Abolition of floating spread band

* In a unified exchange rate, exchange rate is adjusted through the Foreign Exchange Certificate (FXC) market. The FXC is managed by the government and the exchange rate is determined through the selling and buying of the FXC at the foreign exchange market. Thus, in theory the exchange rate is free from government's hand.

Various exchange rates systems were used to promote exports and to keep inflation as low as possible.[29] As shown in Table 6.14, up to 1964, a fixed exchange rate system was employed to promote both targeted imports and exports by maintaining money supply and demand through contraction of money supply, which was oversupplied after the Korean War. However, unstable economic

---

28 For more details, see Chapter 2.

29 There are advantages and disadvantages both in fixed and floating exchange rates. With a fixed exchange rate, firms maintain stable trade without worries about changes in the exchange rate. However, there is no way to solve the problem of trade deficits arising from weakened competitiveness, for example. In contrast, a floating exchange system can restore relative values when trade deficits are accumulated. However, rapid changes of the rate heighten uncertainty of economic activities and stimulate speculation on a floating rate.

environments moved against a fixed exchange rate system and thus, the Korean currency became overvalued. In 1964, a floating, unified exchange rate system was introduced to promote export-related industries and to stabilise exchange rates and in 1974, the won was pegged to the US dollar. Friedman (1953) argued that in a fixed exchange rate system, the adjustment of the rate up or down may not be effective because the adjustment takes place after the trade imbalance has occurred. Indeed, Korea had a systemic problem in adjusting its exchange rates due to high inflation. Higher inflation in Korea than in other countries, particularly Japan, worsened the international competitiveness of Korean exports, resulting in large trade deficits. From 1980 to 1990, the exchange rate was determined within a fixed floating spread band by the movement in the rates of major trading partners and this maintained exchange rates more realistically. However, the exchange rate, which determines actual value for the won was decided by the government. As Seong (1993) argued, this showed that government was still intervening in the exchange market. With sustained economic growth and trade conflicts between trade partners, Korea began to be regarded as a country that manipulates exchange rates. As a result, in 1990, exchange rates have come to move according to market value with a flexible spread band.[30] Such changes of the exchange rate system reflect the extent of government intervention in the financial market in the transition from indicative and regulatory to autonomous market function. Indeed, the progressive change from direct government intervention in the exchange system to a market system is a result of the evolution of financial institutions.

A Changing Political Economy of the Relationship between Government, Chaebol and Financial Institutions in a Growth-Oriented Economic System

The Korean government utilised capital as the most powerful instrument in enlisting firms' cooperation for economic development. All private banks were nationalised and remained under government control until the mid 1980s. Although these controls were gradually relaxed, government intervention in the financial market remains. In the process of economic development, the government induced chaebol with various incentives, of which privileged access to bank credit was one of the most important. Chaebol were forced on the whole to rely on bank loans to mobilise funds for business expansion until the mid-1980s. Cole and Park (1984) said that government control of the financial institutions to guide and to regulate chaebol was central to financial policy. Also, Kim (1990) pointed out that financial institutions, mainly commercial banks, were the main source of government-directed loans to chaebol. Financial institutions functioned

---

30 In this exchange rate system, the exchange rate is basically determined at foreign exchange market traded by banks. In other words, it is determined by the extent of demand for and supply of foreign exchange. However, a spread band was introduced to prevent violent fluctuations in prices.

like blood vessels in supplying finance to chaebol which lay at the heart of the Korean economic system.

The government intervened heavily in the financial sector and continued supporting chaebol by setting real interest rates close to zero or even at a negative rate, thus producing the additional borrowing needed to finance the selected industries.[31] The excess demand for bank credit created a need for credit allocation and as pointed out by Song (1996), it gave the government room to control the amount of loans and their repayment terms. In addition, policy loans and tax reduction played an important role in taming chaebol and these other financial privileges created rent-seeking. On the other hand, small and medium firms had to turn to the curb market. They were weak in borrowing money and had little chance of being chosen for the selected industries. Moreover, they were always disadvantaged by the higher interest rates charged in the curb market. Yet government intervention in the financial market brought about a growth of curb market borrowing amounting to well over 20 per cent of GDP in the 1990s.

Before the launching of real-name accounting in 1993, the government could not grasp the relationship between the curb market and chaebol because a false-name accounting system was allowed. In addition, it was difficult for government to monitor capital flows between the affiliated firms in chaebol because there were many internal dealings between the affiliated firms (Kang 1996). If an affiliated firm took a loan, chaebol could use it for a different purpose, for example, land speculation.

Sometimes, however, the government forced big chaebol to buy indebted firms and then assisted them with special privileges (Kim 1997).

The production sector and the financial sector have institutional complementarity contributing to rapid and sustained growth (Figure 6.4). Increased investment in exports leads to an increase in production, a decrease in production costs, and an increase in sales; in turn, creating further stimulation of the production sector by the financial sector, pushing up an economy to the advanced stage of industrialisation. This has been the consistent growth strategy of the Korean government which has sought to reinforce institutional complementarity, which is a key strength of the Korean economy.

However, government intervention disturbed financial autonomy. Banks formed a triangular system along with government and chaebol, and this paralysed the market mechanism. Indeed, in the 1980s, over-borrowing and excess investment, mainly by chaebol, led to a rapid increase in non-performing bonds and brought about a debt crisis (Cho 1989). Naturally, the government had focused on the restructuring of the financial sector. However, it faced a dilemma: the pursuit of growth-oriented economic development or fundamental reform. The government did not hesitate to choose to fend off the debt crisis, rather than leave chaebol to sink or swim in the market. The detailed restructuring of the financial sector was postponed.

---

31 It is true that some portions of the borrowed money went to speculation, particularly land in order to hedge capital losses caused by inflation.

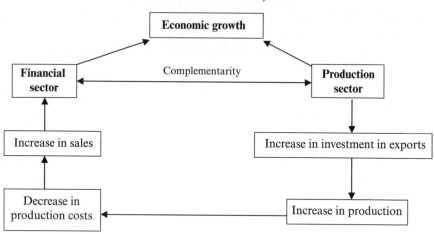

Figure 6.4   Institutional complementarity between the production sector and financial sector in growth-oriented economic system

Figure 6.5 illustrates the changing relationship between government, financial institutions and business before and after the mid-1980s. Up to the mid-1980s, businesses were managed by their owners who exerted all business rights over affiliated firms because the owner had control of decision making through payment guarantees and internal dealing between the affiliated firms (Kang 1998). The owner could ignore minority shareholders rights. The government exerted absolute power over the financial sector and could write off firms' debt under various policies (ibid.). Banks were not in control of their own affairs. Government had to maintain this pattern as long as it favoured a growth-oriented policy centred on chaebol.

However, since the mid-1980s, as a result of trade surpluses, financial liberalisation has been rapidly promoted. In particular, globalisation and the expansion of the scale of the financial sector has been a trigger for industry to relocate abroad (Kojima 1997). In addition, as a result of joining the OECD, the Korean system has been challenged in various ways and exposed to rapidly changing economic environments in particular. To meet the standards of OECD, the financial market has been rapidly opened (Park 1996). This weakened the structure of financial institutions, while strengthening the real sector that has undergone globalisation one step earlier than the financial sector. As a result, financial institutions have not been able to compete with other foreign institutions. As shown in Figure 6.5, mutual payment guarantees and internal dealings between affiliated firms have been gradually eliminated. The management of financial institutions has changed from that of an in-house governing body to an outside governing body. If non-performing loans in a chaebol (or chaebol related firm) increase beyond a critical amount, the chaebol (the affiliated firm) has to resolve the matter without the help of government. However, chaebol and financial institutions can not catch up with such rapidly changing circumstances.

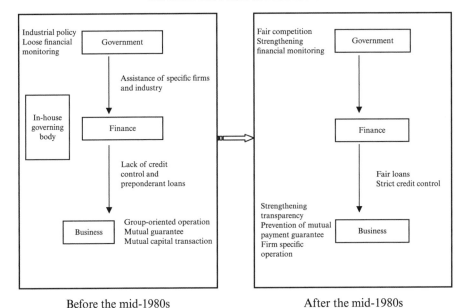

Before the mid-1980s   After the mid-1980s

Figure 6.5   The changing relationship between government, finance and business

In adjusting an existing system, practical reality in the short-term is often ahead of the ideal remedy based on a long-term view. Yet, the goal of stability for the financial institutions in Korea offers stability for the whole economy.

Chapter 7

Japan's Influence on the Formation of the Korean Economic System

In the process of Korea's industrialisation, economic dependence on the Japanese economy was the prerequisite for Korean economic development. Without the assistance of the Japanese economy, the policy of economic development through dependence by the Korean government would probably have failed. In order to continue to sustain economic development, the import of production goods as well as technology transfer from Japan were necessary for Korea's economic development. In other words, the essential materials needed for industrialisation were supplied by Japan. The Korean economic structure is based on the principle that the more Korea exports to world markets, the more Korea must import from Japan.

Over time, the Japanese economy has been increasingly instilled into the Korean economy, while establishing a virtuous circle that Korea imports intermediate and capital goods and technology from Japan, and then exports goods through an assembly-process, generating further exports as well as improving productivity. As the Korean economy progressed, however, the Korean economic system began to reflect the changing economic environments.

As the Korean economy moved progressively into light industry, heavy and chemical industry and high-tech industry, the Japanese economy has been gradually embedded into the Korean economy so that the Korean economy has come to fluctuate according to the changing Japanese economy creating a 'zero sum relationship'. In each industrial stage of Korea, Japanese economic influence has shifted from capital and direct investment to technology, and naturally Japanese loans, direct investment and technology have been gradually instilled into the Korean economy. Thus, the process of Korean economic development is closely linked with the pattern of Japan's influences on Korea.

The Changing Industrial Stages in Japan and Korea

As Kosai and Ogino (1984) pointed out, the restructuring of industry means that labour and capital, invested in certain industries are transferred to other countries in response to changes in demand and the price-cost structure.

In the 1950s, Japan experienced rapid economic growth. Between 1951 and 1957, real GNP rose by 108 per cent per annum, accompanied by rapid increases in labour costs (Nakamura 1993). Rising wages began to change the production structure. Not only did rapid industrial expansion itself increase the overall demand for workers and therefore wages, but also, and more importantly, as workers were attracted and absorbed into more productive and higher-paying jobs in the expanding sector, wages in the contracting sector rose simultaneously (Ozawa 1979).

During the early 1970s, the oil shock and the appreciation of the yen were other factors that brought about the restructuring of industry. The appreciation of the yen increased imports and lowered the international competitiveness of exports (Kosai and Ogino 1984). Consequently, Japan had to either shift into capital-intensive industries, or transfer those parts of the production process which were labour-intensive to offshore sites where labour was cheaper. Japan itself had to concentrate more on high-value products (Argy and Stein 1997).

With the prospect of an end to US economic aid, Korea adopted a development policy dependent on the inflow of foreign capital and technology (Jung 1987). Furthermore, the Park government declared a sizable currency devaluation to promote export-led policy (Shin 1994). To create job opportunities at home and promote exports and industrial growth, Korea provided various incentives to attract foreign firms, including the opening of a free export processing zone.

The complementary nature of the Japanese and Korean economies, a function largely of the different historical timing of each country's industrialisation, deepened economic complementarity between the two countries.

Table 7.1   Development phase of Japan and Korea and type of Japanese advance into Korea in the course of Korea's economic development

	Japan	Korea	Major types of Japanese advance into Korea
1950s	Labour-intensive industry	Primary products (import substitution)	Indirect advance via US aid
1960s	Capital-intensive industry (downstream) (steel, shipbuilding, chemicals)	Labour-intensive industry (textile, clothing)	Advance through commercial loans
1970s	Capital- and knowledge-intensive (upstream)	Capital-intensive industry (downstream) (steel, shipbuilding, chemicals, electronics)	Advance through foreign direct investment (FDI)
1980s	Knowledge-intensive industry	Capital- and knowledge-intensive industry (upstream)	Advance through FDI and technology transfer
1990s– 2002	Knowledge-intensive and high-tech industry	Knowledge-intensive and high-tech industry	Advance through FDI and technology transfer

Table 7.1 shows the different timing of the two countries' development and Japan's advance into Korea. In the 1950s, Korea concentrated on reconstruction, following the Korean War, while Japan was drawing international attention not

only by expanding labour-intensive industries aimed at exporting to the US market but also by rebuilding heavy industries aimed at regional markets (Castley 1997). During this period, Japan exported various consumer goods and military supplies to Korea with the help of the US, since official trade between Japan and Korea was forbidden by the Korean government until 1965.

In the 1960s, Japan passed a turning point in the labour market and Japanese firms were seeking to relocate labour-intensive manufacturing process centred on exports (Minami 1994). Export-promotion industrialisation in Korea centred on manufacturing industry was launched in 1962, helped by the long-term links between the US and Korea which permitted access to the US market on favourable terms (Shin 1994). In this period, Japan advanced in Korea through commercial loans, which were very significant for the Korean economy at the time.

It was no coincidence that the economies of Japan and Korea met each other. As Castley (1997) noted, it was an obvious trend for Japan's manufacturing investment in Korea to shift from labour-intensive industries to heavy industry and machinery manufacture. At the same time, Korea wished to attract foreign capital to promote labour-intensive export industries. The aims of both countries were achieved by marrying Japanese capital and technology to Korea's cheap labour.

In common, with most developing countries, the production capacity in Korea of primary input materials, intermediate, and capital goods was not suitable for export-led industrialisation. Many of the ingredients essential to export production such as capital, technology, technical entrepreneurial skills and materials, were lacking. This enabled Korea to turn to Japan, where the industrial structure was at a more advanced stage. The differential between the two countries gave a basis for the adoption by Korea of an export-led industrialisation policy.

In the early 1970s, Japan was transferring from being a latecomer to being an advanced industrialised country and an influential economic powerhouse under the mood of détente in Asia as US economic influence in the region declined.[1] Japan sought an outlet abroad for the survival of its labour-intensive industry (Kojima 1977; Ozawa 1979). This new situation caused Japanese firms to turn to Korea, which was a labour-abundant country.

As the Japanese economy moved from labour-intensive to capital-intensive, knowledge-intensive and knowledge-based high-tech industries, through progressively more advanced stages of industrialisation, the labour-intensive and other industries that were discarded by Japan were passed on to Korea which was waiting for them. This is explained by the words of Cummings (1987: 46) that 'Korea has historically been a receptacle for declining Japanese economy'. Indeed, as Petri (1988) pointed out, the changing structure of Japan provided Korea with a niche enabling Korean firms to produce light industrial goods and in turn, heavy industrial goods at the lower end of the market in each industrial stage.

---

1 In terms of defence, the US had continued to take the initiative in the area. The role of Japan in this period was to prop up economic assistance by replacing the US, which faced a difficult economic situation.

As Japanese industrial restructuring moved into the knowledge-intensive industry Japan discarded downstream capital-intensive industry and the pattern of its economic advance into Korea changed from commercial loans to direct investment. Through this step-by-step process, Japanese investment in Korea enabled Korea to move up the industrial ladder and to enhance the quality of its production.

Doran (1993) pointed out that in the 1980s the cooperation between Japan and Korea based on security rather than an economic relationship shifted to emphasise economic cooperation[2] and thus, Japanese advance through technology was implemented. Accordingly, the parts and capital goods industries in Korea, which were classed as upstream industries, were promoted. Over time, the Japanese economy became increasingly embedded into the Korean economy leading to the formation of a unique Korean economic system. In the 1990s, the pattern continued, reflecting the changing economic relationship between the two countries.

Clearly, Korea's economic relationship with Japan has been dependent and uneven. As Eckert (1990), Castley (1997) and Lee (1996) argued, the Park government intentionally sought to promote an 'organic division of labour' between Japan and Korea that would marry Japanese capital and technology to cheap and non-unionised Korean labour. Castley (1997) notes that Korea's own economic growth has now become structurally linked to Japan's, both through the product cycle and through an exceptional Korean reliance on imported Japanese intermediate and capital goods and technology. Thus, the more Korea's industrialisation progresses, the more parts and components she purchases. In this regard, as Castley (1997) pointed out, it can be said that 'Korea has developed more in conjunction than in competition with the Japanese economy.'

As the Korean economy moved first from agriculture to labour-intensive industry, and later from light industry to more capital-and technology-intensive industry, so the Japanese economy itself has shifted its own industrial and technological frontiers forward, thus maintaining its economic dominance of Korea. Indeed, the model of the Japanese economy has been increasingly embedded in elsewhere in Korea through what is referred to as the 'demonstration effect.' Castley (1997) argued that for Korea, the economic relationship with Japan is not that of a competitor but rather that of a model, where Korea wants to follow in the footsteps of Japanese economic growth. However, Castley (Ibid.) underestimated the changing relationship between the two countries over time. Korea has been watching, learning and mimicking Japan but in doing so, its economic relationship with its neighbour has gradually become a competitive one.

---

2   Japanese-Korean security and economic cooperation was emphasised by the US in building up Korea-Japan-US military alliance by reinforcing Korea, which was the weakest link for the alliance.

Foreign Capital, Direct Investment, Technology and Trade in Korean Economic Development

The Role of Foreign Capital and Direct Investment

Foreign capital usually supplements shortages of domestic capital in the process of industrialisation in developing countries and the need to bring in foreign capital is imperative since capital is always centred to economic analysis in any country. In particular, as an economy progresses, the introduction of foreign capital becomes more important to supplement limited domestic savings, since the traditional agriculture sector and domestic purchasing power cannot create sufficient capital for industrialisation.

The availability of foreign capital enables a recipient to consider an alternative development pattern. As Sano (1977) pointed out, the most important role of foreign capital is to widen the development choices available to developing countries.

Numerically, it is hardly possible to measure the influence of foreign capital on Korea's economy because there is on the one hand no universal or unified yardstick and because there are on the other hand many influences at work both positive and negative and direct or indirect. On a macro level, the direct influence of foreign capital on the host country is on its international balance of payments and on a micro level, on its employment and income. Park (1989) notes that foreign capital plays an important role in the dispersion of technology, the improvement of management and the prevention of monopoly by existing domestic enterprises. Ozawa (1976) points out that an increase in the income of factories and other production units through investment in raw materials contributes to higher economic growth. In addition, foreign capital also works as an incentive for domestic industry to learn new management skills.

Watanabe (1996) argued that the rapid economic growth of Korea was achieved by great expansion of production. This was made possible by an increase in the supply of production equipment for which investment was required.

Figure 7.1 shows investment as a proportion GNP from 1953–1996 and confirms that Korea's rapid economic growth was accompanied by a sharp increase in investment accounting for nearly 40 per cent of GNP at its highest. Investment is a mix of domestic savings and foreign capital. As shown in Figure 7.1, the period from 1953 to 1965 is characterised by a low level of savings and investment, which was insufficient to support Korea's industrialisation. During this period a large amount of investment was the result of US aid.

In the 1960s, the inflow of foreign capital enabled Korea to move into labour-intensive light industries and then into capital-intensive heavy industries in the 1970s. The Ministry of Finance and Economy (MOFE) and the Korea Development Bank (KDB) (1993) noted that foreign funds in Korea were mostly used to build the basic production facilities resulting in the increase of production capabilities. Lee (1994) pointed out that foreign loans and investments were used in heavy and chemical industrialisation and its supporting infrastructure. This

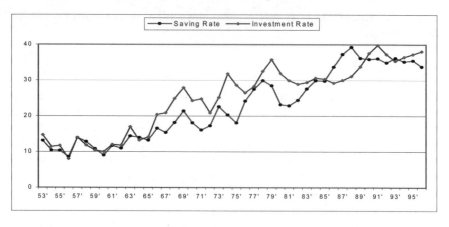

Figure 7.1   Savings and investment rates as a proportion of GDP between 1953–1996

Sources: BOK (1999); National Statistical Office of Korea (various years).

was focused on the export trade, which brought in the foreign exchange needed to initiate and sustain further growth of the manufacturing sector.

During the rapid economic development period, it was not possible for Korea's domestic investment to be based on domestic savings. The level of domestic investment exceeded domestic savings and the difference had to be made up with foreign capital. In particular, during the period of the first and second economic five-year plans, over half of all investment was made with foreign capital, and in the period of heavy and chemical industrialisation, foreign capital accounted for over a third. Between 1965 and 1972 foreign capital accounted for more than 60 per cent of the investment in the textile industry (Hattori 1997).

As shown in Figure 7.1, between 1965 and 1985, the period of rapid and sustained economic growth, foreign capital especially from Japan, played an essential role. Between 1986 and 1989, Korea recorded the first trade surpluses in its economic history so that the level of domestic savings at last exceeded the level of domestic investment. However, since 1991 the role of foreign capital has risen again, although its impact is less significant than in the past.

As shown in Table 7.2, Cho and Kim (1997) estimated the effect of foreign capital on Korea's economic growth between 1962–1982, when foreign capital had a significant impact on the Korean economy. The Table shows that without foreign capital, GNP would have grown by an average of only 4.9 per cent during the period, compared with an actual growth rate of 8.2 per cent.[3] It can be calculated from Table 7.2 that approximately 40 per cent of the average growth from 1962 to 1982 was attributable to external borrowing.

---

3   According to the White Paper on Foreign Debt, the same result was calculated by the Economic Planning Board.

Table 7.2   Growth effect of foreign capital (%): 1962–1982

	1962–66	1967–71	1972–76	1977–82	Total (1962–82)
GNP growth rate (A)	7.9	9.7	10.2	5.6	8.2
ICOR[1]	2.3	3.1	3.4	5.0	3.4
GNP growth rate without foreign savings (B)	3.8	4.9	6.9	4.1	4.9
Growth effect of foreign capital (A)–(B)	4.1	4.8	3.3	1.5	3.3

Notes
ICOR represents Incremental Capital Output Ratio and total capital includes domestic gross fixed formation, increase in inventories and statistical discrepancy.
GNP is calculated at 1975 constant prices.
1   ICOR measures the additional capital that creates an additional unit of output. According to Cho and Kim, the growth of GNP is equal to the reciprocal of ICOR multiplied by the increase in investment. The reciprocal of ICOR multiplied by the domestic saving ratio generates the economic growth with no external debt. However, as they pointed out, the results of estimation should be interpreted carefully because it assumes that ICOR is regarded as constant no matter what the size of investment is, and that all foreign capital is used only for capital formation. For more details, see Cho and Kim (1997).

Source: Economic Planning Board, White Paper on External Debts, 1988, quoted in Cho and Kim (1997): 103.

As the Korean economy grew, the importance of borrowing decreased gradually, but still accounted for 27 per cent of growth during 1977 and 1982. However, this calculation may be an underestimate because, as pointed out by Park (Ibid.), there are various components of contribution, not all of which can be measured in appraising the influences of foreign capital.

On the other hand, foreign direct investment transfers not only capital but also a package of managerial resources, including technology, management know-how, sales capacity, and plants (Kojima 1977; Lall 1992). Accordingly, the transfer of technology and its embodiment, machinery, plants, and equipment is essential. Although no direct investment was made in Korea by Japanese firms before 1965, when the normalisation treaty[4] was signed, subsequent Japanese investment and

---

4   The normalisation treaty between Japan and Korea was materialised for common benefits among Korea, Japan, and the US. Up to the early 1960s, Korea as a whole suffered from economic instability. President Park, who captured power through military coup, was eager to pursue economic development in order to strengthen the political legitimacy of his regime, and to appease the people's complaints about the military government. The US government refused a request for $25 million in economic assistance and cut drastically the amount of existing aid. Park sought investment from Japan through diplomatic normalisation. Japan also needed to help Korea's economic development for its security by

planning contributed immensely to Korean growth (Sano 1977).[5] After the foreign direct introduction law was amended in 1966, direct investment from Japan to Korea showed a rapid increase.

Electronics, textiles and other light industries are typically labour-intensive. Castley (1997) pointed out that Japanese investment was concentrated on Korea's key industries. In the late 1960s, Japanese investment poured into clothing and textiles; and in the 1970s it concentrated on textiles, electronics, machinery and chemicals; and in the 1980s it went to upstream industries in electronics, and machinery and chemicals, to replace of textile industry, which was typical of light industry.

Figure 7.2 shows the virtuous cycle of economic development created by Japanese direct investment in Korea. Increase in Japanese investment with advanced technology encouraged Korea to promote domestic products. Improved productivity raised domestic sales and strengthened competitiveness in the international market. In addition, incomes increased through the expansion of domestic sales and exports and as a result induced further Japanese investment accelerated by the multiplier effect.

The Role of Technology in Economic Development

Technology, along with labour and capital is one of the crucial elements in the course of economic development through industrialisation because it enables an economy to raise productivity, improve competitiveness, and sustain economic

---

utilising Korea as a shield against communism since she was unable to take direct military action under the Article 9 of the constitution and the Yoshida Doctrine. Also, the US was in serious economic difficulties, being forced to curtail aid to Korea and thereby the diplomatic normalisation between Korea and Japan became inevitable.

5   There are several factors attracting an outflow of Japanese capital to Korea. Firstly, trade surplus of Japan increased tremendously. Thus, Japanese government shifted its policy to encourage the export of capital overseas. Secondly, with the results of overvaluation of yen to the dollar as well as wage increase caused by labour shortage, price competitiveness in overseas markets decreased and thus, small-medium scale industry vulnerable to the changing economic environments came to relocate their industrial sites seeking cheap labour. Thirdly, pollution emerged as a heavy burden in Japan. Fourthly, combined with the rise of land price, the Japanese inevitably sought to relocate their industrial sites offshore. Sixthly, the Japanese industry reached a turning point requiring industrial restructuring and thus she turned her eyes for a new outlet in order to strengthen her competitiveness. On the other hand, Korea needed Japanese capital not only to supplement the low level of domestic savings but also to implement the consecutive five-year economic plan. Secondly, Korea has an abundant supply of cheap and relatively well-educated labour. Thirdly, the sites of industrial compounds already under construction in Korea meet the demand of Japanese capital. Fourthly, although national sentiment against Japan has not been erased, Korea is geographically close to Japan and the sentiment of the Koreans to Japanese capital is not so much pointed as can be witnessed in other countries in Southeast Asia offering the optimal conditions as an investment site for Japan. Fifthly, foreign capital introduction law passed in 1966 offered the providers of foreign capital a number of preferential benefits such as tax exemption, guarantee of remittance of interest and favour for the use of land.

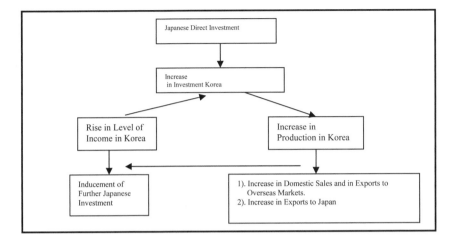

Figure 7.2   The effect of Japanese direct investment on the Korean economy

development, thus upgrading the entire economy.[6] In particular, as an economy moves up, the importance of technology becomes more important since, as emphasised by Chung (1992), it keeps the competitiveness of products afloat by inputting constant technical progress in the form of invention, innovation and diffusion of new techniques (Enos 1988).

Kim and Seong (1997) note that there are various ways for developing countries to acquire other means of technology transfer, such as joint ventures, joint R&D, technology licensing, management contracts, subcontracting, formal and informal technology transfer by FDI, and strategic technological alliances. As Dahlman and Kim (1992) pointed out, these various means of technology transfer have increased rapidly since the 1960s, enabling industrial structure in developing countries to move a more advanced stage.

Foreign direct investment is the main outlet for technology transfer. It is the dominant form of resource and technology transfer from advanced countries. In addition, as Lall (1985) and Litvak and Maule (1973–1974) pointed out, it is transferred with a package of technology by combining the provision of capital with technical know-how, equipment, management, access to overseas markets and other skills. In general, they are all interrelated. In particular, new organisational and technical skills, the ability to generate and to gather information, the development of inter-firm specialisation, and the consolidation of linkages with suppliers, buyers and institutions have occurred in the process of technology transfer, adaptation, absorption and diffusion (Park 1992; Jung 1996; Wong 1996). In this regard, as Lal (1983) stressed, technology transfer and other determinants to affect its linkages with others have important effects on the process of industrialisation.

---

6   In particular, technology-related FDI is concerned with long-term capital inflows so that increased FDI inflows can mitigate the shortage of short-term foreign capital.

The role of the recipient of technology is as important as that of the technology supplier. Enos (1988) pointed out that a developing country needs to possess at least a minimal level of indigenous technological capability to absorb imported technologies. In particular, he explains technology capability in two ways: macro and micro level. On a macro level, capability development is decided by government, for example, through investment in skills, information flows, infrastructure and supporting institutions. On a micro level, it is decided by individual firms.

Lal (1983) distinguished the form of technology transfer into two broad categories: internalised and externalised. According to him, the internalised form refers to technology-related investment where control is possessed by foreign partners normally associated with FDI in its traditional forms, while the externalised form refers to all other forms, primarily licensing, international subcontracting, and joint-ventures with local control. Thus, as noted by Hong (1998), the characteristics and volume of technology transfers are good indicators of the technological level of the country and the direction of technological change, meaning that the country has needed much closer contacts, stressing the upgrading of technologies and skills in manufacturing industries.

The purchase of capital goods is another channel of technology transfer along with training by foreign firms. Indeed, much of modern technology is embedded in the imported capital goods whose purchase and installation comprise investment. Technology is also acquired through license agreements, joint-ventures, turn-key, informal contacts, and subcontracting to companies holding more advanced technology. The subcontracting includes original equipment manufacturing (OEM) when a local firm produces a finished product to the specification of a foreign buyer (Castley 1997).

The Role of Trade in Economic Development

No country has succeeded in attaining economic development without exposure to other economies. Unlike the traditional wisdom that factors of production do not move between countries, trade not only serves as a substitute for this mobility but also leads towards an optimum utilisation of resources across the world. As Kuznets (1994) asserted, trade is critical for modern economic growth, and without trade Korea could not have achieved its high growth rates for a sustained period.

Kuznerts (1988) noted that trade can be the most important determinant of industrial growth for countries with a small domestic market since it makes them more reliant on the external market.

Figure 7.3 shows changes in leading exports from Korea. Kojima (1997) argued that the rapid expansion of exports over a period of time was made possible because new export products were created before the old ones began to decline. The textile industry became a major foreign exchange earner, which enabled reinvestment in related industries. Textiles were joined by other light industrial goods, and together they comprise the second product cycle in Figure 7.3.

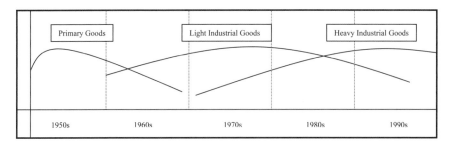

Figure 7.3   Changes in leading exports from Korea over time

In 1985, the export of light industrial products was surpassed by that of heavy industrial products. Heavy industry became more important as Korea developed, becoming particularly vital in the 1970s when the heavy industrialisation programme was deliberately fostered by the government. The push towards heavy industry was further accelerated during the 1980s. Under the protection and financial assistance of the government, heavy industry expanded its production and eventually became the centre of Korean manufacturing industry. Export demand, through the multiplier mechanism, led to an increase in domestic demand, and the contribution of both greatly stimulated economic growth (Castley, 1997).

Korea's Economic Growth through Dependence on the Japanese Economy[7]

Growth through Dependence on the Japanese Economy

Korea adopted its export-led industrialisation policy despite the fact that parts, intermediate goods, and machinery and equipment, which are essential for industrialisation were lacking. Korea had to import production goods from Japan, yet the principal philosophy of Korea throughout the entire economic development period was to attain a self-reliant economy and to break away eventually from dependence on the Japanese economy. However, it was not possible for Korea to industrialise without placing itself in a dependent position on advanced economies, and especially Japan. Not only has Korea introduced capital and technology from Japan, but has also maintained a high degree of trade dependence. By placing herself in a dependent position, Korea has searched for a different development path, which rejects the dependency emphasised by many dependency scholars, while following a trend of economic growth through

---

7   Contrary to what the dependency economists argue, it cannot be said that Korea has been exploited by Japan since the economic relationship between them has delivered favourable economic benefits to both countries. The dependency perspective that the advance of the core into the peripheries caused underdevelopment or stagnation of the peripheries cannot be accepted in this case because the dynamic process of Korea's capital accumulation has been sustained and rapid economic development has been achieved.

dependence. In other words, by internalising such a dependent position, Korea succeeded in industrialisation. This structure has enabled the Korean economy to form a unique relationship with Japan: the closer the self-reliant economy, the closer the industrial structure is that of Japan.

As many have pointed out, it is a better policy for a country with poor capital accumulation and a small domestic market to adopt an outward looking policy than an import substitution policy.[8] Petri (1988) argued that Korea deliberately followed the Japanese development model, regarding it as the successful example of an export-oriented strategy for economic development by adopting Japanese technologies, policies, and commercial institutions, and the exploitation of externalities generated by the Japanese penetration of global market.

The cooperative security relationship between Korea, Japan and the US in the 1960s began to expand towards the economic dimension. However, American consumers' tastes had become used already to Japanese goods and thus Korea needed to manufacture to at least a similar quality as that of Japan, in order to penetrate the American market. However, with the low level of technology and capital shortage it was not possible to gain consumer confidence in Korean goods in the US market. Korea had to import high quality intermediate and capital goods, with a view to satisfying consumers' tastes.

Due to its small domestic market, Korea needed to develop an export market to achieve the economies of scale in production. As long as Japan was one step ahead of Korea, Korea did not need to worry too much about the changing economic environment. Korea was able to invest in promising industries because, as Castley (1997) and Lee (1996) pointed out, the country could minimise uncertainty on factors such as the direction of future technology development, the supply and demand for raw materials, and the anticipation of market change by watching the progress of the Japanese economy. 'Watching out' allowed Korea to maximise economic opportunities while minimising possible risks.

Japan provided the model the Korea needed. Japan supplied capital, intermediate and capital goods, and the technology needed for export development, it also helped to distribute Korea's exports to the US market (Yamazawa 1985). In other words, Japan was the source of supply for industrial goods and at the same time, a key absorber and distributor of exports.

Economic Development through Technology Dependence on Japan

Korea has pursued economic development through the introduction of Japanese capital, Japanese direct investment and technology transfer, especially since 1965. Choi and Cho (1996) noted that the Korean government sought to intervene in the technological process to bring down the costs and improve the conditions for Korean firms. As pointed out by Lal (1983), the thrust of government policies was to increase the externalised technology transfer in order to boost local capability development, often behind high protective barriers.

---

8   For argument on export promotion policy, see Ballasa (1983), Kim (1975) and Keesing (1967) and for import substitution policy, see Frank (1979) and Dos Santos (1970).

Table 7.3   Trends of Korea's technology introduction from Japan and royalty payment to Japan (no. of cases of technology introduction, $m, %)

Year	Total no. of cases (A)	No. of cases from Japan (B)	(B/A)×100	Total payment (C)	Payment to Japan (D)	(C/D)×100
1961–80	1,730	1,017	58.8	457.8	168.3	36.8
1981	247	108	43.7	107.1	35.4	33.1
1982	308	164	53.2	115.7	29.3	25.3
1983	362	201	55.5	149.5	37.1	24.8
1984	437	217	49.7	213.2	53.1	24.9
1985	454	228	50.2	295.5	74.6	25.2
1986	517	264	51.1	411.0	129.5	31.5
1987	637	307	48.2	523.7	181.4	34.6
1988	751	354	47.1	676.3	214.7	31.7
1989	763	343	45.0	888.6	273.9	30.8
1990	738	333	45.1	1,087.0	341.4	31.4
1991	592	277	46.8	1,183.8	372.5	31.5
1992	533	232	43.5	850.6	266.3	31.3
1993	707	285	40.3	946.4	352.9	37.3
1994	430	124	28.4	1,276.6	399.2	31.3
1995	236	69	29.2	1,947.0	694.8	35.7
1996	189	41	21.7	2,297.2	723.9	31.5
1997	173	31	17.9	2,414.6	605.2	25.1
1998	92	15	16.3	2,386.6	609.4	25.5
1999	83	12	14.5	2,686.8	615.6	22.9
2000	80	20	25	3,062.8	527.4	17.2
2001	74	10	13.5	2,642.7	392.1	14.8
2002	60	5	8.3	2,721.6	403.0	14.8

Note: after 1994 only reported cases are counted.

Sources: Ministry of Science and Technology (various years); Korea Industrial Technology Association (various years).

Table 7.3 shows technology transfer from Japan to Korea, each year from 1981 to 1996. Before 1980, technology introduction from Japan was less important than capital and direct investment. Nevertheless, up to 1980, around 59 per cent of total cases of technology introduction came from Japan. With the active policy of technology introduction by the Korean government, between 1981 and 1990 technology transfer from Japan to Korea gradually increased. During the 1990s and the early 2000s, technology transfer from Japan declined due in part to the result of Korea's efforts to develop technology at home and in part to Japan's reluctance to transfer technology to Korea resulting from the growing influence of the Korean economy in the world economy.

Over the whole period from 1981–2002, the share of Japanese technology from the total cases of technology transfer has been high reflecting the heavy dependence of Korea on Japanese technology. Importantly, a technology recipient tends to depend on the technology first employed, leading to snowballing dependence on the technology. In this sense, as the dependency scholars argued, it is impossible for the recipient to break away from the chain of already-used technology.

Table 7.4   Trends of technology transfer accompanying patent and trademark rights from Japan: 1985–1994 (no. of cases)

| | Cumulated technology transfer | | | | | |
| | From all countries | | | From Japan | | |
	Technology introduction	With patent	With brand	Technology introduction	With patent	With brand
1985	454	238	104	228	116	49
1987	637	281	160	307	137	54
1989	763	365	189	343	158	63
1990	738	333	157	333	139	51
1991	582	266	148	277	110	67
1992	533	246	111	232	97	69
1993	707	334	175	285	85	72
1994	430	250	69	124	80	68

Source: MITI (various years).

Up to 1996, Korea introduced 9,520 cases of technology of which 48.5 per cent came from Japan and 20.5 per cent from the US. As shown in Table 7.4, technology introduction with accompanying patent, which represents the transfer of core technology from Japan to Korea, decreased from 116 cases in 1985 to 80 cases in 1994. Relatively, technology from the US accounts for large and more expensive projects (Kojima 1979; Lee 1992), and thus royalty per technology transfer from Japan is, as argued by Kojima (1985) and Hattori (1988), lower than that of the US.[9] It is misleading to say that technology transferred from Japan to Korea is at a lower stage than that transferred from the US. In general, as Hattori (1988; 1997) argued, for Japanese companies technology itself is seen as a business item, which is available to raise profits. Some factors such as tied-goods accompanied by technology transfer, market penetration to the recipient country and securing marketing information in the recipient country are mainly considered as determining factors that affect the decision whether to transfer technology to developing countries (Hattori 1988). The receipt of a royalty payment is just one of the factors that affects the total profits in transferring technology.[10] The concern about securing market share is of much greater interest than that of technology transfer alone (Hattori 1988).

---

9   For more details, see Y.-H. Kim (1995), H.-J. Lee (1996), K.-U. Lee (1988), C.-N. Kim (1992), Park (1990), Kojima (1977; 1997), and Rhu (1993). In particular, for comparison of Japanese type of technology transfer and that of the US in Korea, see Kojima (1977, 1997).

10 Of course, for Japanese companies, it is better to receive a large amount of royalty payment for technology transfer. However, royalty payment itself is not the only factor that determines technology transfer. Accordingly, it is not reasonable to argue that Japanese technology is at a low stage, although the amount of royalty paid for technology transfer is not high.

Table 7.5 Technology transfer from Japan by industry between 1962 and 1994 (no. of cases, %)

	Total cases from all countries (A)	Total cases from Japan (B)	(B/A)×100
Agro-livestock	43	23	53.5
Food	282	119	42.2
Pulp, paper	39	17	43.6
Textile, fabric	71	23	32.4
Synthetic	427	148	34.7
Sericulture, cement	236	138	58.5
Oil refining, chemicals	1,453	726	49.9
Pharmacy	224	60	26.8
Metal	443	253	57.1
Electric and electronics	2,389	1,096	45.9
Machinery	2,424	1,437	59.5
Shipbuilding	240	57	23.8
Telecoms	153	48	31.4
Electricity	103	20	19.4
Construction	163	70	42.9
Others	518	218	42.1
Total	9,196	4,453	48.5

Source: Ministry of Science and Technology (various years).

Table 7.5 represents the total cases of technology introduced from Japan by industry between 1962 and 1994. Electric and electronics, and chemicals, which made a major contribution to the expansion of Korea's exports together accounted for the majority of the total cases of technology introduced from Japan but the largest single sector was the machinery industry which accounted for nearly 60 per cent of all transfers from Japan between 1962 and 1994. Although the number of cases is much smaller, the proportion in cement and agro-livestock show a dependence on Japanese technology that is quite high. Overall, as shown in Table 7.6, Korea's development has been helped significantly by Japanese technology during the past four decades.

Such dependence on Japan in various sectors has been caused by industrialisation that followed the Japanese model for economic development as well as the different industrial stages between the two countries. It can be said that Korea's industrialisation has been pursued and kept afloat by Japanese technology transfer and as a result, the industrial structure of Korea now looks similar to that of Japan. In particular, Hopday (1995, 1998) noted that OEM have been one of the most crucial mechanisms of technological learning in the course of Korea's economic development.

Because of the deep dependence on Japan, other countries have not played such a major part in introducing technology to Korea. Kim (1993) and Hattori (1988) note that it is standardised technology in Japan that has been transferred to Korea. This means that Korea has had to produce standardised goods, for which Japan had previously enjoyed a monopoly. The transfer to Korea was caused by the different technological development stages between Japan and Korea.

Table 7.6   Stages in technological development between Japan and Korea

	Japan	Korea
1950s	Incremental process: changes for quality and speed of production	Basic production capabilities
1960s	Full production skills Process innovation Product design capability	Basic production capabilities Assembly skills Imitation
1970s	Begins R&D for products and processes	Incremental process: changes for quality and speed Minor innovation
1980s	Competitive R&D capabilities Advanced product and process innovation	Quasi-full production skills Process innovation Product design capability Begins R&D for products and processes
1990s	Advanced new product innovation	Competitive R&D capabilities New product innovation

Hobday (1995; 1998) notes that technological progress reflects the stages of economic development. As shown in Table 7.6, as the Japanese economy moved up to new industrial and technological frontiers, so the Korean economy shifted first from industry needing low technology discarded by Japan, then to middle stream technology, and later from middle stream to upper stream technology.

Figure 7.4 shows diagrammatically the changing pattern of Korean economic development as the economy progressed. Technology plays an important role in producing goods and in particular, as the economy moves to a higher stage of the industrial ladder, the level of technology becomes even more important (Hobday 1995; Castley 1997). The vertical axis represents the level of technology at the three stages: pre-matured, standardised, and advanced technology.

The horizontal axis shows the level of skill in producing goods. As Hattori (1988) pointed out, the distinction between assembly or processing technology is important in deciding the level of technology since it is closely related to the formation of skilled labour. He pointed out that the higher processed products needs the more advanced technology, which in turn requires higher levels of accumulated skill.

Figure 7.4 shows that Korea's economic development has been attained and sustained with a high level of assembly technology. The assembly-processing industry needs a skilled labour force. In particular, as Hattori (1988) and Taniura

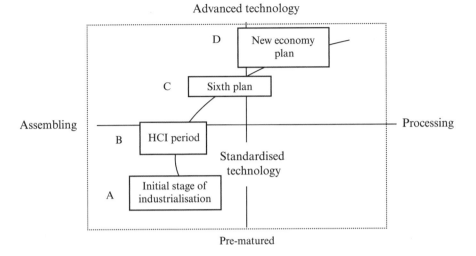

Advanced technology

Figure 7.4   Technology development and the pattern of Korea's industrialisation

Note
Major leading industry:
A: Food and beverages, textiles, toys, miscellaneous, plywood, radio assembling;
B: Textiles, paper products, radio, TV sets, shipbuilding, steel, electronics, semi-conductors;
C: Chemical products, steel, electronics, semiconductors, computers, cars;
D: Semiconductors, machinery, metal products (parts and components).

Source: Compiled from Hattori (1987): 277.

(1989) state, the higher the industrial stage, the more skill is needed. For example, in moulding processing, skill plays an important role in both quality and the volume of production. Most of the technologies introduced in Korea have been standardised and already embedded in production equipment (Hattori 1988; Kim 1993; Lee 1993). The equipment investment ratio in Korea is outstandingly high because investment is needed not only to increase the supply of but also to introduce the latest production equipment (Taniura 1989).

Simple labour-intensive industries such as miscellaneous, shoes, radio, black and white TV sets, clothing, and textiles mainly assembled with Japanese technology and parts emerged in the 1960s and intermediate goods relying on Japanese goods were promoted.[11] Although Korea moved rapidly towards the advanced stage of industrialisation, as shown in Figure 7.4, it is clear that the upward trend lies mainly in assembly rather than processing. During the 1970s, in heavy and chemical export industries such as electronics, steel, construction and shipbuilding, the pattern has

---

11 For more detail on the electric and electronics industry of Korea, see Korea Electronics Industries (1987) and Samsung (1998).

changed little.[12] Indeed, Korea did not hesitate to import parts and the required technology from Japan, both being essential for production.

In the 1990s, Korea came to produce the highly integrated semiconductor, but as shown in Figure 7.4, the stage of technology is somewhere between standardised and advanced technology. Even in the semiconductor industry, the equipment that assembles the products has come mostly from Japan (Yanagimachi 1994). Other products such as medicines and purifiers for air and water have been mostly imported from Japan (Kim et al. 1993). Korea has tended to import for assembly industries, which do not necessarily need highly skilled technology.

This pattern has brought about a unique economic structure in which the more Korea exports, the more it needs to import from Japan, creating a 'cormorant economic structure'.[13] Hattori (1988) points out that the technology of the parts and machinery industry should keep pace with the speed of the required advanced technology in the assembly-processing industry. In Korea the balance between the technology of the parts and machinery industry and the required technology in the assembly-processing industry has deteriorated because Korea urged rapid expansion of exports resulting in a shortage of skilled labour, and because there has been a reassuring supplier, Japan.

Independent large firms[14] whose industries are centred on assembly industries have also chosen to import Japanese parts, components and capital goods due to their high quality, exact delivery date, and reliable after-sales service rather than to promote domestic industries requiring a painstaking learning process and a strong element of risk.

The Light Industrialisation Period of Korea and its Dependence on Japan

Although rapid economic development in Korea was attained under consecutive five-year economic plans from the early 1960s onwards, export-oriented economic development was first planned and promoted in the late 1950s (see Table 7.7).

Lower growth in some sectors was experienced from 1958-61 because foreign aid after the late 1950s was being gradually reduced at this time. Between 1954 and 1957 economic growth was led by consumer goods such as food and textiles and between 1958 and 1961 it was led by intermediate and production goods such as fertilisers, cement and glass. The former years marked a stage when growth was mainly in consumer goods, within a self-reliant economy that was being helped by foreign aid. The latter years, however, were a stage of warming-up for the

---

12 For the electronic industry, see Kang et al. (1993), for the parts industry, see Kim et al. (1993), for general literature on technology relations with Japan, see Lee, et al. (1993), Kim et al. (1993), Park and Moritani (1993) and Yoon and Lee (1998).

13 Chinese fishermen along the Yangtze River catch fish by using cormorants whose necks are tied so as not to swallow fish they catch. As a result, the fish is given to the fishermen. By the same token, Korean industries that do not produce advanced goods, but are in an assembly-processing stage are similar to those cormorants that provide fishes for their masters.

14 This refers to large firms independent of the chaebol.

Table 7.7   Growth rate of industry by sector (annual average, %): 1954–1961

	1954–57	1958–61
Food	12.8	9.0
Textile	25.1	-0.9
Chemicals	14.9	20.2
Ceramics	22.9	18.2
Metal goods	24.0	21.1
Machinery and equipment	18.3	19.0
Total manufacturing	18.1	6.7

Source: Bae (1970): 7.

promotion of export-led industrialisation centred on intermediate and production goods, although the growth of the total manufacturing sector from 1958–1961 was 6.7 per cent, compared with 18.1 per cent in the period 1954–1957 (Table 7.7).

Attempts by the Korean government to attract foreign capital before 1965 were unsuccessful (Cho 1994). After the normalisation treaty between Korea and Japan in 1965, commercial loans poured into Korea from Japan. The normalisation treaty signalled the beginning of the second period of major Japanese influence on the Korean economy since the Korea-Japan Kanghwa Treaty of 1876 that had first opened Korea's ports for international trade (McNamara 1990). The 1965 treaty brought about widespread Japanese activity in Korea, and the results in terms of economic ties between the two countries were immediate and dramatic (Castley 1997). Indeed, from this moment, the Korean economy began to take on a vertical linkage with the Japanese economy. Korea-Japan trade had been growing since the 1950s despite the lack of formal diplomatic relations, but until 1965, the US was the major trading partner.

However, within little more than a year after the signing of the treaty, Japan surpassed the US as Korea's most important trading partner and continued to hold this position throughout the period of rapid growth of the 1960s to the 1990s. Japan has dominated Korea's economy by capturing it with surplus products, services, capital and technology.

The benefits of normalisation for Korean economic growth were enormous. The treaty was an economic imperative for President Park of Korea, who had justified his military coup of 1961 by promising the Koreans the establishment of a 'self-reliant nation' (Song 1996). At a time when American aid was being reduced and the Park government was desperately seeking alternative sources of capital to finance its new development plans, the treaty with Japan provided Korea with $300 million in grants, $200 million in public loans, and $300 million in commercial credits (raised to $500 million in 1967) over a ten-year period.[15]

---

15 Korea had attempted to attract foreign capital needed for its successive Five-Year Economic Plans. The efforts to introduce foreign capital were almost in vain. Requests were made to the US, World Bank, IMF, Italy, France, Britain and Germany. Except for Germany, all were rejected. However, the loan from Germany was not an easy one. Until

The bulk of the funds flowed into such key manufacturing industries as textiles, fertiliser, cement, steel and transportation and into major infrastructure projects (Sano 1977).

Thus, the normalisation treaty between Japan and Korea marked a watershed in the sense that Korea received public loans as well as commercial loans from Japan, resulting in the attraction of further foreign funding from other countries. In 1965, Japan accounted for over 90 per cent of the total commercial loans, amounting to $70.8 million (see Table 7.8).

With the introduction of Japanese capital, foreign capital in Korea started to climb sharply. Commercial as well as public loans increased rapidly from 1966 onwards. Public loans in general were used to finance social overhead investment and, commercial loans were for the promotion of private firms (Sashipnyunsa 1993). In fact, the government encouraged private firms to draw on commercial loans to expedite economic development. Table 7.8 shows the extent of this lending loans between 1965 and 1972 and it continued through the 1970s and 1980s.[16]

As Castley (1997) pointed out, how to channel funds into the productive sectors is more important than how to attract them. As shown in Table 7.9, between 1959 and 1971, commercial loans went mainly into manufacturing industry, especially labour-intensive industries such as textiles and petrochemicals. The majority of public loans, amounting to $87m, went into social overhead investment and services.

Japan was a major contributor of commercial loans to Korea, at favourably low interest rates. At the same time, Japanese firms were moving into Korea, mainly dominated by the GTCs, the core of the keiretsu. By 1975 149 Japanese firms were established in Korea, in a wide range of industries, from marine products to manufacturing (Byun and Kim 1988).

Developing countries in the 1960s were not free to export their goods to lucrative markets because of their inability to provide competitive export-credit facilities. Korean firms were able to overcome this problem by allowing the Japanese GTCs to export their products through joint-ventures and subcontracting arrangements (Castley 1997). Indeed, as Yoshihara (1981) argued, between the

---

then, Korea had been denied access to loans for her development plans due to her inability to provide the credit facilities. She was not a country that traded on credit. The Korean government itself was not seen as sound security for loans. No country and no international institutions guaranteed Korea's borrowing. At that time, Germany had a significant labour shortage, especially in hardworking fields. In the end, the government succeeded in borrowing $30 million on condition that Korea supplied 5,000 mining workers and 2,000 nurses. Korea could borrow on the security of human resources. However, the amount accounted for only 30 per cent of the required foreign capital. By the end of 1969, Japan had provided $123 million in grants and $75 million in government loans. The amount of Japanese commercial loans ($380 million by the end of 1969) exceeded the originally pledged sum of $300 million over ten years. See also Lee and Sato (1982) and Kim (1999).

16 Japanese firms were encouraged by the Japanese government to find offshore industrial sites by removing various restrictions on foreign investment. In addition, the Korean government provided them with the government's guarantees in order to induce Japanese capital into Korea.

Table 7.8   Introduction of public and commercial loans from Japan: 1959–1972 ($m)

	Japan	
	Public loan	**Commercial loan**
1959–63	–	–
1964	–	0.4
1965	–	70.8
1966	44.9	67.1
1967	29.9	36.3
1968	18.6	110.0
1969	11.2	71.9
1970	13.1	82.5
1971	101.9	62.9
1972	63.5	101.9
Total	192.1	543.7

Source: Sashipnyunsa (1993).

Table 7.9   Foreign capital introduction by industry: 1959–1971 (arrival base, $m)

	1959–66			1967–71		
	Public	**Commercial**	**Subtotal**	**Public**	**Commercial**	**Subtotal**
Primary industry	–	39	39 (16.2)	342 (42.2)	49	391 (18.1)
Manufacturing	24 (20%)	132 (75.0)	156 (52.7)	68	752 (55.6)	820 (3.9)
Food, drinks	–	–	–	3	21	24
Textile, clothing	4	37 (13.9)	41 (13.9)	7	148 (7.0)	155 (7.2)
Wood, paper	–	1	1	–	37	37
Petro-chemicals	14	61 (25.3)	75 (25.3)	43	262 (14.2)	305 (14.2)
Non-ferrous metal	6	24	24	24	117	120 (5.6)
Primary metal	–	4	4	9	104	113 (5.2)
General machinery	–	–	–	3	2	
Electric electronics	–	6	6	–	18	18
Transportation equipment	–	5	5	–	42	42
Others		–	–	–	1	1
SOC and services	87 (72.5)	5 (2.8)	92 (31.1)	401 (49.4)	552 (40.7)	953 (44.0)
Grand total	120	176	296	811	1,353	2,164

Note: figures in parentheses are the percentage share of total foreign capital.

Source: EPB (1981).

Table 7.10   Japanese firms in Korea (end of 1975, case)

	Mitsui	Mitsubishi	Sumitomo	Fuji	Daiichi	Sanwa	Kogin	Total
Marine product	–	–	–	–	–	–	1	1
Construction	1	–	–	1	–	–	–	2
Food	1	1	1	–	1	–	1	5
Textile	3	1	2	–	–	2	2	10
Chemicals	5	6	1	1	1	3	5	22
Glasses	1	1	2	1	–	–	1	6
General machinery	2	1	5	4	3	–	4	16
Electric equipment	9	4	13	5	4	–	1	35
Other mfg	2	4	2	3	4	–	2	17
Other commercial	5	4	6	2	1	2	–	20
Total	32	23	35	20	14	8	17	149

Source: Byun and Kim (1988).

late 1960s and the early 1970s the Japanese GTCs handled more than 50 per cent of the total exports of Korea. Although the role of the Japanese GTCs decreased over time, they were still handling over 20 per cent of the total Korean exports until the late 1970s, according to Yamazawa and Kohama (1981).

In the late 1960s, Japanese investment in Korea went into clothing and textiles; in the 1970s it was concentrated on textiles, electronics, machinery and chemicals; and in the 1980s it went into more upstream industries in electronics, machinery and chemicals replacing the clothing and textile industries, which were a typical of light industry (Hattori 1987; Taniura 1989). Many Korean firms preferred to enter into joint ventures with Japanese firms, agreeing a 50 per cent or less holding, not only to generate spreading effects to local firms but also to spread the indirect benefits of production methods, managerial skills and marketing systems (Castley 1997). Step by step, the growth of light industries supported by Japanese capital and direct investment in the 1960s helped to finance heavy and capital industries in the 1970s and Japanese firms provided a model for marketing skill and marketing access in penetrating overseas markets.

Heavy and Chemical Industrialisation Period of Korea and its Dependence on the Japanese Economy

The HCI programme in Korea was announced in 1973, although it was planned in 1971. The programme was focused on promoting defence-related industries such as iron and steel, non-ferrous metal, shipbuilding, machinery, electric and electronics, and chemicals.[17]

In 1979, the share of heavy and chemical industry in the industrial structure of Korea was 52 per cent, and in 1980 it accounted for 41.5 per cent of all exports, compared with 12.8 per cent in 1970. Throughout the 1970s, the capacity of

---

17 In fact, the biggest Changwon machinery industrial site established for the purpose of the promotion of machinery industry had been run by the Department of Defence for long time. The machinery industry, together with iron and steel industry, was called a flower of the defence industry.

production and the volume of exports in heavy and chemical industry sharply increased (see Table 7.11).

Table 7.11   The changing industrial structure during the heavy and chemical industrialisation period: 1970–1980 (%)

	Share of industrial structure		Share of export	
	HCI	Light industry	HCI	Light industry
1970	37.8	62.2	12.8	69.7
1971	–	–	–	–
1972	–	–	–	–
1973	–	–	–	–
1974	40.5	59.5	23.7	63.4
1975	46.4	53.6	25.0	57.4
1976	46.8	53.2	29.1	58.8
1977	48.5	51.5	32.2	53.6
1978	48.8	51.2	34.6	54.4
1979	51.2	48.8	38.4	51.4
1980	52.6	47.4	41.5	49.4

Source: BOK (various years).

Lee (1996) argued that the strategic industries of Korea needed Japanese firms for their capital, technology, managerial and marketing skills. Dependence upon this instrument became more prominent because Korea was seeking to achieve economies of scale by increasing its productive capacity.

To accelerate HCI industrialisation, joint-ventures in Korea were established with Japan. However, as some pointed out, Japanese loans were often conditional on the import of Japanese capital goods.

Japanese capital began to shift from commercial loans in the mid-1060s and the early 1970s to direct investment during and after heavy and chemical industrialisation and the process deepened Korea's dependence on Japan. The Korean economy began to form a unique industrial structure influenced by the changing economic environment in Japan.

As shown in Table 7.12, from 1962 to 1966 the US accounted for most of the direct investment in Korea in both the number of cases and the amount of investment. However, from 1967–1971, Japan came to dominate direct investment. From 1972 to 1976 Japan's dominance in FDI in Korea accounted for 86.8 per cent of cases and 71.3 per cent of all FDI by value.

The Parts Industry and its Dependence on Japan

The parts industry in Korea can be characterised by the increase in overseas dependence derived by the HCI programme centred on assembly-processing exports in the 1970s (Kim et al. 1993; Lee 1996; Yoon and Lee 1998). Through

Table 7.12   Foreign direct investment in Korea by country of origin ($m, %)

	1962–66		1967–71		1972–76		1977–81	
	Case	Amount	Case	Amount	Case	Amount	Case	Amount
Japan	**5**	**8,329**	**241**	**89,688**	**739**	**627,059**	**132**	**300,851**
	(12.8)	**(17.6)**	**(68.9)**	**(41.0)**	**(86.8)**	**(71.3)**	**(54.1)**	**(41.7)**
US	25	24,984	85	95,340	78	134,955	67	235,660
	(64.1)	(52.7)	(24.3)	(43.6)	(9.2)	(15.3)	(27.5)	(32.7)
Europe	4	10,841	10	9,891	24	38,775	38	95,311
	(10.3)	(22.9)	(2.9)	(4.5)	(2.8)	(4.4)	(15.6)	(13.2)
Others	5	3,257	14	23,701	10	78,636	7	88,827
	(12.8)	(6.9)	(4.0)	(10.8)	(1.2)	(8.9)	(2.9)	(12.3)
Total	39	47,411	350	218,620	851	879,425	244	720,649
	(100.0)	(100.0)	(100.0)	(100.0)	(100.0)	(100.0)	(100.0)	(100.0)

Note: Figures in parenthesis represent the share of amount and the number of cases by period.

Source: Ministry of Finance (1982).

the promotion of HCI in the 1970s, the domestic division of labour between light and heavy industry increased and intra-industry in heavy and chemical industries decreased.

As the heavy and chemical industry expanded in the 1970s, trade deficits with Japan increased, as they had done during the expansion of export-led light industry in the 1960s. Among production process in heavy and chemical industry, final assembly-processing production, which is labour-intensive was grafted onto Korea and the means of production such as parts and components were provided through imports.

Accordingly, it is obvious strategy that Korean economy not only reduces induced imports brought about by assembly-processing heavy and chemical industrialisation but also overcome the limits of exports for consumer goods-oriented production (BOK 1992; Lee 1996). Thus, parts industrialisation policy in the 1980s was to achieve not only import substitution for parts but also export substitution for final goods in the heavy and chemical industry by promoting the parts industry, which is the means of production for assembly-processing heavy and chemical industry. However, unlike assembly-processing, the parts industry is technology-intensive and needs broad complementarity between large, small and medium firms. Accordingly, Korea shifted its policy to improve small and medium firms in the parts industry and to improve technology, often through promoting R&D (Jung 1996).

As Korean industry progressed, the dependence of the Korean economy on Japan shifted again from capital dependence to technology dependence by deepening and expanding technology cooperation between Korea and Japan, both qualitatively and quantitatively.

The Electronics Industry of Korea and its Dependence on Japan

The electronics industry in Korea developed through the interplay of government policy, the chaebol and foreign capital. Along with the machinery industry, the electronics industry represents a typical case of development through dependence. Basically, the trend of imports from Japan in the electronics industry in Korea has followed the business cycle. When business is booming in Korea, the volume of imports from Japan increases and when business is in decline, the volume of imports from Japan also declines (see Table 7.13).

As shown in Table 7.13, total trade balances in the electronics industry with world from 1986–1991 were in surplus and those with Japan were in deficit. The import of electronic parts from 1986–1991 is the main cause of trade deficits with Japan in the electronics industry. This is the result of export-oriented industrial policy that neglected complementary development between final goods and parts (Lee 1995).

Table 7.13   Trend of trade balance with Japan in the electronics industry: 1986–1991 ($m, %)

		1986	1987	1988	1989	1990	1991
Total trade balance in electronics industry	Exports	7,249	11,133	15,731	16,564	17,224	19,334
	(%)		(53.6)	(41.3)	(5.3)	(4.0)	(12.3)
	Imports	4,343	5,797	8,128	8,926	9,849	11,246
	(%)		(33.5)	(40.2)	(9.8)	(10.3)	(14.2)
	Balance	2,906	5,336	7,603	7,638	7,375	8,088
	(%)		(83.6)	(42.5)	(0.5)	(–3.4)	(9.7)
Trade balance with Japan in the electronics industry	Export to	544	1,008	1,599	1,961	2,201	1,820
	(%)		(85.6)	(41.6)	(22.6)	(12.2)	(–17.3)
	Import from (%)	2,682	3,398	4,458	4,437	4,575	4,785
			(26.7)	(31.2)	(–0.5)	(3.1)	(4.6)
	Balance	–2,138	–2,390	–2,859	–2,476	–2,374	–2,965
	(%)		(11.8)	(19.6)	(–13.4)	(–4.1)	(24.9)

Note: Figures in parentheses are the percentage rate of increase vis-à-vis the previous year.

Source: EIAK (various years).

Dependence on Japanese products in the electronics industry should be understood in terms of capital and technology rather than in terms of trading performance. Technology introduction and direct investment in Korea from Japan has two facets: in the short term, it deepens technology dependence but in the long-term, it heightens the level of technology and enables localisation.

The Korean Economic System

Table 7.14 shows technology introduction in the electronics industry between 1962 and 1991 in Korea. From 1961–1991, home appliances accounted for 25.9 per cent of the total cases, and computer and peripheral equipment for 25.3 per cent, electronic parts for 22 per cent, semiconductors for 11.4 per cent, and telecommunications equipment for 9.5 per cent. The total cases of technology introduction in the electronics industry over the period 1962 to 1991 was 1,467, of which 660 (45 per cent) were from Japan.

Table 7.14   Technology introduction in the electronics industry: 1962–1991 (cases, %)

All countries	'62–79	'80–85	86	87	88	89	90	91	Total
Home appliances	57	116	21	23	45	37	44	35	378
Telecom. equipment	19	40	10	7	12	18	27	6	139
Semiconductors	12	37	12	23	15	33	20	15	167
Computers and peripheral equipment	8	59	36	38	56	44	77	51	369
Electronic parts	78	66	26	31	27	38	22	42	330
Others	8	10	5	10	15	20	9	7	65
Total	182	328	110	132	170	190	199	156	1,467
Japanese technology introduction	120	142	48	56	75	79	80	60	660
Dependence on Japan (%)	65.9	43.3	43.6	42.4	44.1	41.6	44.2	38.5	45.0

Sources: 'Annual Report Technology Introduction' 1995; EIAK (various years).

From 1962 to 1979, Japan accounted for 66 per cent of technology introduction in the electronics industry in Korea. Since then, as shown in Table 7.14, the percentage has been gradually reduced. In the 1980s, along with technology diversification policy by the government, the share of technology sourced from overseas has been gradually shifted from Japan to the US. This is a reflection of the fact that on the one hand, firms mainly chaebol in Korea have tried to diversify technology in order to reduce heavy dependence on Japanese technology and on the other hand, Japanese companies have increasingly hesitated to transfer technology as Korea has emerged as an influential and competitive industrial force.

In the 1970s, Japanese direct investment in Korea in the electronics industry accounted for most foreign investment in Korea (Castley 1998). It continued to increase until the late 1980s, when Japan withdrew due to rapid increases in wages in Korea (Kojima 1997).

The electronics industry has become a key industry for export-led industrialisation. The industry grew by assembling imported goods, a process which has become institutionalised, for example, in home appliances, which can be assembled by mass production. However, as in other sectors, the dependence

Table 7.15   Japanese direct investment in the Korean electronics industry: 1969–1990

	Joint venture	Japanese firm	Amount of investment	Share of Japan	Major item
1969	Korea Elec.	Toshiba	3,184	6.1	Electric and electronic parts
	Samsung Elec.	NEC	21,302	12.8	Electronic parts
1970	Gold Star	Mitsubishi	5,806	19.6	Electric tool
	G-S Alps	Alps Elec.	17,900	50	Electric, electronic, telecom. parts
	Korea Dongkwang	Toko	25,157	100	Electronic parts
1971	Korea Tokyo Elec.	Tokyo Sanyo	37,609	100	Electronic products
	G-S Cable	Hitachi Cable	14,707	12.9	Wire, cable
1972	Romu Korea	Romu	14,509	86	Resistors
	Samyoung Elec.	NCC	2,307	33.45	Electrolytic condenser
	Kor. Tokyo Silicon	Sanyo	12,960	100	Electronic parts
	Korea Sung Jun	Hoshiden	2,800	100	Electronic parts
	Korea Showa	Showa	6,007	100	Electronic parts
	Electronic Parts Ind.	Shenbei EandM	2,300	20.1	Speaker system
	Korea Nakagawa	Nakagawa	2,300	100	Electric machinery and tools
	Korea Taiyo	Taiyo	10,349	100	Electronic parts
	Korea Toyo Tele.	Toyo	5,746	100	Electronic products
1973	Korea Star	Star Precision	2,850	100	Machine tools
	Korea TDK	TDK	10,426	99.1	Electronic parts
	Saejin	Futaba	2,280	50	Electronic parts
	Korea Sanyon	Sanken	8,744	100	Electronic products
	Korea Sammi	Mitsumi	7,528	100	Electronic products
1974	G-S	Fuji Elec.	14,045	29.5	Sensor parts
1975	Sebang Elec.	Yuasa	2,637	34.3	Condenser
1976	Korea TT	Tokyo Sanyo	3,793	100	Electronic products
1977	Taepyongyang	Tokyo Mag.	2,549	40	Permanent magnet
1981	Korea Kisho Elec.	Kisho Elec.	25,020	94.3	Sound tools
1983	G-S Micronics	Dai Nippon	2,921	20	Shadow mask
1984	Korea Sanyo	Sanyo	4,204	49	Sound tools
1986	Dongwoo Hit Equip	Tokyo Hit	3,509	45	Hit treatment products
	Magne Trio	Sansei Shokai	4,840	97.2	Parts and trading
	Korea Sankyo	Sankyo Seiki	6,991	80	Small motor
	Jinhae Mitsumi	Mitsumi	5,625	90	Charger
	Korea Ilshin	Yamaichi	2,918	100	Microwave oven
	Korea Hokushin	Lee	4,775	100	VTR parts
1987	Sambo Computer	Seiko	10,777	12.3	Computer hard-wear
	Changwon Hoshide	Hoshiden	2,375	95	Electronic parts
	Korea Shinei	Shinei Sankyo	15,995	100	Fax, computer related parts
	Korea Shinko	Shinko Denki	15,995	100	Lead frame
	Korea Alps	Alps Elec.	69,011	95	Computer peripheral tools
	Korea Kashio	Kashio	2,351	95	Watch
1988	Samnam Elec.	Nam	2,424	100	Lead frame
1989	Woo Jin Precision	Fuji Elec.	4,179	70	Laser gun
1990	ITT Canon Korea	ITT Canon	2,040	51	Electric and electronic products

Note: the table represents companies that invested over $2m in Korea.

Source: Ministry of Finance (1991).

of the electronics industry on imported parts makes it vulnerable to circumstances affecting suppliers abroad.

Yanagimachi (1994) notes that the electronics industry in Korea deepened its technology dependence as a result of exporting based on the assembly processing of parts. Firms that assemble and then produce final goods in Korea remain at the stage of imitation of Japanese products due to the shortages of design technology within Korea (Kim et al. 1993; Castley 1997).

The electronics industry developed because the Korean government encouraged the introduction of foreign capital and technology under its export-led industrialisation policy. Japanese firms in the parts industry advanced into Korea during this period. This was accelerated through joint ventures with Japanese firms in Korea and Japan. In the process, the electronics industry in Korea has progressively come to imitate the model of Japan. Its fortunes fluctuate according to these affecting of Japanese industry. As pointed out by Fukagawa (1997), the strong yen was favourable to Korea, generating large trade surpluses. A weak yen, by contrast, was unfavourable to the Korean economy.

For example, for Samsung, Japan was the supplier of updated information, and of capital as well as technology. Japan's impact on Samsung has continued through its entire life. Samsung depended on Japanese technology, management, and production-equipment as well as capital through joint-ventures with Japanese companies, which held the most advanced technology in the industry when decisive investment was needed.

Samsung's electronics industry shows much greater dependence on Japan than other industries in Samsung. As described by Lee (1986), the founder of Samsung himself was influenced by Toshio Iue, the Chief Executive of Sanyo who emphasised the major characteristics of value added in the electronics industry when he finally decided to invest in this industry. As a result, Samsung and Sanyo first established a joint-venture in 1969, followed by other companies related to the electronic industry (see Table 7.16). Sanyo offered licences, technology assistance, production equipment, raw materials and know-how to Samsung. Throughout this process, Samsung followed Japan in the timing of its investment, plant construction and technology transfer.[18]

----

18 In addition, Samsung copied Japanese GTCs, which play a crucial role in contributing to Japan's striking development by dealing with a wide range of export goods from miscellaneous to missiles. Furthermore, Lee, the founder, used to stay in Tokyo every New Year to discuss new business projects with Japanese specialists in each business sector, and to obtain up-to-date information on business trend. Moreover, Samsung copied Toshiba and Matsushita models in establishing its strategic technology research institute (Toshiba model) and an educational training centre (Matsushita model), which educates all the new members of staff compulsorily for 24 days.

Table 7.16   Japanese technology assistance in Samsung's electronic sector

Company (Japan)	Year	Technology transfer
Sanyo	1969	According to the agreement of technology transfer, starts black and white TV assembly
NEC	1969	Produces CRTs' electronic parts
Torei	1973	Starts synthetic fibre production
Toyo Engineering	1978	Establishes industrial plant factory for exports
Toshiba	1981	Introduces microwave oven technology licence
Toshiba	1983	Introduces technology licence for air-conditioner
Sony	1983	Introduces technology licence for VCR
JVC	1983	Introduces technology licence for VCR
Toshiba	1984	Introduces technology licence for word processing, facsimile and washing machine
Sanyo	1984	Introduces technology licence for vending machine
Ikegami	1984	Supplies technology for broadcasting camera
Sanyo	1984	Introduces technology licence for microwave
Matsushita	1985	Introduces technology licence for magneton
Denkin	1989	Co-develops VCR
TRD	1990	Co-develops camcorder camera
Toshiba	1993	Concludes 8-year contact of flash memory
NEC	1994	Exchanges research data for 256MB DRAM

Sources: Samsung Chonja (1989: 371–4; Clifford (1994): 319; Hopday (1995): 66, 70, 86; Samsung (1998).

The Changing Economic Relationship between Korea and Japan

From Dependent Development to Post-Dependent Development

Korea has attained rapid and sustained economic growth through export-led industrialisation since the early 1960s (Watanabe 1996). Korea exports mainly non-durable consumer goods based on textile products and basic industrial materials based on metal and chemical products while importing capital goods based on machinery and raw materials for industrial use, mainly from Japan. As Korea's industrial structure has advanced, its dependence has deepened on production goods from Japan.

Trade imbalance between Japan and Korea has been caused by the difference in the industrial structure of both countries. Japan has a full industrial structure, which is able to produce almost all kinds of manufactured goods. Japan's imports are low and its exports are high. Korea, on the other hand, has high exports

without being self-sufficient in capital goods. Korea depends on imports to sustain
its export activity.

The neoclassical school notes that a country with the rate of high economic
growth but a small domestic market represents heavy dependence on trade vis-à-vis
GNP. Not only did Korea have little comparative advantage in primary goods, but
also had vulnerable industrial structure, being dependent on the import of parts
and intermediate and capital goods. With a weak self-supporting economy, Korea
needed to take a transitional development path by importing parts, intermediate
and capital goods and then exporting final goods after assembly and processing.
In this way, as long as technology is embedded in imported capital goods, their
import can be beneficial to Korean economy. Indeed, technology transfer from
Japan to Korea accounted for 48.5 per cent of the total imported technology
between 1962 and 1996. Of this, more than 61 per cent was introduced in the
period from 1962 to 1978, when industrialisation was being rapidly promoted.
In addition, a number of other means of acquiring technology, such as joint
ventures, licensing, management contracts subcontracting have increased
significantly and have enabled the Korean economy to upgrade technology and
skills in manufacturing industries.

The main reason for trade deficit in machinery, which accounts for the largest
share of the whole of the Korean trade deficits with Japan, is that Korean
industrialisation started with dependence on Japanese production goods such
as machinery and intermediate goods – representing typical behaviour of a
'latecomer'. Accordingly, Korea has depended on imported machinery from
Japan in order to produce non-machinery goods resulting in vertical division of
labour between Japan and Korea.

In the initial stage of economic take-off, Korea started with assembly
processing products when industrial base for parts and components were not
well-established (Hattori 1988; Taniura 1989). Assembly processing deepened
dependence on Japanese capital and intermediate goods and was facilitated by
geographical proximity of the two countries, understanding of the Japanese
language, the colonial experience, the low price of machinery, parts and
components, punctuality of delivery date and convenience and reliability of the
after-sale service system (McNamara 1990; Eckert 1990).

Korea promoted an export-drive policy at the initial stage of industrialisation.
The policy needed a high quality of exports to be maintained. However, in
Korea, there was no supply basis for production goods to meet such demand,
which forced Korea to import those products in order to improve productivity
and quality. Accordingly, as production and exports over the whole industry
developed, imports of machinery, particularly from Japan, increased along with
the increase in the volume of exports.

The pattern of Korean economic development can be understood in terms
of the synergy between internal and external factors. For Korea, with a small
domestic market, poor supply of capital and limited technology, it was relevant to
seek resources and markets from Japan to industrialise itself through dependence
on Japan. The truth, however, is that Korea intentionally adopted the path to

dependence[19] and thereby a unique economic system was created that rejects the structure of *dependency* and places Korea at the centre of a *dependent* position in the process of economic development. Mardon's explanation (1990) supports the Korean case, arguing that the effects of foreign capital on economic development in a country vary according to the role of the recipient government and domestic businesses in the country.

Korean economic development shows a trend from dependent to post-dependent.[20] In particular, substitution for production goods by domestic industry has come about through technological advances, which have enabled Korea to break its dependency on the core. The technology accumulated in the process of industrialisation has also helped small and medium firms at home to produce parts, intermediate goods and equipment, and to improve their productivity. As a result, large firms have increased their procurement from small and medium-sized companies in Korea, rather than importing the goods they need from Japan.

In the process of economic development, domestic capital has been accumulated which, in turn, has improved the ability of foreign capital. This has also helped small and medium firms, which were often excluded from the industrialisation process, to participate in the expanding market. This has created a more balanced industrial structure including large, medium and small firms.

The Changing a Zero-Sum Relationship

Since 1985, the sustained strong yen has enabled rapid globalisation of the Japanese economy. Korea has followed Japan by investing actively in overseas markets. With the help of Japan, Korea has maintained an outward-looking economy throughout the entire economic development period. As stated already, Japan has supplied intermediate and capital goods for Korea and the US provided a market for Korean goods. Korea has benefited from these relationships.

Korea's industrialisation has created a complementary relationship between Korea and Japan in terms of inter-and intra-industry relations (Watanabe 1996; Castley 1997). Japan did not hesitate to help Korea grow in various ways. As Watanabe argued (1986), by importing parts, intermediate and capital goods from Japan, Korea could specialise in labour-intensive assembly-processing industries, which needed less in the way of advanced technology and skills.

---

19 Indeed, Korea does not have followed the entire character of dependence. For example, there are three types of foreign capital: aid, loan and FDI. As pointed out by many dependency writings about Latin American countries, foreign capital synonymous with FDI from MNCs involved foreign control resulting in diminishing the independent decision making by the domestic firms and by the recipient government. Thus, as Kim (1997) argues, dependency on foreign capital as well as technology hinders long-run economic growth in developing countries by generating a circle of permanent dependency of the borrower to the lender.

20 However, post-peripherisation in production cannot necessarily accompany economic development through dependence structurally and systematically. Indeed, most developing countries have forced adverse trend, that is, development underdevelopment.

At the same time, the US market became a strong customer for Korea's exports in the 1960s and 1970s, just as the US was for Japan in the 1950s (Castley 1997). In the late 1980s, however, Korea set out to restructure its economy, owing to the rapid growth of exports, and to changes in demand and the price-cost structure, as noted by Kosai and Ogino (1984). There was new focus on domestic demand rather than export-led industrialisation.

Japan, too, was changing its policy, notably by beginning to relocate some major industries in Southeast Asia and China, rather than Korea, where labour costs were beginning to rise significantly (Fukagawa 1997). Labour-intensive production from Korea that had competed with Japan in the lucrative US market began to move to ASEAN countries where the value added for Japan was considerably higher than for production carried out in Korea (Sohn, Yang and Yin 1998). As a result, Korea's exports to Japan fell between 1988 and 1995.

From the early 1990s, the economic relationship between Japan and Korea began to change. The diversification of Korean industry progressed rapidly and the weight of Japan and the US became less significant than before (Fukagawa 1997). In the late 1980s, Asian NIEs and ASEAN countries had emerged as attractive export markets and in 1995 they accounted for 26 per cent of total exports from Korea, while exports to Japan and the US declined by 33 per cent, of which Japan accounted for 24.5 per cent (BOK 1999). The role of the US as an absorber of Korean exports has declined since the late 1980s but the role of Japan as a supplier of intermediate and capital goods to Korea has not changed.

Figure 7.5 shows the trade relationship between Japan, Korea, and the US in 1985 and 1995. During this period, Japanese yen increased sharply in value. In 1988, a trade structure that imported equipment and intermediate goods and in turn exported these goods through assembly-process to the US worked in Korea's favour. By 1995, however, it was unfavourable to Korea because of the much higher cost of imports from Japan to Korea.

As pointed out by Fukagawa (1997), until 1988, the economic relationship between Japan and Korea was a zero-sum relationship. The strong yen had worked in Korea's favour and had helped Korea to increase its exports to the US.[21] However, by the mid 1990s and despite the continuing strength of the yen, Korea's exports to the US were only slightly higher than in 1985 while the value of Japan's exports to Korea had increased considerably.

---

21 Importantly, during the strong yen period Korea's imports from Japan has been increased significantly because of the high leakage effect resulting in strong inducement of imports. However, increase in the volume of Korea's exports has traded off the amount of imports from Japan. Nevertheless, it is inevitable that such strong leakage effect caused by the different level of technology as well as the different timing of industrial structure between Japan and Korea reduces the profits of Korean firms.

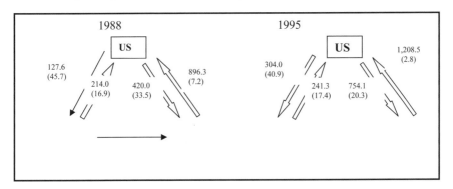

Figure 7.5   The changing trade structure among Japan, Korea and the US (%, million)

Note: Figures in parenthesis represent increase rate vis-à-vis the previous year (%).

Source: Compiled from Korea Statistics of the Customs Clearance and Japan Statistics of the Customs Clearance, quoted in Fukagwa (1997): 276.

From Bilateral to Global Relationship

From the late 1980s, the relationship between Korea and Japan has been changing from a bilateral to a global relationship (Lee 1996). At this time, Korea, like Japan, began to relocate some of its industrial production to ASEAN countries and China and expanded exports to the world market, helped in part by the strong yen, which made Korean goods more competitive than in the past.

During this period, the volume of Korea's exports increased, generating a large trade surplus of Korea for the first time (Shon et al. 1998). Korean products increased their share in the US market, but not at the expense of exports from Japan.

Korean products increased their shares in the US market while Japanese goods being strongly regulated under the VRA (Voluntarily Regulation Agreement) since the late 1980s. Korea's exports such as textile, steel, colour TV, VTR, microwave oven, and automobile have been significantly increased (Fukagawa 1997).

Table 7.17 shows for 1990 to 1995 the market share of the major industries of Korea and Japan in the US, Europe (the European Union) and China. It can be seen that there are no Korean products threatening the share of Japanese products in these markets, except for textiles and colour TVs. As Fukagawa (1997) has pointed out, it is not correct to say that Japan has lost market share as a result of the impact of Korean exports to the US and the EU.

Despite the appreciation of the Japanese yen, the volume of Korea's imports from Japan had continued to increase because of the unique economic structure in Korea where increasing exports leads to more imports from Japan. However, as industrial structure of Korea moves towards convergence with Japan, Korean

Table 7.17   Share of Korea's selected manufacturing and service industries in total FDI between 1962 and 1996 (%)

	1962–86	1987–90	1991	1992	1993	1994	1995	1996
Manufacturing	67.4	63.3	80.0	75.3	67.6	35.4	43.2	56.2
Food	3.4	4.5	1.3	13.5	2.0	0.5	1.1	1.8
Textile and Clothing	9.9	4.5	0.9	2.7	0.4	0.5	3.0	1.2
Chemicals	14.2	12.4	15.5	28.5	33.7	11.0	10.0	10.1
Medicine	2.8	3.6	4.8	3.8	1.8	3.2	1.1	1.1
Petroleum	3.3	1.5	33.5	0.2	2.8	0.5	9.3	9.3
Machinery	4.2	7.7	9.5	5.9	3.3	7.0	5.9	5.9
Electricityand Electronics	14.7	17.9	9.1	7.1	3.6	3.7	10.2	12.2
Transport Equipment	11.2	10.1	2.0	4.2	11.5	3.1	3.4	10.8
Services	31.9	36.3	20.0	24.4	32.4	64.6	56.8	43.8
Wholesale and Retail	0.6	0.1	0.4	1.4	0.7	2.5	4.3	14.3
Trading	0.0	1.7	4.5	6.8	11.6	9.5	8.0	4.8
Hotel	18.7	20.7	3.1	1.1	7.1	20.8	4.3	5.0
Financing	7.1	9.5	6.2	5.7	4.5	20.5	26.3	7.7
Insurance	0.1	2.4	3.7	5.4	1.2	0.8	4.0	1.4
Others								
US	32.0	26.2	22.2	33.2	31.7	21.5	25.2	17.1
Japan	49.1	49.1	17.7	25.7	21.9	32.8	24.8	12.3
EU	6.9	12.4	53.2	28.9	30.1	33.3	27.2	35.8
Other countries	12.0	12.3	8.9	14.2	16.3	14.4	22.8	34.8
Total	100.0	100.0	100.0	100.0	100.0	100.0	100.0	100.0

Notes: Based on actual investment. For 1962–86 and 1987–90, figures are annual averages.

Source: Ministry of Finance and Economy (1998).

goods are beginning to compete with Japanese goods within the Japanese market (Ann and Kim 1997).

These trends put pressure on Japan but Korea is similarly pressured from below. The relocation of industry by both Korea and Japan in ASEAN countries and China means that Korea can see growing competition from lower wage economies that are catching up with it. However, despite the fact that Korea has lost competitiveness since 1994, its exports, including exports within the region, continued to increase.

Towards Economic Horizontalisation

This chapter concludes with a brief examination of some of the way in which the Korean and Japanese economies were beginning to converge in the period from the late 1980s until just before the 'Asian economic crisis' of 1997, which is where this study ends.

Korea has always had a trade deficit with Japan. This is because of its position 'one step behind' Japan in the process of achieving economic development and maturity. Japanese investment in Korea reached a peak in 1988 of $697.3 million.[22] Thereafter, it began to decline, following wage increases in Korea that made investment less profitable than before. As shown in Table 7.17, lower Japanese investment, from 1991 onwards, was supplemented by investment from the European Union and from other countries. This change made it inevitable that Korea would deal in future with many countries, in addition to its long-standing links with Japan.

Although Korea lost competitiveness with Japan through rising labour costs between 1987 and 1993, it emerged as a partner holding capital and with relatively advanced technology. Korea still has a technology gap with Japan but the relationship between the two countries by the mid 1990s was on a much more level footing than in the past and was approaching the horizontal investment type between advanced countries, where capital moves according to market characteristics and demand factors (Dunning 1997). This is exemplified by Korea's admission in 1996 as a member of OECD.

A key factor in the economic convergence between Korea and Japan is relative technological strength of the two countries. Table 7.17 shows that the share of technology-related FDI has increased over time as Korean firms have increasingly embraced technology-intensive industry, including the knowledge-intensive service sector. Hong (1998) notes that in 1994, FDI in the service sector began to exceed FDI in the manufacturing sector and Table 7.17 show this pattern continued in both 1995 and 1996.

In response to the upward pressure on technology protection by advanced countries, Korean firms strengthened strategic alliances[23] with foreign firms in the 1990s (Hong 1998). Home appliances and semiconductor products in both Korea and Japan have played a leading role in supplying these goods to world markets. In particular, Fukagawa (1997) says that Korea by the mid 1990s has achieved the first-class level in the semiconductor industry. These developments have resulted in various types of horizontal strategic alliances such as joint technical cooperation, marketing cooperation including third countries, production agreement, and horizontal OEM between big companies in both Japan and Korea.

Strategic alliances between Samsung Electronics-Nitsuden and Toshiba, LG Electronics and Hitachi, Hyundai Electronics and Fujitsu are important examples of cooperation. Indeed, as Hong (1998) pointed out, increased investment between the alliances improves the quality and access to complementary assets, in particular the technological capabilities of firms and the infrastructure needed for a knowledge-based economy. In 1996, the number of strategic alliances of

---

22 The amount is based on approval. See MOF (1990).

23 Hong (1998) noted that strategic alliance refers to a way of transaction on a spectrum somewhere between market transactions and mergers. Joint technological collaboration, joint ventures, production agreement, marketing cooperation and manufacturing on an OEM basis are categorised in the example. As pointed out by Dunning (1997), strategic alliances are regarded as the advanced type of FDI in order not only to improve exploitation of global production efficiency but also to secure complementary assets. For more details, see Dunning (1997).

Korean firms was 265, a substantial increase from 209 in the previous years (Hong 1998). Many Korean firms in the electronics industry have sufficient international competitiveness and technological competence to pursue alliances with firms not only in Japan but also in the US and Europe.

Convergence is closer in some sectors than in others. Table 7.18 presents Korea's Trade Specialisation Index (TSI), which shows the relative dependence of Korea in world trade and in trade with Japan.

Table 7.18   Korea's Trade Specialisation Index (TSI) by commodity: 1990 and 1995

	World		Japan	
	1990	**1995**	**1990**	**1995**
Foodstuffs	−0.26	−0.40	0.92	0.87
Industrial materials	−0.39	−0.29	−0.25	−0.34
Chemicals	−0.49	0.13	−0.65	−0.53
Iron and steel	0.05	−0.12	−0.02	−0.15
Others	−0.49	−0.64	−0.15	−0.31
Capital goods	−0.13	0.07	−0.61	−0.60
General machinery	−0.43	−0.34	−0.85	−0.83
Precision	−0.53	−0.62	−0.80	−0.83
Transportation equipment	0.26	0.45	−0.45	−0.74
Electronic parts	0.14	0.36	−0.30	−0.19
Semiconductor	0.04	0.42	−0.24	0.81
Braun tube	0.56	0.87	−0.61	0.19
Home appliances	0.78	0.70	0.01	0.18
Sound tools	0.61	0.33	−0.18	0.00
CTV	0.95	0.98	0.63	0.97
VTR	0.95	0.92	0.33	0.31
Shipbuilding	0.75	0.56	−0.88	−0.84
Textiles	0.92	0.62	0.91	0.89

Note: TSI can be obtained by the formula (exports − imports)/(exports + imports). If Korea entirely specialises in exports to or imports from another country with respect to a commodity category, the TSI is either + 1 or − 1 respectively. The closer the TSI to zero, the more horizontal is the industrial specialisation between the two countries.

Source: Korea Trade Association (various years), based on MITI (various years).

The closer the TSI is zero, the more horizontal is the industrial specialisation between Korea and the comparator. In trade with Japan, Korea still showed vertical specialisation in most industries in both 1990 and 1995 but in some industries such as semiconductors and home appliances, there is a high degree of horizontal specialisation, which supports the strategic alliances that were established in the mid 1990s.

This chapter has traced the evolving economic relationship between Korea and Japan. It shows that Japan has had a major influence on Korea's economic development and that the relationship between the two countries, beginning as one of dependency on the part of Korea became one of growing interdependence, at first through Japan's contribution to export-led industrialisation in Korea and more recently through the development strategic partnership in selected industries where, increasingly, Korea and Japan have become equal players on the world stage.

Chapter 8

Conclusion

What is the best way to explain economic development? This has been one of the major concerns of economists since the birth of the argument. There have been mainly three views to explain the process of economic development: the neoclassical, the developmental-state and the dependency view. None of these theories is sufficient, in itself, to explain the successful economic development of Korea. Indeed, there is considerable controversy over the factors that have most contributed to it. This research has argued for a different explanation by combining and modifying elements in the existing theoretical perspectives to fit the special features of the Korean case. A middle way is followed, based on a cautious use of the developmental-state view, which is seen as particularly relevant to Korea, since most of the internal factors affecting development have been chosen and determined by government.

The analysis presented in the thesis has shown the importance of the institutions of development rather than the selection of specific factors considered most relevant to economic development. It was argued that economic development comes about through the evolution of institutions, which comprise both internal and external factors. Over time, institutions work together in pursuit of a certain goal or goals and though they may begin by doing so in a complementary fashion, a more competitive relationship eventually develops. Where government is involved, what begins as a top-down relationship with other institutions becomes blurred, reflecting a shift in the balance of power. The study has suggested that there are many possible types of institutions, which result in bolstering up economic development other than those implied in conventional views. As the economy develops, a new partner, for example financial institutions, emerges as a response to economic development; and as this evolutionary process continues, other partners emerge and their strategic complementarity is gradually strengthened. This pattern was seen in the changing relations between government and the chaebol and between government and financial institutions in Korea.

The study has also shown the importance of external factors in contributing to economic development. As I argued, a developing economy cannot achieve growth without the help of external factors. Government and private sector institutions provide incentives to attract external attention, and both internal and external interests can be served in this process. As the economy develops, both internal and external factors become intertwined. The influence of Japan on the evolution of the Korean economic system was shown to follow this pattern.

The Evolution of the Korean Economic System in Action

In the 1960s, the authoritarian developmental government led by President Park chose the chaebol as a strategic partner to help bring about economic development in Korea. The government also nationalised the private banks, partly to keep them out of the hands of the chaebol and partly to maintain its control of all the principal levers of economic power. An export-led industrialisation policy was adopted and after the normalisation of relations with Japan in 1965, Japanese capital began to flow into the Korean economy, to be followed later by direct investment on the part of many Japanese companies. This brought technological 'know-how' as well as foreign investment into Korea, enabling it to expand its export activities. The more Korea exported, for example to the United States, the more it needed to import from Japan to sustain the export-led economy. Thus, Korea and Japan became strongly inter-dependent but with Korea always 'one step behind' Japan, at least until the mid 1990s when there were signs of convergence in the important semiconductor and domestic appliances industries.

The role of the Korean government began to change under President Chun, who took over in 1980. The financial institutions were denationalised but government continued to guarantee loans to the chaebol to enable them to go on expanding without risk of bankruptcy or job losses. Since the mid-1980s, however, further deregulation has left the chaebol much more exposed to the market, as recent events (post-1997) have shown. However, this process freed the chaebol from much of the close government attention that characterised their early relationship and has created a situation where government and chaebol are able to follow different policies and even to compete, where necessary.

The present structure of the Korean economy as it has evolved over the last 50 years, and particularly in the period from 1960 to 1997, is illustrated in Figure 8.1. The figure shows on the left the government sector and on the right, the private sector, which consists of the chaebol and the financial institutions. The overseas market and the Japanese economy form part of the inter-relationships and inter-dependencies that characterise the present-day Korean economy. Unlike the situation 40 years ago, the government, although it remains important, is no longer the dominant actor in the Korean economy. The relationship with Japan remains critical to Korea but, as was argued in the previous chapter, it is no longer a dependency relationship but rather one of mutual benefit to both countries

In summary, there was a strategic alliance between government and chaebol in the market system. The alliance was complementary to begin with but became competitive over time. It played as an independent variable that affected the whole economy in the process of economic development. The existence of the strategic alliance went against arguments in the three views of development, that government and market have a zero-sum relationship with one group's interest being at the expense of the other's. In addition, as the economy became mature, the financial institutions emerged as another independent variable. Their denationalisation had beneficial effects on the process of economic development. This view stands in contrast to Amsden's model (1989), in which independent factors were fixed, without room for another independent variable to emerge.

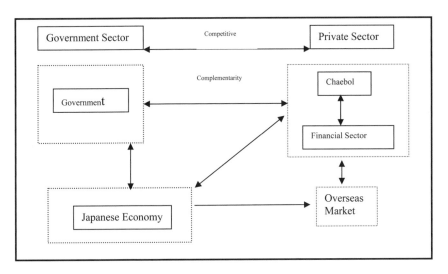

Figure 8.1   The changing function of the Korean economic system

Moreover, the relationship between government, chaebol and financial institutions was not a constant one. It changed in the process of economic development - again with beneficial effects for the Korean economy. This view is different from that in earlier studies which suggests that the relationship between them was always 'top-down', where government indicated and chaebol followed. Furthermore, institutions developed and evolved through competition and in turn, their evolution contributed to economic development. This view is strengthened by the time span adopted for this study. The most important external factor is Japan. Its contributions of both 'hardware' and 'software' (business culture and know-how) have had a great influence on the formation of the economic system in Korea; and they have become embedded into the economy. However, the relationship with Japan has changed over time, reflecting and influencing changes in the economies of both countries. This conclusion differs from that of Castley (1997) who did not emphasise the changing influence of Japan on the formation of the Korean economic system.

In particular, although the neo-institutionalists analyse how an institution in an economy has evolved over time, they clearly neglected a process of how external factors have affected the formation of the economic system. In addition, they do not consider the evolutionary process of institutions that enables another institution to emerge as the economy becomes mature and do not see the complementary relationship between institutions and government. Furthermore, they do not see that the evolutionary process of institutions needs an advanced market mechanism and at the same time, the advanced market mechanism requires further development of institutions. It is through these complementary relationships that economic development is achieved. The present research has overcome these limitations, using Korea as a case study.

A Correlation of the 1997 Korean Financial Crisis with the Changing Korean Economic System

The government-chaebol relationship was initially the most important factor in the process of economic development in Korea. Over time, the financial institutions grew in importance and affected the direction of the Korean economic system. Their role was however, to bolster up the chaebol to sustain rapid economic development. The bankruptcy of a financial institution would bring about the bankruptcy of chaebol and other firms and vice versa, creating instability in the whole economy. In this system, continual complementarity among government, chaebol and financial institutions has been required to maintain rapid and sustained economic growth. In addition, as chaebol heightened their economic power by increasing their market share, for banks it was difficult to supervise the management of chaebol because they limited abilities to screen the viability of their lending. Moreover, the chaebol became more successful than the government in terms of acquisition of information and fund-raising and thus the chaebol became more independent of the government. With their increasing financial independence, the chaebol become more aggressive so that the government could hardly monitor chaebol's decision making in the allocation of resources. As the economy has grown and been exposed more to globalisation, the government-chaebol relationship has become less effective and efficient. As I noted, the economic system has been gradually formed through time and the complementarity of institutions needs time to be recognised as a part of the economic system. However, with the result of a rapidly changing economic environment, the Korean economic system has fallen into a transitional period. Institutions have become interdependent and chaos in the economic system has generated economic inefficiency. For the government with relatively weakened authority it was difficult to control the market mechanism as they did in the past, in particular, as each institution has begun to have its own voice. Korea began to experience a contradiction between institutions brought about by rapid economic growth.

Furthermore, Korea followed in the footprint of Japanese economic development. Korea had adopted Japanese technologies, economic policies and the mechanism of commercial institutions. As long as Japan is one step ahead of Korea, Korea could minimise uncertainty such as trend of technology and forecast of market fluctuations and thus, she could invest intensively in profitable sectors created by the leader, Japan. Watching out and witnessing was itself a living example that minimised potential risks and maximised economic opportunities. In this process, Japanese economic influence was gradually internalised in each institution whose conditions have been more or less affected by the changing Japanese economic environment. However, since the mid-1990s Japan has failed to provide clear industrial relationship as she did in the past. With no significant technology development but with modified existing technology mainly introduced by Japan, its rapid and sustained economic growth has been questioned. Korea that neglected to develop technology and promote its own industries has also lost a sense of direction where to go alongside the struggling Japanese economy. All these structural problems provided a triggering effect for market signal represented by a market phenomenon and as a result, the market signal made bad structural conditions worse, leading a crisis of the real economy.

The Evolutionary Process of the Korean Economic System since the Crisis

Since the crisis, the government has assisted venture companies in the way that she did for the chaebol in the past as an alternative player for economic development substituting chaebol-led economic system, causing the majority of the chaebol to become bankrupt. However, the government has not abandoned a chaebol-led growth structure, rather more competitive and complementary relationships between chaebol, venture companies and the government has been needed. Although most of commercial banks have been nationalised again by the government, the financial institutions have been completely exposed to global standards so that a very competitive environment has been created, giving less room for the government to control as she did in the past. As a result, the crisis has brought about many structural changes in the Korean economic system: in industrial structure, it has changed from an expansion-oriented structure to a profit-oriented structure; in financial management, from debt financing to equity financing and cash flow orientation; in personnel management, from cronyism to ability orientation. On the other hand, the long-lasting weak economic performance of Japan has exposed its own economic problems, causing less impact on the Korean economy. Unlike before the 1997 crisis, the won has not moved to the opposite direction to the yen, blowing out the zero-sum game between the yen and the won. Rather, both currencies in Korea and Japan have moved toward the same direction; the weak yen, the weak won and the strong yen, the strong won, giving little benefit to Korean exports. Indeed, this reflects that the two countries have become competitive and complementary in their economic relationship.

Since the 1997 crisis, each institution and government in the Korea economic system has moved toward more complicated and sophisticated relationships and at the same time the market mechanism has been streamlined to support these relationship. In this process, institutions have continued to evolve through more comprehensive and competitive relationships, reflecting economic development.

Other Considerations

These conclusions are the result of a detailed case study of the evolution of the Korean economic system which has drawn on material published in English, Korean and Japanese, including data from Korean business and trade organisations that has not been used before in a study of this kind. The research, therefore, is a contribution that crosses language boundaries as well as academic and analytical boundaries. A long timescale was adopted for the study, beginning after World War II and continuing until 1997. The research was started in 1997 and does not, therefore, deal with or address issues arising from the so-called 'Asian Financial Crisis' that began in Thailand in 1997 and spread to certain other Asian countries, including Korea.

The research was at both micro and macro level and largely desk-based. Although time was spent on bibliographic work in both Tokyo and Seoul, there was no fieldwork with any of the institutions covered in the study. This was a decision that had to be made quite early on in the research but it means, for example, that no work could be undertaken with government departments, financial institutions or individual firms on their specific behaviour in the market. Work with firms, especially in the light of the knowledge gained during this study, would be a potentially rewarding area for further research. At an institutional level, too, work involving labour unions and citizen's groups could be of interest and would add another dimension to the story of Korea's economic development. Much emphasis has been given in this study to the influence of Japan but a similar detailed analysis of the influence of the United States on the Korean economy would also be illuminating.

Despite these possible suggestions, it is believed that this study has cast new light on the process of economic development and the evolution of the Korean economic system, looking in particular at the roles of government, the chaebol, the financial institutions and the influence of Japan. In particular, Korea can serve as a useful model, breaking away from the conventional three views. What is required is an empirically relevant theory of both the general paradigm of developing countries and its special independent factors – especially as found in Korea. It is toward the development of such a theory that this book is dedicated.

Bibliography

Aarnio, O. 1998. 'The Strains of Economic Growth in Korea: Isn't Broad-based Growth Enough After All?', *Asia Pacific Business Review*, Vol. 4, No. 2, 149–56.

Ahn, C.-Y. 1988. 'Economic Development of South Korea, 1945–1985: Strategies and Performance', *Korea and World Affairs*, Vol. 10, No. 1, Spring.

Ahn, C.-Y. and S. Nakamura, eds. 1989. *Economic Structure of Modern Chosun*, Seoul: Bibong Press (in Korean).

——, eds. 1993. *Study on Industrialisation of Modern Chosun*, Seoul: Bibong Press (in Korean).

Ahn, C.-Y. and J.-H. Kim. 1997. 'The Outward-looking Trade Policy and The Industrial Development of South Korea', in D.-S. Cha and D.H. Perkins, eds, *The Korean Economy, 1945–1995: Performance and Vision for the Twenty-first Century*, Seoul: KDI.

Akamatsu, K. 1962. 'A Historical Pattern of Economic Growth in Developing Countries', *The Developing Economies*, No. 1, March–August.

Amin, S. 1974. *Accumulation on a World Scale: A Critique of the Theory of Underdevelopment*, 2 vols, New York: Monthly Review Press.

Amsden, A. 1986. 'A Technological Perspective on the General Machinery Industry in the Republic of Korea', in M. Fransman, ed., *Machinery and Economic Development*, London: Macmillan.

——. 1989. *Asia's Next Giant: South Korea and Late Industrialisation*, New York: Oxford University Press.

Amsden, A. and L.-S. Kim. 1985. 'The Role of Transnational Corporations in the Production and Exports of the Korean Automobile Industry', *Harvard Business School Working Paper*.

Aoki, M. 1988. *Information, Incentives and Bargaining in the Japanese Economy*, Cambridge: Cambridge University Press.

——. 1992. *Nihon Keizai Seido Bunseki: Zoho, Insenteibu, Kosho Geimu* [*A Comparative Institutional Analysis of Japanese Economy: Information, Incentive, and Negotiation Game*], Tsukuma Shoten (in Japanese).

——. 1995. *Keizai Shistemu no Shinka to Tagensei* [*Evolution of Economic System and Pluralism*), Toyo Keizai Shinposha (in Japanese).

Aoki, M. and R. Dore, eds. 1994. *The Japanese Firm: Sources of Comparative Strength*, Oxford: Clarendon Press.

Aoki, M., and M. Okuno-Fujiwara. 1996. *Keizai Shistemuno Hikakuseido Bunseki* [*A Comparative Institutional Analysis of an Economic System*], Tokyo: Tokyo University Press (in Japanese).

Aoki, M. and M. Okuno-Fujiwara. 1997. *The Role of Government in East Asian Economic Development: Comparative Institutional Analysis*, Oxford: Oxford University Press.

Aoki, T. 1992. 'Foreign Investment and Network Formation', in S. Tokunaga, ed., *Japan's Foreign Investment and Asian Economic Interdependence*, Tokyo: University of Tokyo Press.

Argy, V. and L. Stein. 1997. *The Japanese Economy*, Basingstoke: Macmillan.

Arndt, H.W. 1985. 'The Origins of Structuralism', *World Development*, Vol. 13, No. 2, February.

——. 1987. 'Industrial Policy in East Asia', *Industry and Development*, Vol. 22.

Asia Economic Research Institute. 1967. 'Kankoku no Kigyo' ['Enterprise of Korea'], Singapore: AERI.

Bae, M.-K. 1970. *Future Development and Problems of Industrialisation in Korea*, Singapore: AERI.

——. 1977. 'Soduck Bunbae' ['Income Distribution'], in H.Y. Byun and Y.-H. Kim, eds, *Hakuk Kyongjeron* [*The Korean Economy*], Seoul: Bibong Publishing (in Korean).

——. 1987. 'Business-Labour Relationship', in S. Cho et al., eds, *Theory and Reality of the Korean Economy*, Seoul: Seoul National University Press (in Korean).

Bae, Y.-M. 1994. 'Finance', in Academy of Korean Social Economy, eds, *Lecture of Korean Economy*, Hawool Academy (in Korean).

Balassa, B. 1971. 'Industrial Policy in Taiwan and Korea', *Weltwirtschaftliches Archiv*, Vol. 106, No. 1, 55–77.

——. 1981. *The Newly Industrialising Countries in the World Economy*, Oxford: Pergamon Press.

——. 1982. 'Structural Adjustment Policies in Developing Economies' *World Development*, Vol. 10, No. 1.

——. 1983. 'Outward Versus Inward Orientation Once Again', *The World Economy*, Vol. 6, No. 2.

——. 1988. 'The Lessons of East Asian Development: An Overview', *Economic Development and Cultural Changes*, Vol. 36, No. 3. April, Supplement.

——. 1990. 'Korea's Development Strategy', in Jene K. Kwon, eds, *Korean Economic Development*, Westport, CT: Greenwood Press.

Bank of Korea (BOK). *Economic Statistics Yearbook*, various issues (in Korean).

——. 1990. *Kiup Kyongyong Bunsuck* [*An Analysis of Business Management*) (in Korean).

——. 1993. *Korea's Financial Institution* (in Korean).

——. 1995. *Kiup Kyongyong Bunsuck* [*An Analysis of Business Management*] (in Korean).

Baran, P. 1957. *The Political Economy of Growth*, New York: Monthly Review Press.

Baranson, J. 1970. 'Technology Transfer through the International Firm', *American Economic Review*, Vol. 60.

Barth, J.R., G. Caprio Jr, and R. Levine. 2001, *The Regulation and Supervision of Bank Around the World: A New Database*, in R.E Litan and R. Herring, eds, *Integrating Emerging Market Countries into the Global Financial System*,

Brookings-Wharton Papers on Financial Services, Baltimore, MD: Brookings Institution Press.

Bernard, M. and J. Ravenhill. 1995. 'Beyond Product Cycles and Flying Geese: Regionalisation, Hierarchy and Industrialisation of East Asia', *World Politics*, Vol. 47, No. 2 January.

Bhagwati, J. 1978. *Anatomy and Consequences of Exchange Control Regimes*, New York: National Bureau of Economic Research.

——. 1985. 'Foreign Trade Regimes', in J. Bhagwati, ed., *Dependence and Interdependence*, Oxford: Basil Blackwell.

——. 1987. 'Outward Orientation: Trade Issues'. in V. Corbo, M. Khan and M. Goldstein, eds, *Growth-Oriented Structural Adjustment*, Washington, DC: IMF and World Bank.

Blumenthal, T. and C.-H. Lee. 1985. 'Development Strategies of Japan and the Republic of Korea: A Comparative Study', *The Developing Economies*, Vol. 23, September.

Bradford Jr, C. 1981. 'ADC's Manufactured Export Growth and OECD Adjustment', in W. Hong and L. Krause, eds, *Trade and Growth of the Advanced Developing Countries in the Pacific Basin*, Seoul: KDI.

——. 1987. 'Trade and Structural Change: NICs and Next Tier NICs as Transitional Economies,' *World Development*, Vol. 15, No. 3.

Bumsinsa. 1998. *Act on Foreign Direct Investment and Foreign Capital Inducement*, Seoul: Bumsinsa.

Byun, H.-Y. 1975. 'Chaebol ui Yoonri wa Kyojebalchon' ['Moral Principle of Chaebol and Economic Development'], *Shin Dong-A*, No. 136 (in Korean).

——. 1992. *Hankook Kyeongje ui Sungjang goa Byuncheun* [*Korean Economic Growth and Changes*], Seoul: Bibong Publishing (in Korean).

Byun, H.-Y. and Y.-H. Kim. 1988. *Hankug Kyojeron* [*Principle of the Korean Economy*], Seoul: Bibong Publishing (in Korean).

Cain, P.J. and A.G. Hopkins. 1993. *British Imperialism: Innovation and Expansion, 1688–1914*, London and New York: Longman.

Calder, K. 1993. *Strategic Capitalism: Private Business and Public Purpose in Japanese Industrial Finance*, Princeton, NJ: Princeton University Press.

Caparaso, J. 1978. 'Introduction: Dependence and Dependency in the Global System', *International Organisation*, Vol. 32, No. 1, Winter.

Cardoso, F.H. 1977. 'The Consumption of Dependency Theory in the United State', *Latin American Research Review*, Vol. 12, No. 13.

Castley, R. 1997. *Korea's Economic Miracle: The Crucial Role of Japan*, Bastinstoke: Macmillan.

——. 1998. 'The Korean Industry: The Japanese Role in its Growth', *Asian Pacific Business Review*, Nos 2–3, December.

Cathie, John. 1998. 'Financial Contagion in East Asia and the Origins of the Economic and Financial Crisis in Korea', *Asian Pacific Business Review*.

Cha, D.-S. 1983. *Oija Doip ui Hyokkwa Boonsok* [*An Analysis of Effect of Foreign Capital Inflow*], Seoul: Korea Institute for Economics and Technology (KIET) (in Korean).

Chakravarity, S. 1987. 'The State of Development Economics', *The Manchester School of Economics and Social Studies*, Vol. 55, No. 5, June, 521–31.

Chang, H.-J. 1994. *The Political Economy of Industrial Policy*, London: Macmillan Press.

——. 1998. 'South Korea: The Misunderstood Crisis', in K.S. Jomo, ed., *Tigers in Trouble*, London and New York: Zed Books Ltd.

Chenery, H.B. 1975. 'The Structuralist Approach to Development Policy', *American Economic Review*, Vol. 65, No. 2, 310–16.

Cho, D.-S. 1987. *The General Trading Company*, Lexington, MA: Lexington Books.

——. 1989. 'Diversification Strategy of Korean Firms', in K-H. Chung and H.-C. Lee, eds, *Korean Managerial Dynamics*, New York: Praeger.

——. 1990. *Hankug Chaebol Yongu [Research of Korean Chaebol]*, MaeKyong Economic Newspaper Publishing (in Korean).

——. 1994. *Hankug Chaebol Yongu (Research of Korean Chaebol)*, Maekyong Economic Newspaper Publishing (in Korean).

——. 1997. *Chaebol*, Maekyong Economic Newspaper Publishing (in Korean).

Cho, S. 1991. 'Abchug Sungjangui Shibalgoa Gaebal Chonryaguo Jongchack' ['Take-off of Condensed Growth and Consistent Development Strategy'], in B-H. Koo, ed., *Historical Illumination of Korean Economy*, Seoul: Korea Development Institute (in Korean).

——. 1994. *The Dynamics of Korean economic Development*, Washington, DC: Institute for International Economics.

——. 1996. *Hankug Kyongje Gaejoron [Explanation of Reforming the Korean Economy)*, Tasan Publishing (in Korean).

Chosun Kyongje Tongge Yoram. 1949. *Survey of Chosun Economic Statistics* (in Korean).

Cho, Y. and T. Hellmann. 1993. 'Government Intervention in Credit Markets in Japan and Korea – An Alternative Interpretation from New Industrial Economic Perspective', PRE Working Paper Series, World Bank.

Cho, Y.-B., and Yoo, eds. 1988. *Hankuk Jabonjuui ui Seonggyok Nonjaeng [Debate on Characteristics of Korean Capitalism]*, Dae-Wang Publishing (in Korean).

Cho, Y.-J. 1988. 'The Effects of Financial Liberalisation on the Efficiency of Credit Allocation: Some Evidence from Korea', *Journal of Development Economics*, September.

—— 1989. 'Finance and Development: The Korean Approach', *Oxford Review of Economic Policy*, Vol. 5, No. 4, Winter.

——. 1990. 'The Financial Policy and Financial Sector Developments in Korea and Taiwan', in J.K. Kwon, ed., *Korean Economic Development*, Westport, CT: Greenwood Press.

——. 1997. 'Government Intervention, Rent Distribution, and Economic Development in Korea', in M. Aoki, H.-K. Kim and M. Okuno-Fujiwara, eds, *The Role of Government in East Asian Economic Development*, Oxford: Clarendon Press.

Cho, Y.-J. and J.-K. Kim. 1997. *Credit Policies and the Industrialisation of Korea*, Seoul: KDI.

Choi, S-R. 1998. *Business Conglomerates*, Seoul: CFE (in Korean).

Chou T.-C. 1988. 'American and Japanese Direct Foreign Investment in Taiwan: A Comparative Study', *Hitotsubashi Journal of Economics*, Vol. 29.

Chow, P.C.Y. and Kellman, M.H. 1993. *Trade: the Engine of Growth in East Asia*, New York: Oxford University Press.

Chung, D.-H. and J.-H. Cho. 1999. *Economic Development in East Asia*, Seoul: Sejong Publishing (in Korean).

Chung, K.-H., Lee, H.-C. and K.-H. Jung. 1997. *Korean Management: Global Strategy and Cultural Transformation*, Berlin: Walter de Gruyter.

Chung, U.-C. 1991. *A Financial Reform*, Bupmoonsa (in Korean).

Chung, Y.-I. 1973. 'Japanese Investment in Korea: 1904–1945', in A. Nahm, ed., *Korea Under Japanese Colonial Rule: Studies of the Policy and Techniques of Japanese Colonialism*, Michigan: Centre for Korean Studies Institute of International and Area Studies, Western Michigan University.

Cline, W. 1982. 'Can the East Asian model of Development be Generalised?', *World Development*, Vol. 10, No. 2.

Coase, R.H. 1993. '1991 Nobel Lecture: The Institutional Structure of Production', in O.E. Williamson S.G. Winter, eds, *In the Nature of the Firm: Origins, Evolution and Development*, New York: Oxford University Press.

Colander, D., ed. 1984. *Neoclassical Political Economy*, Cambridge, MA: Ballinger Publishing.

Cole, D.C. and Y.-C. Park. 1984. *Korea's Financial Development, 1945–80*, Seoul: KDI.

Corbo, V. and S.-W. Nam. 1988. 'Korea's Macroeconomic Prospects and Policy Issues for the Next Decade', *World Development*, Vol. 16, No. 1.

Corbo, V. and S.-M. Suh. 1992. *Structural Adjustment in a Newly Industrialised Country: The Korean Experience*, Baltimore, MD: Johns Hopkins University Press.

Cumings, B. 1987. 'The Origins and Development of the Northeast Asian Political Economy: Industrial Sectors, Product Cycles, and Political Consequences', in F. Deyo (ed.), *The Political Economy of the New Asian Industrialisation*, Ithaca, NY: Cornell University Press.

——. 1997. *Korea's Place in the Sun: A Modern History*, New York: W.W. Norton & Company.

Dahlman, C. and L.-S. Kim. 1992. 'Technology Policy for Industrialisation: An Integrative Framework and Korea's Experience', *Research Policy*, Vol. 21.

D'Costa, A.P. 1994. 'State, Steel and Strength: Structural Competitiveness and Development in South Korea', *The Journal of Development Studies*, Vol. 31, No. 1, October.

Deyo, F.C. 1987. 'Coalitions, Institutions, and Linkages Sequencing – Toward a Strategic Capacity Model of East Asian Development', in F. Deyo, ed., *The Political Economy of the New Asain Industrialisation*, Ithaca, NY: Cornell University Press.

Dodaro, S. 1993. 'Exports and Growth: A Reconsideration of Causality', *The Journal of Developing Areas*, Vol. 27, No. 2, January.

Doner, R.F. 1993. 'Japanese Foreign Investment and the Creation of a Pacific Asian Region', in J. Frankel and M. Kahler, eds, *Regionalism and Rivalry: Japan and the US in Pacific Asia*, Chicago: University of Chicago Press.

Doran, C.F. 1993. 'The United State, Japan, and Korea: The New International Political Economy', *Asian Perspective*, Vol. 17, No. 1, Spring–Summer.

Dore, R. 1986. *Flexible Rigidities: Industrial Policy and Structural Adjustment in the Japanese Economy 1970–80*, London: The Athlone Press.

Dornbusch, R. 1992. 'The External Balance', in V. Corbo and S.-M. Suh, eds, *Structural Adjustment in a Newly Industrialised Country: The Korean Experience*, Baltimore, MD: Johns Hopkins University Press.

Dos Santos, T. 1970. 'The Structure of Dependence', *American Economic Review*, Vol. 60, No. 2, May.

Dosi, G., C. Freeman, R. Nelson, G. Silverberg and L. Soete, eds. 1988. *Technical Change and Economic Theory*, London: Pinter Publishers.

Dunning, J.K. 1997. *Alliance Capitalism and Globalisation*, London: Routledge.

Eckert, C.J. 1990. 'Economic Development in Historical Perspective, 1945–1990', in C. Eckert, K.-B. Lee and E. Wagner, eds, *Korea Old and New A History*, Seoul: Ilchokak Publishers.

Economic Intelligence Unit (EIU). 1997. *South Korea – Country Report*, No. 2.

Economic Planning Agency. 1989. *The Philosophy of Prosperity in the Asia-Pacific Region: Japan's Role as Viewed from the Perspective of its Comprehensive National Capability*, Tokyo: Ministry of Finance Printing Bureau (in Japanese).

Economic Planning Board (EPB). *White Paper on Foreign Investment*, various issues (in Korean).

——. *Economic Survey: Annual Report of the Korean Economy*, various issues (in Korean).

——. 1993. 'Major Economic Statistics' (in Korean).

Economist. 1998. 'East Asian Economic Survey: Frozen Miracle', 7 March.

Edwards, S. 1988. 'Financial Deregulation and Segmented Capital Markets: The Case of Korea', *World Development*, Vol. 16, No. 1.

Eggertsson, T. 1990. *Economic Behaviour and Institutions*, Cambridge: Cambridge University Press.

Electronics Industries Association of Korea. 1990. 'Statistics of Electric and Electronics Industries', various years (in Korean).

Enos, J.L. and W.-H. Park. 1988. *The Adaptation and Diffusion of Imported Technology: The Case of Korea*, London: Croom Helm.

Esho, H. 1989. 'Kaihatsu Keizai no Tenkan to Kankoku Moderu', *Keizai Shirin*, Vol. LVII, June (in Japanese).

Evans, P. 1979. *Dependent Development: The Alliance of Multinational, State and Local Capital in Brasil*, Princeton, NJ: Princeton University Press.

Euh, Y.-D. 1987. 'Foreign Debt', in S. Cho et al., eds, *The Theory and Reality of the Korean Economy*, Seoul: Seoul National University Press.

Fair Trade Commission. 1993. *Daegyumo Chibtan Soyu Hyonhwang [Report of Stock Ownership of Big Business]* (in Korean).

——. 1996. *Fair Trade Annual Report* (in Korean).

Fajnzylber, F. 1981. 'The Industrial Dynamic in Advanced Developing Countries', in W.-T. Hong and L. Krause, ed., *Trade and Growth of the Advanced Developing Countries in the Pacific Basin*, Seoul: KDI.

Fields, K.J. 1991. 'Developmental Capitalism and Industrial Organisation: Chaebol and the State in Korea', paper presented at the Conference on Political Authority and Economic Exchange in Korea, East-West Centre, Honolulu, 3–5 January.

——. 1995. *Enterprise and the State in Korea and Taiwan*, Ithaca, NY: Cornell University Press.

Fishlow, A. 1990. 'The Latin American State', *Journal of Economic Perspectives*, Vol. 4, No. 3.

Flath, D. 2000. *The Japanese Economy*, Oxford: Oxford University Press.

Frank, A.G. 1966. 'The Development of Underdevelopment', *Monthly Review*, October.

——. 1967. *Capitalism and Underdevelopment in Latin America: Historical Studies of Chile and Brazil*, New York: Monthly Review Press.

——. 1969. *Latin America: Underdevelopment or Revolution*, New York: Monthly Review Press.

——. 1979. *Dependent Accumulation and Underdevelopment*, New York: Monthly Press Review.

——. 1991. 'Economic Ironies in World Politics: A Sequel to Political Ironies in World Economy', *Economic and Political Weekly*, 27 July.

Fransman, M. 1986. *Technology and Economic Development*, Brighton: Wheatsheaf.

Freeman, C. 1989. 'New Technology and Catching Up', *European Journal of Development Research*, Vol. 1, No. 1.

Frieden, J. 1981. 'Third World Indebted Industrialisation: International Finance and State Capitalism in Mexico, Brazil, Argentina, and South Korea', *International Organisation*, Vol. 35, No. 3.

Friedman, M. 1953. 'The Methodology of Positive Economics', in M. Friedman, *Essays in Positive Economics*, Chicago: University of Chicago Press.

Fruin, M. 1992. *The Japanese Enterprise System: Competitive Strategies and Cooperation Structure*, Oxford: Oxford University Press.

Fukagawa, U. 1997. *Kankoku: Senshinkoku Keizairon [The Theory of the Advanced Economy: the Case of Korea]*, Nihon Keizai Shinbunsha, in Japanese.

Furtado, C. 1976. *Economic Development of Latin America: Historical Background and Contemporary Problems*, Cambridge: Cambridge University Press.

Galtung, J. 1971. 'A Structural Theory of Imperialism', *Journal Of Peace Research*, No. 2.

Gerschenkron, A. 1962. *Economic Backwardness in Historical Perspective*, New York: Frederick.

Goldsmith, R. 1969. *Financial Structure and Development*, New Haven, CT: Yale University Press.

Grajdanzev, A. . 1944. *Modern Korea*, New York: The John Day Company.

Green, A.E. 1992. 'South Korea's Automobile Industry', *Asian Survey*, Vol. 32, No. 5, May.

——. 1994. 'Moving Beyond the State: The Industrial Context of South Korea's Comparative Advantage', in D.-S. Suh, ed., *Korean Studies: New Pacific Currents*, Honolulu: Centre for Korean Studies.

Greenway, D. and D. Sapsford. 1994. 'Export, Growth, and Liberalisation: An Evaluation', *Journal of Policy Modeling*, Vol. 16, No. 2, April.

Griffin, K. 1969. *Underdevelopment in Spanish America*, London: Allen & Unwin.

Grubel, H. 1967. 'Intra-Indusatry Specialisation and the Pattern of Trade', *The Canadian Journal of Economics and Political Science*, Vol. XXXIII.

Guisinger, S. 1991. 'Foreign Direct Investment Flows in East and Southeast Asia', *ASEAN Economic Bulletin*, Vol. 8, No. 1, July.

Guy, J. 1991. *The Motor Industry of South East Asia*, London: Economist Intelligence Unit.

Haggard, S. 1987, 'State and Foreign Capital in the East Asian NICS', in F. Deyo, ed., *The Political Economy of the New Asian Industrialism*, Ithaca, NY and London: Cornell University Press.

——. 1990. *Pathways from the Periphery: Politics of Growth in the Newly Industrialising Countries*, New York: Cornell University Press.

Haggard, S. and C.-I. Moon. 1990. 'Institutions and Economic Policy: Theory and a Korean Case Study', *World Politics*, No. 2, January.

Haggard, S., R. Cooper, S. Collins and S.-T. Ro. 1994. *Macroeconomic Policy and Adjustment in Korea, 1970–1990*, Cambridge, MA: Harvard University Press.

Hall, P. 1987. *Governing the Economy*, Cambridge: Polity Press.

Hamada, K. 1972. 'Japanese Investment Abroad', in P. Drysdale, ed., *Direct Foreign Investment in Asia and the Pacific*, Toronto: University of Toronto Press.

Hamilton, C. 1983. 'Capitalist Industrialisation in East Asia's Four Little Tigers', *Journal of Contemporary Asia*, Vol. 13, No. 1.

Han, B.-H. 1985. 'Korea's Global Policies: Policy Toward Japan', in Y.N. Koo and S.J. Han, eds, *The Foreign Policy of the Republic of Korea*, New York: Columbia University Press.

Hanazaki, M. 1990. 'Deepening Economic Linkages in the Pacific Basin Region: Trade, Foreign Direct Investment and Technology', *Japan Development Bank Research Report*, September.

Harris, L. 1987. 'Financial Reform and Economic Growth: A New Interpretation of South Korea's Experience', in L. Harris, ed., *New Perspective on the Financial System*, London: Croom Helm.

Hashimoto, K. 1996. 'Study on Production of Japanese Firms in Asia', *Ritsumeikan Business Management*, Vol. 34. No. 5, January.

Hattori, T. 1988. *Kankokuno Keiei Hatten* [*Development of Korean Business*], Tokyo: Bunshinto, in Japanese.

——. 1989. 'Japanese Zaibatsu and Korean Chaebol', in K.-J. Lee and H.-C. Lee, eds, *Korean Managerial Dynamics*, New York: Praeger.

——. 1997. 'Chaebol-Style Enterprise Development in Korea', *The Developing Economies*, Vol. 35, No. 4, December.

Hayek, F. 1984. 'Competition as a Discovery Procedure', in N. Chiaki and K.R. Leube, eds, *The Essense of Hayek*, Stanford, CA: Hoober Institution Press.

——. 1989. 'The Pretence of Knowledge', *American Economic Review*, Vol. 79, No. 5.

Hearley, D. 1991. *Japanese Capital Exports and Asian Economic Development*. Paris: Development Centre for the Organisation for Economic Cooperation and Development.

Hewitt, T., H. Johnson and D. Wield, eds. 1992. *Industrialisation and Development*, Oxford: Oxford University Press.

Hirakawa, K. 1992. *NIES: Sekai Shistemu to Kaihatsu [NIES: World system and Development]*, Tokyo: Dobunkan (in Japanese).

Hirata, A. and N. Takashi. 1989. 'Changing Patterns in International Division of Labour in Asia and the Pacific', in S. Miyohei and L. Fu-chen, eds, *Global Adjustment and the Future of Asian Pacific Economy*, Tokyo: Institute of Developing Economies.

Ho, S.P.-S. 1984. 'Colonialism and Development: Korea, Taiwan and Kwangtung', in R.H. Myers and M.R. Peattie, eds, *The Japanese Colonial Empire, 1895–1945*, Princeton, NJ: Princeton University Press.

Hobday, M. 1995. *Innovation in East Asia: the Challenge to Japan*, Cheltenham: Edward Elgar.

——. 1998. 'Latecomer Catch-up Strategies in Electronics: Samsung of Korea and ACER of Taiwan', *Asian Pacific Business Review*.

Honda, K. 1990. *Kakoku Shihonshugi Ronso [Debates on Korean Capitalism]*, Sekai Shoin: Tokyo (in Japanese).

Hong, J.-P. 1997. 'Chaebol and Small-and Medium-sized Companies', in D.-H. Kim and G. Kim, eds, *Reform of Korea's Chaebol*, Seoul: Nanam Press.

Hong, S.-D. 1994. 'Source of Economic Growth in Korea: 1963–1992', *Korea Development Review*, Vol. 16, No. 3, Seoul: KDI, November.

Hong, Y.-S. 1996. 'International Strategic Alliance for Promotion of Global Competitiveness', in K.-Y. Jeong and M.-S. Kwack, *Industrial Strategy for Global Competitiveness of Korean Industries*, Seoul: KERI.

——. 1998. 'Technology-Related FDI Climate in Korea', *KIEF Working Paper 98–15*, Korea Institute for International Economic Policy.

Hong, W.-T. 1976. *Factor Supply and Factor Intensity of Trade in Korea*, Seoul: KDI.

——. 1981. 'Trade, Growth and Income Distribution: The Korean Experience', in W.-T. Hong and L. Krause, eds, *Trade and Growth of the Advanced Developing Countries in the Pacific Basin*, Seoul: KDI.

——. 1987. 'Export-led Growth and the Opening of Trade', in S. Cho et al., eds, *Theory and Reality of Korean Economy*, Seoul: Seoul National University Press.

Hughes, A. and A. Singh. 1991. 'The World Economic Slowdown and the Asian and Latin American Economies: A Comparative Analysis of Economic Structure, Policy, and Performance', in T. Banuri, ed., *Economic Liberalisation: No Panacea*, Oxford: Clarendon Press.

Hur, H. 2002. 'A Study of bank restructuring after the financial crisis', MA thesis, Dongkuk University, Department of Economics (in Korean).

Industrial Technology Association. 1980. *Annual Report on Technology Introduction* (in Korean).

——. 1990. *Annual Report on Technology Introduction* (in Korean).

International Monetary Fund (IMF). 1996. *IMF Survey*, 22 January.

Ireland, A. 1926. *The New Korea*, New York: E.P. Dutton & Company.

Ito, M. 1992. *The Japanese Economy*, Cambridge, MA: MIT Press.

Johnson, C. 1982. *MITI and the Japanese Miracle*, Stanford, CA: Stanford University Press.

——. 1984. *The Industrial Policy Debate*, San Francisco: Institute for Contemporary Studies.

——. 1985. 'Political Institutions and Economic Performance: The Government-Business Relationship in Japan, South Korea, and Taiwan', in R.A. Scalapino, S. Sato and J. Wanandi, eds, *Asian Economic Development – Present and Future*, Berkeley, CA: Institute of East Asian Studies, University of California.

——. 1987. 'Political Institutions and Economic Performance: The Government-Business Relationship in Japan, South Korea, and Taiwan', in F. Deyo, ed., *The Political Economy of the New Asian Industrialisation*, Ithaca, NY: Cornell University Press.

Joo, J.-H. 1983. *Kaihatsu Keizaigaku no Kihon Shiten o Meggute [A Basic Perspective on Development Economics]*, Sekai Keizai Hyoron (in Japanese).

——. 1985. *Chaebol Kyojeron [The Theory of Chaebol Economics]*, Jongeum Munhwasa (in Korean).

Jones, L. and I. Sakong. 1980. *Government, Business and Entrepreneurship in Economic Development: The Korean Case*, Cambridge, MA: Harvard University Press.

Jung, K.-H. 1987. *Hankuk Kieobui Sungjang Jonryaggoa Kyoyoung Kujo [Growth Strategy of Korean Enterprises and Business Structure]*, The Korean Chamber of Commerce and Industry (in Korean).

——. 1989, 'Business-Government Relations in Korea', in K.-H. Chung and H.-C. Lee, eds, *Korean Managerial Dynamics*, New York: Praeger.

Jwa, S.-H. 1999. *Chinhwarongjok Chaebolron [An Evolutionary Theory of Chaebol]*, Seoul: Bibong Publishing (in Korea).

Kang, C-G. 1992. 'Sanup ui Balcheun goa Sanup Jeongcheck' ['Industrial Development and Policy'], in W.T. Lim, ed., *The Understanding of Korean Economy*, Seoul: Bibong Publishing (in Korean).

——. 1998. 'Crisis of Korean Economy and a Suggestion of Overcoming the Crisis', *Dangdae Bipyong*, Spring (in Korean).

Kang, C., J. Choi and J.-S. Chang. 1991. *Cahebol: Sungjangui Chooyoginga Tamyoogui Hwashiinga [Chaebo: A Leader of Growth or A Perfect Picture of Avarice?]*, Seoul: Bibong Publishing (in Korean).

Kang, M.-H. 1996. *Chaebolgoa Hankug Kyungje* [*Chaebol and Korean Economy*], Nanam Publishing (in Korean).

Kang, Y.-K. et al. 1993. *Policy Suggestions for Dependence of Electronics Industry on Japanese Technology*, Policy Study 93–08–03, STEPI (in Korean).

Keesing, D. 1967. 'Outward Looking Policies and Economic Development', *Economic Journal*, Vol. 77, June.

Kim, B.-J. 1987. *The Theory of Korean Economy and Reality*, Seoul: Seoul National University Press (in Korean).

Kim, C.-N. 1992. *A Prospect of Japanese Industry and Trade Structure*, Policy Study, 92–29, KIEP (in Korean).

Kim, E.-H. 1990. 'Financing Korean Corporations: Evidence and Theory', in J.K. Kwon, ed., *Korean Economic Development*, Westport, CT: Greenwood Press.

Kim, E.-M. 1997. *Big Business, Strong State: Collusion and Conflict in South Korean Development, 1960–1990*, New York: State University of New York Press.

Kim, H.-K. 1999. *A Secret History: Glory and Shame of the Korean Economy*, Mae-Kyung Economic Newspaper Press (in Korean).

Kim, H.-J., I-G. Kang and M.-S. Yoon. 1993. *Policy Suggestions for Dependence of Parts Industry on Japanese Technology*, Policy Study 93–08–04, STEPI (in Korean).

Kim, H.-N. 1976. 'Japanese-South Korean Relations in the Post-Vietnam Era', *Asian Survey*, Vol. 16.

Kim, I.-Y. 1998. *Hankugui Kyungje Sungjang* [*Growth of Korean Economy*], CFE (in Korean).

Kim, J.-D. 1999. 'Inward Foreign Direct Investment Regime and Some Evidences of Spillover Effects in Korea', *KIEF Working Paper 99–09*, Korea Institute for International Economic Policy.

Kim, J-I. and L. Lau. 1993. 'The Sources of Economic Growth of the East Asian Newly Industrialising Countries', Asia/Pacific Research Centre, September, Stanford University Press.

Kim, J.-K. 1991. 'An Overview of Readjustment Measures Against the Banking Industries' Non-performing Loans', *Korea Development Review*, Vol. 13, No. 1, Spring (in Korean).

——. 1993. *Kukka Yesan goa Jongchaek Mokpyo* (*National Budget and Policy Aim*], Seoul: KDI (in Korean).

Kim, K.-S. and J.-K. Kim. 1997. 'Korean Economic Development: An Overview', in D.-S. Cha, K.-S. Kim and D. Perkins, eds, *The Korean Economy 1945–1995: Performance and Vision for the Twenty-first Century*, Seoul: KDI.

Kim, K.-S. and M. Roemer. 1979. *Studies in the Modernisation of the Republic of Korea, 1945–75: Growth and Structural Transformation*, Cambridge, MA: Harvard University Press.

Kim, K.-S. 1975. 'Outward-Looking Industrialisation Strategy: The Case of Korea', in W. Hong and A.O. Krueger, ed., *Trade and Development in Korea*, Seoul: Korean Development Institute.

Kim, H.-K. and J. Ma. 1997. 'The Role of Government in Acquiring Technological Capability: The Case of the Petrochemical Industry in East Asia', in M. Aoki, H.-K. Kim and M. Okuno-Fujiwara, eds, *The Role of Government in East Asia Economic Development: Comparative Institutional Analysis*, Oxford: Clarendon Press.

Kim, P.-J. 1990. 'Korea's Financial Evolution', in J.K. Kwon, ed., *Korean Economic Development*, Westport, CT: Greenwood Press.

——. 1997. 'Financial Policies and Institutional Innovation', in D.-S. Cha, K.-S. Kim and D. Perkins, eds, *The Korean Economy 1945–1995: Performance and Vision for the Twenty-first Century*, Seoul: KDI.

Kim, D.-H. and K. Kim. 1999. *Hankug Chaebol Gaehyugron* [*Reform of Korean Chaebol*], Seoul: Nanam Press (in Korean).

Kim, Y.-H. 1988. *Higashi Azia Kogyoka to Sekai Shihonshugi* [*Industrialisation in East Asia and World Capitalism*], Toyo Keizai Shinposha (in Japanese).

——. 1995. 'Dynamics of Industrial Policy: Development of Heavy and Chemical Industries', mimeo.

Kim, Y.-H., et al. 1993. *Study of New Technology-Economic Order between Japan and Korea*, Policy Study 93–08–01, STEPI (in Korean).

Kim, Y.-H., S-J. Shim, J-H. Suh and D.-S. Cho. 1995. *Industrial Restructuring of Japan-Korea Caused by the High Yen and Technology Transfer*, Policy Study 95–16, STEPI (in Korean).

Kim, Y.-S. 1998. 'Global Competition and Latecomer Production Strategies: Samsung of Korea in China' *Asian Pacific Business Review.*

Kim, L.-S. and S.-M. Seong. 1997. 'Science and Technology: Public Policy and Private Strategy', in D.-S. Cha, K.-S. Kim and D. Perkins, eds, *The Korean Economy 1945–1995: Performance and Vision for the Twenty-first Century*, Seoul: KDI.

Kobayashi, N. 1976. 'The Japanese Approach to Multinationalism.' *Journal of World Trade Law*, No. 10.

Kohama, H. 1987. 'Korea's Industrialisation and Promotion of Science and Technology', *Sekai Keizai Hyoron*, 11 (in Japanese).

Kohli, A. 1994. 'Where Do High Growth Political Economies Come From? The Japanese Lineage of Korea's Developmental State', *World Development*, Vol. 22, No. 9.

Kojima, K. 1977. 'Transfer of Technology to Developing Countries: Japanese Type versus American Type', *Hitotsubashi Journal of Economics*, Vol. 17, February.

——. 1985. 'Japanese and American Direct Investment in Asia: A Comparative Analysis', *Hitotsubashi Journal of Economics*, Vol. 25.

——. 1997. 'Foreign Direct Investment-led Economic Growth: Future of East Asian Economy', *Sekai Keizai Hyoron*, No. 3 (in Japanese).

Kong, B.-H. 1995. *Hankuk Kyongjeui Kuenryok Idong* (*Power Shift of Korean Economy*), Changhae (in Korean).

Kong, J.-W. 1993. *Study on Korean Capitalists in the 1950s*, Baesan Suhdang (in Korean).

Koo, H.-G. 1987. 'The Interplay of State, Social Class, and World System in East Asian Development: The Cases of South Korea and Taiwan', in F.C. Deyo, ed., *The Political Economy of the New Asian Industrialism*, Ithaca, NY: Cornell University Press.

Koo, H.-G. and E.-M. Kim. 1992. 'The Developmental State and Capital Accumulation in South Korea', in R.P. Appelbaun and J. Henderson, eds, *States and Development in the Asian Pacific Rim*, Newbury Park: Sage Publications.

Korea Association of Machinery Industry. 1989. *Machinery Industry Trade Statistics* (in Korean).

——. 1993. *Machinery Industry Trade Statistics* (in Korean).

——. 1995. *Machinery Industry Trade Statistics* (in Korean).

Korea Development Bank (KDB). 1997. *Industry in Korea*, Seoul: Korea Development Bank.

KDB and MOF. 1993. *Eoja Doip Sashipnyunsa [A 30-year History of Foreign Capital Introduction]*, Seoul: KDB/MOF.

Korea Development Institute (KDI). 1995. *Chronological Policy Data: A 50-year Korean Economy*, Seoul: Korea Development Institute (in Korean).

——. 1997. *Quarterly Economic Outlook*, Seoul: KDI (in Korean).

Korea Electronics Industries. 1987. *Hankug Chonja Sanup 20 Nyonsa [A 20-Year History of Korean Electronics Industries*, Seoul: KEI (in Korean).

Korea Hyoron [Korea Review], *Nihon Shihon no Taikan Shinshustu to Kankoku Keizai [Japanese Capital and Korean Economy]*, July 1970, January 1971 (in Japanese).

Korea International Trade Association (various years). *Annual Trade Report* (in Korean).

—— (various years). *Trade Statistics* (in Korean).

Korean National Statistical Office. 1985, 1999. *Economic Statistics Yearbook Major Statistics of Korean Economy*, various issues (in Korean)

Kosai, Y. and Y. Ogino. 1984. *The Contemporary Japanese Economy*, London: Macmillan.

Krause, L.B. 'Trade as a Handmaiden of Growth: Similarities between the Nineteenth and Twentieth Centuries', *Economic Journal*, Vol. 53.

Krause, L.B. and K.-S. Kim. 1991. *Liberalisation in the Process of Economic Development*, Berkeley, CA: University of California Press.

Krueger, A. 1978. *Foreign Trade Regimes and Economic Development: Liberalisation Attempts and Consequences*, Cambridge, MA: Ballinger Press.

——. 1980. 'Trade Policy as an Input to Development', *American Economic Review*, Vol. 70, *Papers and Proceedings*.

——. 1981. 'Export-led Industrial Growth Reconsidered' in W.k Hong and L. Krause, eds, *Trade and Growth of the Advanced Developing Countries in the Pacific Basin*, Seoul: KDI.

——. 1983. 'Import Substitution and Export Promotion', *Finance and Development*, Vol. 22, No. 2, June.

——. 1990. 'Government Failure in Economic Development', *Journal of Economic Perspective*, Vol. 4, No. 3.

——. 1997. 'Korean Industry and Trade over Fifty Years', in D.-S. Cha, K.-S. Kim and D. Perkins, eds, *The Korean Economy 1945–1995: Performance and Vision for the Twenty-first Century*, Seoul: KDI.

Krugman, P. 1994. 'The Myth of Asia's Miracle' *Foreign Affairs*, Vol. 73, No. 6, November/December.

Kuznets, P. 1977. *Economic Growth and Structure in the Republic of Korea*, New Haven, CT: Yale University Press.

——. 1982. 'The Dramatic Reversal of 1970–1980: Contemporary Economic Development in Korea', *Journal of Northeast Asian Studies*, 1 September.

——. 1988. 'An East Asian Model of Economic Development: Japan, Taiwan, and South Korea', *Economic Development and Cultural Change*, Vol. 36, No. 3, April, Supplement.

——. 1994. *Korean Economic Development: An Interpretive Model*, New York: Praeger.

Lal, D. 1983 *The Poverty of Development Economics*, London: Institute of Economic Affairs.

Lall, S. 1985. *Multinationals, Technology and Exports*, Basingstoke: Macmillan.

——. 1992. 'Technological Capabilities and Industrialisation', *World Development*, Vol. 20, No. 2.

——. 1993. 'Promoting Technology development: The Role of Technology Transfer and Indigenous Effort', *Third World Quarterly*, Vol. 14, No. 1.

Lawrence, R.Z. 1993. 'Japan's Different Trade Regime: An Analysis with Particular Reference to Keiretsu.' *Journal of Economic Perspectives*, Vol. 7, No. 3, Summer.

Lee, B.-C. 1986. *Ho-Am Jajon* [*Autobiography of Ho-Am*], Garden Grove, CA: Joong-Ang Daily Newspaper Publishing (in Korean).

Lee, B.-K. 1996. *Policy Suggestion for Dependence of Capital Industry on Japan*, Seoul: KERI (in Korean).

Lee, C.-H. 1992. 'The Government, Financial System, and Large Private Enterprise in the Economic Development of South Korea', *World Development*, February.

Lee, C.-H. 1999. 'A Study of the government and chaebols relationship in Korea: a focus from 1993', MA thesis, Yoensei University (unpublished) (in Korean).

Lee, C.-J. and H. Sato. 1993. *US-Japan Partnership in Conflict Management: The Case of Korea*, Claremont, CA: Keck Centre for International and Strategic Studies, Claremont McKenna College.

Lee, H.-C. 1989. 'Managerial Characteristics of Korean Firms', in K.-H. Chung and H.-C. Lee, eds, *Korean Managerial Dynamics*, New York: Praeger.

Lee, H.-G. 1996. *Challenges and Responses in the New Trading Environment: A Korean Perspective*, Seoul: KDI.

Lee, H.-J. 1980. *Kankoku Kogyoka no Rekishiteki Tenkai* [*Historical Development of Korean Industrialisation*], Zeimu Keiri Kyokai, in Japanese.

——. 1989. 'Managerial Characteristics of Korean Firms', in K.-H. Chung and H.-J. Lee, eds, *Korean Managerial Dynamics*, New York: Praeger.

Lee, H.-K. 1994. 'Foreign Direct Investment and Investment Policy', *Study Report 1994–2006*, Seoul: KDI (in Korean).

——. 1999. *Hankuk Chaebol Hyongsungsa* [*The History of Korea's Chaebol*], Seoul: Bibong Press (in Korean).

Lee, K.-T. 1984. 'Government Policy Measures Toward Industrial Concentration and Economic Power Concentration', Korean Economic Policy Case Studies, No. 11, East-West Centre, Honolulu, Hawaii.

Lee, K.-U. 1986. *The Concentration of Economic Power in Korea: Causes, Consequences, and Policy*, Working Paper No. 86–02, Korea Development Institute.

Lee, K.-U. and S.-S. Lee. 1985. *Kiop Kyolhabgwa Kyojeryog Chibjung* [*Enterprise Combination and Concentration of Economic Power*], Seoul: KDI (in Korean).

Lee, M. and J.-S. Shim. 2007. 'The Structural Weakness of Korean Economic Development Model: A Historical Overview', *Current Politics and Economics of Asia and China*, Vol. 16, No. 1, 1–16.

Lee, S.-H. 1998. 'Success and Failure of Development in Semi-peripheral Nations', in Korean Comparative Social Studies, *Success and Failure of East Asia*, Korean Comparative Social Studies (in Korean).

Lee, W.-Y. and Jae-Hyung Kim. 1987. 'Kisul toip daegka ui kyolchong' [Determinants of the Royalty Pasyment in Technology Licencing'], *Hanguk kaebal yongu* [*Korea Development Research*], Korea Development Institute, Vol. 9, No. 1, Spring (in Korean).

Lee, Y.-K. 1990. 'Conglomeration and Business Concentration in Korea', in J.K. Kwon, ed., *Korean Economic Development*, Westport, CT: Greenwood Press.

Lee, W.-K., S.-S. Chang and M.-S. Yoon. 1993. *Policy Suggestion for Technology Acquisition from Japan and its Use*, Policy Study 93–08–02, Policy and Management Institute for Science and Technology (in Korean).

Leibenstein, H. 1963. *Economic Backwardness and Economic Growth*, New York: Wiley and Sons.

Leuddle-Neurath, R. 1988. 'State Intervention and Export-Oriented Development in South Korea', in G. White, ed., *Development State in East Asia*, London: Macmillan.

——. 1988. 'The Experiences and Causes', in P.L. Berger and H.M. Hsiao, eds, *In Search of an East Asian Development Model*, New Brunswick, NJ: Transaction Books.

Lim, H.-C. 1985. *Dependent Development in Korea*, Seoul: Seoul National University Press.

Lim, W.-T. 1987. 'Hankook Kyeoungje Bunseock ui Bangbeobnon' [The Methodology of Korean Economic Analysis'], in W.T. Lim, ed., *The Understanding of Korean Economy*, Seoul: Bibong Press (in Korean).

Linder, S. 1981. 'Cause of Trade in Primary Products Versus Manufactures', in R.E. Baldwin and J.D. Richardson, eds, *International Trade and Finance: Readings*, 2nd edn, Boston, MA: Little Brown and Company, 1981: 40–51.

Lipsey, R.E. 1992. *Direct Foreign Investment and Structural Change in the Asian Pacific Region*, Boulder, CO: Westview Press.

Little, I. 1970. *Industry and Trade in Some Developing Countries*, London: Oxford University Press.

———. 1979. 'An Economic Renaissance', in W. Galenson, ed., *Economic Growth and Structural Change in Taiwan*, Ithaca, NY: Cornell University Press.

———. 1982. *Economic Development: Theory, Policy and International Relations*, New York: Basic Books. .

Litvak, I.A. and C.J. Maule. 1973–74. 'Japan's Overseas Investment', *Pacific Affairs*, Vol. 46.

Love, J. 1994. 'Engines of Growth: The Export and Government Sectors', *The World Economy*, Vol. 17, No. 2, March.

Mae-IL Economic Newspaper, 26 May 1998.

Malecki, E. 1997. *Technology and Economic Development: The Dynamics of Local, Regional and National Competitiveness*, 2nd edn, Boston: Addison Wesley Longman.

Mardon, R. 1990. 'The State and the Effective Control of Foreign Capital: The Case of South Korea', *World Politics*, Vol. 43, No. 1.

Mason, E.S. et al. eds. 1980. *The Economic and Social Modernisation of the Republic of Korea*, Cambridge, MA: Council on East Asian Studies, Harvard University.

McNamara, D. 1990. *The Colonial Origins of Korean Enterprise, 1910–1945*, New York: Cambridge University Press.

Meier, G.M. 1987. *Pioneers in Development: Second Series*, Oxford: Oxford University Press.

Michell, A. 1984. 'Administrative Traditions and Economic Development in South Korea', *IDS Bulletin*, Vol. 15, April.

Minami, R. 1994. *The Economic Development of Japan: A Quantitative Study*, 2nd edn, London: Macmillan.

Ministry of Finance. 1991. *Companies of Foreign Direct Investment*, Seoul: MOF (in Korean).

Ministry of Finance (various years). White Paper on Foreign Direct Investment (in Japanese).

Ministry of Finance and Economy and Korea Development Institute. *Economic Bulletin*, various issues, Seoul: MFE and KDI.

Ministry of Foreign Affairs. 1994. *Japan's ODA: Annual Report*, Tokyo: Association for the Promotion of International Cooperation, March (in Japanese).

Ministry of Finance and Economy. 1998. *Trends in International Investment and Technology*, Seoul: MOFE (in Korean).

Ministry of International Trade and Industry (MITI). 1990. *Kaigai toshi tokei soran* [*Comprehensive Statistics on Japanese Foreign Investment*], Tokyo: MITI (in Japanese).

———, various years. *Wagakuni kigyo no kaigai jigyo katsudo* [*Overseas Business Activities of Japanese Firms*], Tokyo: MITI (in Japanese).

———. 1994. Tsusho Hakusho [White Paper on International Trade], Tokyo: MITI (in Japanese).

———, various years. 'Export-Import Statistics' (in Japanese).

Ministry of Science and Technology, various issues. *Science and Technology Annual* (in Korean).

——, various issues. 'Report of Research Activity in Science and Technology' (in Korean).

Miyashita, K. and D. Russell. 1994. *Keiretsu: Inside the Hidden Japanese Conglomerates*, New York: McGraw-Hill.

Mizoguchi, T. 1975. *Taiwan, Chosen no Keizai Seicho* [*Economic Growth of Taiwan and Korea*], Tokyo: Iwanami Shoten (in Japanese).

——. 1979. 'Economic Growth of Korea under the Occupation: Background of Industrialisation of Korea', *Journal of Economics*, Vol. 2.

Mizoguchi, T. and Y. Yuzo. 1984. 'Capital Formation in Taiwan and Korea', in R.H. Myers and M.R. Peattie, eds, *The Japanese Colonial Empire, 1895–1945*, Princeton, NJ: Princeton University Press.

Moon, C.-I. 1988. 'The Demise of a Developmental State? Neoconservative Reform and Political Consequences in Korea, *Journal of Development Studies*, Vol. 4.

——. 1994. 'Changing Patterns of Business-Government Relations in South Korea', in A. MacIntyre, ed., *Business and Government in Industrialising Asia*, Sydney: Allen & Unwin.

Morikawa, H. 1992. *Zaibatsu: The Rise and Fall of Family Enterprise Groups in Japan*, Tokyo: University of Tokyo Press.

Morishima, M. 1982. *Why Ha Japan Succeeded? Western Technology and the Japanese Ethos*, Cambridge: Cambridge University Press.

Morris-Suzuki, T. 1992. 'Japanese Technology and the New International Division of Knowledge in Asia', in S. Tokunaga, ed., *Japan's Foreign Investment and Asian Economic Interdependence : Production, Trade and Financial System*, Tokyo: University of Tokyo Press.

Myint, H. 1964. *The Economics of the Developing Countries*, New York: Praeger.

——. 1971. 'Dualism and the Internal Integration of Underdeveloped Economies', in *Economic Theory and the Underdeveloped Countries*, New York: Oxford University Press.

——. 1985. 'Organisational Dualism and Economic Development', *Asian Development Review*, Vol. 3, No. 1.

——. 1987. 'The Neoclassical Resurgence of Development Economics: Its Strength and Limitations', in G.M. Meier, ed., *Pioneers in Development: Second Series*, Oxford: Oxford University Press.

Myrdal, G. 1957. *Economic Development and Underdevelopment Regions*, London: Duckworth.

——. 1968. *Asian Drama: An Inquiry into the Poverty of Nations*, New York: Vintage Books.

Nakagawa, N. 1987. 'Azia Shinko Kogyokokka Toshite no Kankoku Keizai' [Korean Economy as the Asia NIES'], in S. Okumura, ed., *Prospect of Asia NIES*, Tokyo: Tokyo University Press (in Japanese).

Nakakita, T. 1988. 'The Globalisation of Japanese Firms and Its Influence on Japan's Trade with Developing Nations', *Developing Economies*, Vol. 26, No. 4, December.

Nakamura, T. 1993. *Japanese Economy: Growth and Structure*, Tokyo: Tokyo University Press (in Japanese).

Nam, C.-H. 1981. 'Trade and Industrial Policies, and the Structure of Production in Korea, Trade and Growth of the Advanced Developing Countries in the Pacific Basin', in W. Hong and L. Krause, eds, *Trade and Growth of the Advanced Developing Countries in the Pacific Basin*, Seoul: KDI.

Nam, S.-W. 1989. 'Liberalisation of the Korean Financial and Capital Markets', unpublished paper, KDI.

——. 1992. 'Korea's Financial Reform since the Early 1980s', KDI Working Paper No. 9207, Korea Development Institute, March.

Nam, S.-W. and J.-I. Kim. 1997. 'Macroeconomic Policies and Evolution', in D.-S. Cha, K.-S. Kim and D. Perkins, eds, *The Korean Economy 1945–1995: Performance and Vision for the Twenty-first Century*, Seoul: KDI.

National Statistical Office. 1995. *An Economic Diary since 1945*, Seoul: NSO.

——, various years. *Major Statistics of Korean Economy*, Seoul: NSO.

Naya, S. and R. Schatz. 1972. 'Trade, Investment, and Aid: The Role of the US and Japan in Asian Economic Development', in H.B. Malmgren, ed., *Pacific Basin development*, Lexington, MA: Heath.

Naya, S. and E. Ramstetter. 1988. 'Policy Interactions and Direct Foreign Investment in East and Southeast Asia', *Journal of World Trade*, Vol. 22, No. 2, April.

Nihon Keizai Shinbun, 'Ajia Toshi ni Dai San no Nami' ['The Third Wave of Asian Investment'], 7 July 1992 (in Japanese).

Nishida, M. 1989. 'Appropriation and Spillover of Technology and International Industrial Organisation', *OCU Economic Review*, Vol. 24. No. 1, January.

Noble, G.W. 1989. 'The Japanese Industrial Policy Debate', in S. Haggard and C.-I. Moon, eds, *Pacific Dynamics: The International Politics of Industrial Change*. Boulder, CO: Westview Press.

Noland, M. 1997. 'Has Asian Export Performance Been Unique?', *Journal of International Economics*, Vol. 43.

North, D. 1990. *Institutions, Institutional Change and Economic Performance*, Cambridge: Cambridge University Press.

——. 1992. *Transaction Costs, Institutions, and Economic Performance*, San Francisco, California: International Centre for Economic Growth.

Nurkse, R. 1954. *Problems of Capital Formation in Underdeveloped Countries*, Oxford: Basil Blackwell.

——. 1959. *Patterns of Trade and Development*, Stockholm: Almquist and Wicksell.

Odagiri, H. 1992. *Growth Through Competition, Competition Through Growth: Strategic Management and the Economy in Japan*, Oxford: Clarendon Press.

——. 1996. *Country Economic Surveys. Korea*, Paris: OECD.

Ohkawa, K. 1970. *Economic Development and Experiences of Japan*, Tokyo: Daimeido (in Japanese).

Okimoto, D. 1989. *Between MITI and the Market: Japanese Industrial Policy for High Technology*, Stanford, CA: Stanford University Press.

Okuno-Fujiwara, M. 1997. 'Toward a Comparative Institutional Analysis of the Government-Business Relationship', in M. Okuno-Fujiwara, ed., *the Role of Government in East Asian Economic Development*, Oxford: Clarendon Press.

Olge, G.E. 1990. *South Korea: Dissent within the Economic Miracle*, London: Zed Books.

Organisation for Economic Cooperation and Development (OECD). 1988. *The Newly Industrialising Countries: Challenge and Opportunity for OECD Industries*, Paris: OECD.

Orru, M., Biggart, N.C. and G. Hamilton. 1997. *The Economic Organisation of East Asian Capitalism*, London: SAGE Publications.

Ozawa, T. 1972. 'Multinationalism, Japanese Style', *Columbia Journal of World Business*, Vol. 7.

——. 1976. 'Commodity Trade and Factor Mobility: Comment', *American Economic Review*, Vol. 66.

——. 1979. 'International Investment and Industrial Structure: New Theoretical Implications from the Japanese Experience', *Oxford Economic Papers*, Vol. 31.

Pack, H. and L. Westphal. 1986. 'Industrial Strategy and Technological Change: Theory versus Reality', *Journal of Development Economics*, Vol. 22.

Paeck, Y.-H. and W.-H. Cho. 1996. 'Globalisation of Financial Industry', in C.-Y. Ahn, ed., *Towards New Direction of Korean Economy in Twenty-first Century*, Seoul: Nanam Press (in Korean).

Page, S. 1989. 'The Role of Trade in the New NICs', *Journal of Development Studies*, Vol. 27, No. 3.

Palmer, G. 1978. 'Dependency: A Formal Theory of Underdevelopment or a Methodology for the Analysis of Concrete Situation of Underdevelopment?', *World Development*, Vol. 6, Nos 7–8.

Papanek, G. 1990. 'The New Asian Capitalism: An Economic Portrait', in P.L. Berger and H.M. Hsiao, eds, *In search of an East Asian Development Model* New Brunswick, NJ: Transaction Books,.

Park, C.-U. 1997. 'Retrospect and Prospect of Economic System', in *An Academic Society of Comparative Economics, Comparative Economic System*, Seoul: Parkyoungsa (in Korean).

Park, D.-C. 1994. 'Trend of Korean Economy', in Academy of Korean Social Economy, *Lecture of Korean Economy*, Seoul: Hanwool Academy (in Korean).

Park, D.-S. 1992. *Leaders of Chaebol in Korea*, Toyo Keizai Shinposha (in Japanese).

Park, E.-Y. 1985. 'Foreign Economic Policies and Economic Development', in Y.-N. Koo and S.-J. Han, eds, *The Foreign Policy of the Republic of Korea*, New York: Columbia University Press.

Park, J.-S. 2004. 'Changes in Competition Structure as a Result of Restructuring of the Financial Industry after the Financial Crisis', Issue Paper, 2005.7.29 (in Korean).

Park, I. 1990. 'Kakokuno Kogyoka to Shihai Santaisei' ['Industrialisation of Korea and Tripartite System of Governance'], *Sekai Hyoron*, No. 4 (in Japanese).

Park, K.-J. et al., 1998. *Korea: Neo-liberalism and Asian Economic Crisis*, Pusan National University Press (in Korean).

Park W.-H. 1989. *Kankokuno Gijuttsu Hatten* [*Technological Development of Korea*], Bunshinto (in Japanese).

Park, W.-H. and Y.-H. Bae. 1996. *Hankug ui Kisul Balchon* [*Technological Development of Korea*], Kyungmunsa (in Korean).

Park, W-H. and M. Moritani. 1993. 'Basic Direction of Technology Cooperation and International Division of Technology between Japan and Korea towards Twenty-first Century', *Policy Studies, 93–35*, KIEP (in Korean).

Park, Y.-C. 1981. 'Export Growth and the Balance of Payments in Korea, 1960–78', in W. Hong and L. Krause, eds, *Trade and Growth of the Advanced Developing Countries in the Pacific Basin*, Seoul: KDI.

——. 1986. 'Foreign Debt, Balance of Payments and Growth Prospects: The Case of the Republic of Korea 1965–1988', *World Development*, Vol. 14, No. 8.

——. 1990. 'Growth, Liberalisation and Internationalisation of Korea's Financial Sector, 1970–1989', *American Economic Review*, Vol. 180, No. 2.

Park, Y.-C. and D.-W. Kim. 1994. 'Korea: Development and Structural Change of the Banking System', in H. Patrick and Y-C Park, eds, *The Financial Development of Japan, Korea, and Taiwan*, New York: Oxford Press.

Park, S.-G. 1991. *A Root and Fruit of Korean Economy*, Seoul: Dolbegae (in Korean).

Patrick, H. and H. Rosovsky. 1976. 'Japan's Economic Performance', in Patrick and Rosovsky, eds, *Asia's New Giant: How the Japanese Economy Works*, Washington, DC: The Brookings Institution.

Perkins, D.H. 1997. 'Structural Transformation and the Role of the State: Korea, 1945–1995', in D.-S. Cha, K.-S. Kim and D. Perkins, eds, *The Korean Economy 1945–1995: Performance and Vision for the Twenty-first Century*, Seoul: KDI.

Petri, P. 1988. 'Korea's Export Niche: Origins and Prospects', *World Development*, Vol. 16, No. 1.

Prebisch, R. 1950. *The Economic Development of Latin America and its Principal Problems*, New York: United Nations.

——. 1965. *The Economic Development of Latin America: A Structural Approach*, New Haven, CT: Yale University Press.

Radelet, S. and J. Sacks. 1997. 'Asia's Re-emergence', *Foreign Affairs*, Nov/December.

Ranis, G. 1979. 'Industrial Development', in W. Galenson, ed., *Economic Growth and Structural Change in Taiwan*, Ithaca, NY: Cornell University Press.

——. 1989. 'The Role of Institutions in Transition Growth: The East Asian Newly Industrialising Countries', *World Development*, Vol. 17, No. 9.

Ranis, G., and J. Fei. 1975. 'A Model of Growth and Employment in the Open Dualistic Economy: The Case of Korea and Taiwan', in F. Stewart, ed., *Employment, Income Distribution and Development*, Frank Cass: London.

Rhee, J-C. 1994. *The State and Industry in South Korea: The Limits of the Authoritarian State*, London: Routlege.

Riedel. 1988. 'Economic Development in East Asia: Doing What Comes Naturally? In Hughes, H, ed., *Achieving Industrialisation in East Asia*, Cambridge University Press: Cambridge.

Ro, S-T. 1994. 'Korean Monetary Policy', in S. Haggard, R.Cooper, S. Collins, C.-S. Kim and S.-T. Ro, eds, *Macroeconomic Policy and Adjustment in Korea 1970–1990*, Cambridge, MA: Harvard Studies for International Development.

Rosenberg, N. 1976. *Perspectives on Technology*, Cambridge: Cambridge University Press.

——. 1982. 'The International Transfer of Technology: Implications for the Industrialised Countries', in *Inside the Black Box: Technology and Economics*, Cambridge: Cambridge University Press.

Rostow, W.W. 1958. *The State of Economic Growth: A Non-Communist Manifesto*, Cambridge: Cambridge University Press.

Rowley, C. and J.-Seok B. 1998. 'Conclusion: Korean Business and Management – The End of the Model?', *Asia Pacific Business Review*, Vol. 4.

——. 1998. 'Introduction: The Icarus Paradox in Korean Businesses and Management', *Asia Pacific Business Review*, Vol. 4, Nos 2/3.

Rozman, G., ed. 1991. *The East Asian Region: Confucian Heritage and Modern Adaptation*, Princeton, NJ: Princeton University Press.

Sachs, J. 1987. 'Trade and Exchange Rate Policies in Growth-oriented Adjustment Programmes', IMF-IBRD Symposium on Growth-oriented Adjustment Programmes, Washington, DC, February.

Sakakibara, E. 1993. *Beyond Capitalism: The Japanese Model of Market Economics*, Lanham, MD: University Press of America.

Sakamoto, Y. 1986. 'Korea in Japan's Foreign Policy-making', *Korean Journal for Japanese Studies*, Vol. 5.

Sakong, I. 1993. *Korea in the World Economy*, Washington, DC: Institute of International Economics.

Salvatore, D. and T. Hatcher. 1991. 'Inward Oriented and Outward Oriented Trade Strategies', *The Journal of Development Studies*, Vol. 27, No. 3.

Samsung. 1989. *Samsung Chonja 20 Nyosa* [*A 20-Year History of Samsung*] (in Korean).

——.1998. Samsung 60 Nyonsa [*A 60-Year History of Samsung*], Samsung Secretariat (in Korean).

——, various issues. *Samsung Annual Report* (in Korean).

Sano, J.R. 1977. 'Foreign Capital and Investment in South Korean Development', *Asian Economies*, No. 23, December.

Schmitz, H. 1984. 'Industrialisation Strategies in Less Developed Countries: Some Lessons of Historical Experience', *Journal of Development Studies*, Vol. 21, October.

Sekai Shuho. 1969. 'Nihon Kigyo no Kaigai Shinshutsu: Asia' ['Overseas Expansion of Japanese Enterprises: Asia'], Tokyo: Sekai Shuho (in Japanese).

Sekiguchi, S. 1983. 'Industrial Adjustment in East Asia's Resource-poor Economics', *The World Economy*, Vol. 6, No. 2, March.

Seong, S.-M. 1993. *Economic Development and Policies for Small and Medium-sized Enterprises in Korea*, KDI Policy Monograph 93–06, KDI.

Shafer, D.M. 1990. 'Sectors, States, and Social Forces: Korea and Zambia Confront Economic Restructuring', *Comparative Politics*, January.

Shin, Y.-H. 1984. *Characteristics and Problems of Korea's Firms*, Seoul: Seoul National University Press.

Shin, J.-S. 1996. *The Economics of the Latecomers: Catching-up, Technology Transfer and Institutions in Germany, Japan and South Korea*, London: Routledge.

——. 1999. *Hakug Kyungje Jesamui Gil* [*Third Way of the Korean Economy*], Joong-Ang M & B (in Korean).

Shin, K.-S. and Seong, S.-M. 2002. 'Korea's Competition Policy After the Economic Crisis', *The Korean Journal of Industrial Organization*, Vol. 10, No. 1.

Shinsanup Kyongyongwon. 1996. *97 Nyon Pan Hankuk 30 Dae Chaebol Jaemu Bunsok* [*Financial Management Analysis of Korea's 30 Largest Chaebol*] (in Korean).

Singer, H.W. 1950. 'The Distribution of Gains between Investing and Borrowing Countries', *American Economic Review*, May.

Small and Medium Industry Promotion Corporation. 1988. *The Present Analysis of International Industrial Co-operation of Small and Medium Enterprises* (in Korean).

Sohn, C.-H., J.-S. Yang and H.-S. Yim. 1998. 'Korea's Trade and Industrial Policies: 1948–1998: Why the Era of Active Policy is Over', KIEF Working Paper 98–05, Korea Institute for International Economic Policy.

Song, B.-N. 1990. *The Rise of the Korean Economy*, Oxford: Oxford University Press.

——, ed. 1993. *Korean Economy*, Seoul: Parkyoungsa (in Korean).

——. 1996. *The Rise of the Korean Economy*, Oxford: Oxford University Press.

Suh, S-C. 1978. *Growth and Structural Changes in the Korean Economy: 1910–1940*, Cambridge, MA: Harvard University Press.

Srinivasan, T.N. 1985 'Neoclassical Political Economy, the State and Economic Development', *Asian Development Review*, Vol. 3, No. 2.

Stern, J., J.-H. Kim, D. Perkins and J.-H. Yoo. 1995. *Industrialisation and the State: The Korean Heavy and Chemical Industry Drive*, Cambridge, MA: Harvard University Press.

Steven, R. 1990. *Japan's New Imperialism*. Armonk, NY: M.E. Sharpe.

Stewart, C.T. 1985. 'Comparing Japanese and US Technology Transfer to Less-Developed Countries', *Journal of Northeast Asian Studies*, Spring.

Stiglitz, J.E. 1989. 'The Economic Role of the State', in A. Heertje, ed., *The Economic Role of the State*, London: Basil Blackwell.

——. 1993. 'The Role of the State in Financial Markets', *Proceedings of the World Bank Annual Conference on Development Economics*, Washington, DC: World Bank.

Streeten, P. 1982. 'A Cool Look at "Outward-looking" Strategies for Development', *The World Economy*, Vol. 5, No. 2, March.

Suzuki, N. 1974. *Ajia no Keizai Hatten to Yushutsu Shiko Kogyoka* [*Asia's Economic Development and Trade-Oriented Industrialisation*], Singapore: AERI.

Tahara-Domoto K. and H. Kohama. 1989. *Machinery Industry Development in Korea: Intra-industry Trade between Japan and Korea*, Tokyo: International Development Centre of Japan.

Taniura, T. 1978. 'Development of Manufacturing Industries in Korea', *Asia Economy*, Vol. 19, No. 7 (in Japanese).

——. 1989. *Kankokuno Kogyokato Kaihatsu Taisei* [*Korea's Industrialisation and Development System*], Asia Economic Institute, Tokyo: Asia Economy Press (in Japanese).

Tho, T. Van. 1988. 'Foreign Capital and Technology in the Process of Catching up by the Developing Countries: The Experience of the Synthetic Fiber Industry in the Republic of Korea', *World Development*, Vol. 26, No. 4.

Tsiang, S.C. 1964. 'Tax, Credit and Trade Policies to Promote the Production and Export of Manufactures of Developing Countries', *The Journal of Development Studies*, Vol. 1, October, No.1.

Urata, S. 1993. 'Changing Patterns of Direct Investment and Implications for Trade and Investment', in C.F. Bergsten and M. Noland, eds, *Pacific Dynamism and the International Economic System*, Washington, DC: Institute for International Economics.

US Government Agency for International Development, 'US Overseas Loans and Grants and Assistance from International Organisations', 1 July 1945–30 September 1976.

Vernon, R. 1966. 'International Investment and International Trade in the Product Life Cycle', *Quarterly Journal of Economics*, Vol. 80.

Vogel, E. 1991. *The Four Little Dragons: The Spirit Industrialisation in East Asia*, Cambridge, MA: Harvard University Press.

Wade, R. 1990. *Governing the Market*, Princeton, NJ: Princeton University Press.

Wade, R. and F. Veneroso. 1998. 'The Asian Crisis: The High Debt Model versus the Wall Street-Treasury-IMF Complex', *New Left Review*, Vol. 219.

Wall, D. 1976. 'Export Processing Zones.' *Journal of World Trade Law*, No. 10.

Wallerstein, I. 1974. *The Modern World System I: Capitalist Agriculture and the Origins of the European World-Economy in the Sixteenth Century*, San Diego: Academic Press.

Watanabe, T. 1981. 'An Analysis of Structural Dependence between Korea and Japan', *Trade and Growth of the Advanced Developing Countries in the Pacific Basin*, in W. Hong and L. Krause, eds, *Trade and Growth of the Advanced Developing Countries in the Pacific Basin*, Seoul: KDI.

——. 1982. *Gendai Kankoku keizai Bunseki* [*An Analysis of Contemporary Korean Economy*], Keiso Shobo: Tokyo (in Japanese).

——. 1986. *Seicho no Asia, Teitai no Asia* [*Growth and Stagnation in Asia*], Tokyo: Tokyo Keizai Shinposha (in Japanese).

——. 1986. *Kankoku Bencha Capitalizumu* (*Korea: Venture Capitalism*), Kodansha (in Japanese).

——. 1990. *Gaisetsu Kankoku Keizai* [*The Korean Economy*], Arihikyaku (in Japanese).

Watanabe, T. and C.-N. Kim. 1996. *Kankoku Keizai Hattenron* [*Principle of Korean Economic Development*], Keisho Shobo (in Japanese).

Watanbe, T., and C.-N. Kim. 1997. *Hyundae Hankug Kyoje Balchonon* [*Theory of Modern Korean Economic Development*], Yoopung Publishing (in Korean).

Weiss, L. and J.M. Hobson. 1995. *States and Economic Development: A Comparative Historical Analysis*, Cambridge: Polity Press.

Westphal, L.E. 1978. 'The Republic of Korea's Experience with Export Led Industrial Development', *World Development*, Vol. 6, No. 2.

——. 1990. 'Industrial Policy in an Export-propelled Economy: Lessons from South Korea's Experience', *Journal of Economic Perspectives*, Vol. 4, No. 3, Summer.

Westphal, L.E., Y.-W. Rhee and G. Pursell. 1984. *Source of Technological Capability in the Third World*, London: Macmillan.

Westphal, L. Y.-W. Rhee, L. Kim and A. Amsden. 1984. 'Republic of Korea', *World Bank*, Vol. 12, Nos 5/6.

Whang, I.-J. 1991. 'Government Direction of the Korean Economy', in G. Caiden and B.W. Kim, eds, *A Dragon's Progress – Development Administration in Korea*, West Hartford, CT: Kumarian Press.

——. 1997. *Economic Transformation of Korea, 1945–95: Issues and Responses*, Seoul: The Sejong Institute.

Wong, P.-K. 1996. 'Technological Transfer and Development Inducement by Foreign MNCs: The Experience of Singapore', in K.-Y. Jeong and M.-S. Kwack, eds, *Industrial Strategy for Global Competitiveness of Korean Industries*, Seoul: KERI.

Woo, J.-E. 1991. *Race to the Swift: State and Finance in Korean Industrialisation*, New York: Columbia University Press.

World Bank. 1986. *World Development Report*, New York: Oxford University Press.

——. 1987. *Korea: Managing the Industrial Transaction*, vols 1 and 2, Washington, DC: World Bank.

——. 1993. *The Eastern Asian Miracle*, New York: Oxford University Press.

——. 1996. *World Development Report*, New York: Oxford University Press.

Yagahmaian, B. 1994. 'An Empirical Investigation of Exports, Development, and growth in Developing Countries: Challenging the Neoclassical Theory of Export-led Growth', *World Development*, Vol. 22, No. 12.

Yamamura, N. 1979. 'Asia's New Economic Giant in the 1980s', *The World Economy*, Vol. 2, No. 1, January.

Yamazawa, I. and H. Kohama. 1985. 'Trading Companies and the Expansion of Foreign Trade: Japan, Korea, and Tailand', in K. Ohkawa and G. Ranis, eds, *Japan and the Developing Countries*, Oxford: Basil Blackwell.

Yanagimachi, K. 1994. 'Technological Development of Semiconductor's Company: the Case of Samsung Group', in M. Takuro, ed., *The Crossroads of Korean Business Management*, Nagoya City: Nagoya University Press (in Japanese).

Yasuoka, S. 1989. 'Japanese Zaibatsu and Korean Chaebol', in K.-H. Chung and H.-C. Lee, eds, *Korean Managerial Dynamics*, New York: Praeger.

Yong, Y. 1972. 'Foreign Investment in Developing Countries: Korea', in P. Drysdale, ed., *Direct Foreign Investment in Asia and the Pacific*, Toronto: University of Toronto Press.

Yoo, J.-H. 1990. 'The Trilateral Trade Relation among the Asian NIEs, the US and Japan', KDI Working Paper No. 9005, Korea Development Institute, April.

Yoo, S.-C. 1997. 'Possibility and Limit of Confucian Capitalism', *Tradition and Contemporary*, No. 1, Summer (in Korean).

Yoo, S.-J., and S.-M. Lee. 1987. 'Management Style and Practice of Korean Chaebols', *California Management Review*, Vol. 29, Summer.

Yoo, S.-M. 1995. *Chaebol in Korea: Misconceptions, Realities, and Policies*, Seoul: KDI.

Yoo, S.-M. and S.-S. Lee. 1997. 'Evolution of Industrial Organisation and Policy Response in Korea: 1945–1995', in D.-S. Cha, K.-S. Kim and D. Perkins, eds, *The Korean Economy 1945–1995: Performance and Vision for the Twenty-first Century*, Seoul: KDI.

Yoon, C.-H. and J.-W. Lee. 1998. 'Study on Trade Competitiveness and Technology in Manufacturing Industry of Korea', *Working Paper, 98–11*, STEPI (in Korean).

Yoon, Y.-K. 1990. 'The Political Economy of Transition: Japanese Foreign Direct Investments in the 1980s', *World Politics*, Vol. 43, No. 1.

Yoshihara, Hideki. 1988. 'Nihonteki Seisan Shisutemu no Kaigai Iten' ['The Overseas Transfer of the Japanese Production System'], in Y. Hideki, H. Kiichiro and Y. Kenichi, ed., *Nihon Kigyo no Gurubaru Keizai* [*The Global Economy of Japanese Firms*], Toyo Keizai Shinposha (in Japanese).

Young, A.K. 1974. 'Internationalisation of the Japanese General Trading Companies', *Columbia Journal of World Business*, Vol. 9.

Index